Praise from Job Seekers for the Knock 'em Dead Books

"I got the position! I was interviewed by three people and the third person asked me all the questions in *Knock 'em Dead*. I had all the right answers!"
— B.M., Massapequa, New York

"I just finished writing the letter I have dreamed of writing for three years: my letter of resignation from the Company from Hell. Thanks to you and the book, *Kno_____ed*, I have been offered and have accepte__ __ exc____nt p___tion with a major international ser___e corporation."
— C.C., Atlanta, Georgia

"Thank you for your wonderful book! I read it before attempting to secure a position in an industry that I had been out of for fourteen years. The first company I interviewed with made me an offer for more money than I had expected."
— K.T., Houston, Texas

"My previous employer asked me to resign. Your book got me through my depression, and in only four weeks, got me four job offers. This is the first time in my career I have this many options to choose from."
— D.H., North Canton, Ohio

"I credit you as being the number one source of information on this issue, and recommend you every time I hear that someone is in the job market. The cost of the book is the best money I've ever spent."
— T.S., Atlanta, Georgia

"After college graduation, I searched and searched for a job, and ended up taking a few low-paying ones I was overqualified for. Finally, I read your book and have been offered every job I have applied for since."
— L.E. (no address given)

"I followed the advice in *Knock 'em Dead* religiously and got more money, less hours, a better hospital plan, and negotiated to keep my three weeks vacation. I start my new job immediately!"
— A.B., St. Louis, Missouri

"My job search began a few months ago when I found out that I would be laid off because of a corporate buyout. By following your advice, I have had dozens of interviews and have received three very good job offers. Your excellent advice made my job hunt much easier."
— K.C., St. Louis, Missouri

"I fou__ yo__ b___ _o be absolutely invalu-__ during m_ ____ ___ search. Since then I have had a chance to spe__ __th my interviewer, who informed me that it was my strong interview that landed me my job offer. He went on to outline what had turned him off about other candidates, and it was some of the very same mistakes I used to make before reading your book!"
— D.D., Houlton, Maine

"Every time I've used your book, I've gotten an offer! This book is incredible. Thanks for publishing such a great tool."
— W.Z., Columbia, Maryland

"Just a quick note to let you know how much your book has helped me. I was chosen for my job out of more than 100 applicants! I later loaned the book to a friend and circled the things that had helped me. She interviewed on a Thursday, and she was offered the position that Thursday night! Thanks for writing such a helpful book."
— S.G., Sacramento, California

"Your book is simply fantastic. This one book improved my yearly income by several thousand dollars, and my future income by untold amounts. Your work has made my family and myself very happy."
— M.Z., St. Clair Shores, Michigan

"Thank you for all the wonderfully helpful information you provided in your book. I lost my job almost one year ago. I spent almost eight months looking for a comparable position. Then I had the good sense to buy your book. Two months later, I accepted a new position. You helped me turn one of the worst experiences of my life into a blessing in disguise."
— L.G., Watervliet, New York

"I was out of work for four months—within five weeks of reading your book, I had four job offers."
— S.K., Dallas, Texas

"Yesterday I received two job offers in the space of fifteen minutes. I am now using the 'Negotiating the Offer' chapter to evaluate these positions."
— W.B., Thornhill, Ontario

"I read every page in the book and, after a two-month search, got ten interviews with top-performing companies and six offers (five of which I declined)."
— M.V., Millington, Tennessee

"I was sending out hordes of resumes and hardly getting a nibble—and I have top-notch skills and experience in my field. I wasn't prepared for this tough job market. When I read your book, however, I immediately began applying some of your techniques. My few nibbles increased to so many job interviews I could hardly keep up with them!"
— C.S., Chicago, Illinois

"I read the book, cover-to-cover, and then flew to California to complete fourteen intense interviews in a two-day period. Although I was interviewing for an entry-level position with a high-tech firm, I faced few technical questions. Most of them were behavioral questions, exactly the types your book prepared me for. I had the enviable position for making a choice of which job to take!"
— S.T., San Jose, California

"I got two job offers within a twenty-four-hour period. The information you've provided is as valuable as the air you breathe."
— J.M., Greensboro, North Carolina

"I will always remain a student of yours. Since the first edition to the last, I got every copy, and with each I learn more. I have had several interviews, all of which were generated by the tactics of your book."
— M.R., Beaumont, Texas

"It was as if the interviewer had just put the same book down! After being unemployed for more than a year, I am grateful to say that I've landed the best job I've ever had."
— E.M., Honolulu, Hawaii

"I read and used your book, *Resumes That Knock 'em Dead*, as I searched for a job. I was called for an interview and was up against ten applicants. To make a long story short, I interviewed on Monday morning, and by Monday afternoon knew I had the job."
— E.H. (no address given)

"I just received the offer of my dreams with an outstanding company. Thank you for your insight. I was prepared!"
— T.C., San Francisco, California

"After reading your book, *Resumes That Knock 'em Dead*, I rewrote my resume and mailed it to about eight companies. The results were beyond belief. I was employed by one of the companies that got my new resume, and received offers of employment or requests for interviews from every company. The entire job search took only five weeks."
— J.V., Dayton, Ohio

COVER LETTERS

KNOCK 'EM DEAD
THAT

Martin Yate

Adams Media
Avon, Massachusetts

To your good fortune, that intersection of preparation, effort, and opportunity.

Acknowledgments

Knock 'em Dead is now in its nineteenth year of publication, and it has become a staple for job hunters around the world. This is due to the ongoing support of countless people on the team of Adams Media, both past and present.

Published by
Adams Media, an F+W Publications Company
57 Littlefield Street, Avon, MA 02322 U.S.A.
www.adamsmedia.com

ISBN: 1-59337-107-1

Printed in the United States of America.

J I H G F E D C B

Library of Congress Cataloging-in-Publication Data
Yate, Martin.
Cover letters that knock 'em dead / Martin Yate.-- 6th ed.
p.   cm.
ISBN 1-59337-107-1
1. Cover letters. 2. Résumés (Employment) I. Title: Cover letters that knock them dead. II. Title: Knock 'em dead. III. Title.

HF5383.Y378 2004
650.14'2--dc22
2004016366

This publication is designed to provide accurate and authoritative information with regard to the subject matter covered. It is sold with the understanding that the publisher is not engaged in rendering legal, accounting, or other professional advice. If legal advice or other expert assistance is required, the services of a qualified professional person should be sought.
— From a *Declaration of Principles* jointly adopted by a Committee of the American Bar Association and a Committee of Publishers and Associations.

Many of the designations used by manufacturers and sellers to distinguish their products are claimed as trademarks. Where those designations appear in this book and Adams Media was aware of a trademark claim, the designations have been printed with initial capital letters.

This book is available at quantity discounts for bulk purchases.
For more information, call 1-800-872-5627.

READ THIS FIRST

There's a cruel paradox at work when it comes to writing cover letters. We strive to excel in our professions, spending our energies to become top-notch accountants, truck drivers, brain surgeons . . . and we spend little or no time learning to promote ourselves on the printed page. When suddenly our livelihood depends, in the first instance, on our ability to create a compelling professional profile, we find ourselves in dire straits.

In the technological revolution that brought us computers and e-mail we all started writing once more, but at the same time found our writing skills long since rusted. Although packaging our professional selves for evaluation by others has such enormous impact on all aspects of the quality of our lives, most of us have simply never made the development of adequate written communication skills a top priority. This task is made the more difficult because we are creating a sales document, and a document where we are the subject. If you are like most people, packaging and pitching yourself to others is both an uncomfortable and difficult prospect.

Sometimes, more senior professionals hire others to craft these messages. The rest of us, well, we just send these all-important sales documents (for that is what they are) out into the world far weaker than they could be, with the result that we stay longer in that dead end job, or longer unemployed.

If you find yourself in this situation at the most inopportune time imaginable—during your job search—take heart. *Cover Letters That Knock 'em Dead* has helped millions of people around the world craft personal, unique, and hard-hitting job-hunting letters of all types, and it can do the same for you. Use it exactly as I recommend in the pages that follow. If you do, you will reap a number of benefits, the most important of which is this:

- Your job hunt will get a tremendous boost, because your letters will look great, pack a punch, get read, and position you as a mover and shaker worth interviewing, and worth remembering.

This book will enable you to have templates on hand for all kinds of useful letters which you can use in a productive job hunt—not only cover letters of every conceivable type, but letters for every situation, including follow-up letters, acceptance letters, and those oh-so-happy letters of resignation. These letters were all designed to keep your candidacy forefront in the minds of employers. They are real letters written by real job hunters, and also by professional resume and letter writing professionals. They will give you that extra edge in a highly competitive job market, as you will have the advantage of proven tools, customized to your own needs.

There are other advantages:

- You won't waste a moment of precious time conceiving letters from scratch, because you will have a wide selection of templates to rework for your own needs.
- You'll have the satisfaction of knowing that you've made a tough, intricate, and vitally important professional challenge a little easier and more enjoyable than it is for most people in your shoes (your competitors, for example).
- Once settled in a new position, you will be able to adapt the techniques you learn here to other on-the-job written communications that are part of the underpinnings of any successful career.

◆ ◆ ◆

Employers go through four distinct stages in reaching a hiring decision.

1. *Long-list development.* Advertising and other sources develop the biggest possible field of qualified candidates.
2. *Short-list development.* The long list is screened to rule out also-rans. Those who make the cut are invited in for an interview.

3. *Short-list prioritization.* Through a series of two or three interviews, candidates are weeded out. Those still standing are ranked according to various criteria. (To learn how to successfully make it through the interview process, see the "The Five Secrets of the Hire" chapter in *Knock 'em Dead: The Ultimate Job Seeker's Resource.*)

4. *Short-list review.* After the dust settles, each candidate's strengths and weaknesses are reviewed for one last time before the final decision. The information in the dossier created for every short-list candidate plays a key role here. This dossier will contain all the knowledge the company has about you. This will include your resume, cover letter, and any follow-up letters you have been smart enough to send during the interview process.

In each of these steps, letters have a role to play in taking you to the next level. For example, a resume without a cover letter often gets no further than the trash can. The reader feels you are obviously not interested enough in their specific job to write a cover letter, while on the other hand your competition is providing concrete evidence of commitment and communication skills.

A "To Whom It May Concern" letter fares little better. A letter with a salutation by name gets read and kept. As will letters following up on meetings that make comments on the discussions and issues addressed.

It's estimated that the average piece of business correspondence initially receives less than thirty seconds of the reader's attention; just a quick scan to reject or save for more careful consideration. A great cover letter will get you much more; it will get a second more careful reading, and it will get your resume read with serious attention. In crafting your cover letter, you are not aiming to win a place next to a favorite novel on the reader's bedside table. A powerful cover letter will win that momentary flash of genuine interest and get your resume read carefully. Once that's accomplished, you can use the models in this book for the follow-up letters that will help you to step upward on the four-tiered ladder to the job offer.

Letters help you move through each phase of the hiring cycle by supporting your candidacy and reminding employers of your relevant skills, continued existence, and interest in the job, all the way to the offer. It's a well-known fact, in headhunting circles, that when there is nothing to choose between two top candidates, the offer will always go to the most enthusiastic; professional follow-through with your letters makes that enthusiasm clear.

In the fourth step (the short-list review) the interviewer recalls what happened in each phase of the interview cycle. All notes and documentation in the applicant dossier are reviewed for each candidate. This means that as you pass through each step of the cycle, you are presented with a heaven-sent opportunity to advance your candidacy for when that moment of truth finally arrives. You can seize the opportunity to include all manner of pertinent information that will identify you as the unquestioned prime choice when that last, most critical evaluation is taking place.

Your written record (all the different types of letters you can create during the interview cycle to advance your candidacy) demonstrates writing skills, attention to detail, professionalism, and that all-important enthusiasm; each letters adds yet another meaningful plus to your candidacy. And remember that these pluses are being made when you aren't there to speak up for yourself.

◆ ◆ ◆

I took a commonsense approach to putting this book together: I collected more than 4,000 successful job-hunting letters from the most cynical professionals in the country: corporate human resources people and professional headhunters. I approached more than 1,000 of these people and asked them to provide the truly impressive letters they came across—the letters that made a difference, grabbed attention, and advanced someone's candidacy against tough competition. The cream of the crop can be found within these covers. Over the years, this book has become the standard against which the others in the field are judged, and it is updated on a regular basis to incorporate new ideas and letter samples that add to its breadth, depth, and efficacy.

From these letters, and from my discussions with professionals in the field, I learned which things work—and which don't—when putting together a cover letter. These qualities are explored in detail later on in the book, but there is one overriding factor that virtually all the successful letters shared, and it's worth exploring here.

All but a handful of the letters were only one page long. Yours probably should be too. Why is brevity so important? My sources on the hiring side of the desk, where I also spent a number of years, feel that:

1. They don't have time to wade through dense patches of text, and they view those who can't get to the point in a dim light.
2. Second pages get detached and often lack sufficient contact information. (For that matter, first pages often fall short in the same category.)

A strong mail dimension to your job-hunting campaign can double and triple your effectiveness. Throughout this book, whenever you read the word "mail" it has a double meaning—regular mail and e-mail. The most effective job-hunting campaign will always use the two mediums in tandem. For maximum impact you will want to follow-up each mailing with a telephone call to the recipient; for more information on this part of the job search, my book *Knock 'em Dead: The Ultimate Job Hunter's Resource* will help you with advice on how to turn these calls into interviews, and where no openings exist, referrals for further opportunities.

If you use the letter samples simply as they are, as noncustomized templates, you may open a few doors. But the "real" you will be so different from the letters that the interviewers will eventually be left with a nagging doubt that you aren't all you appear to be. Besides, when it is so easy to customize these samples, why not make the effort as a gift to your career? Then, with small changes, you'll be able to use them again and again throughout your career.

Browse through the wide variety of letters in the second half of this book. Not all of them will fit your needs at this moment, but take a look anyway. You will see, on every page, proven methods of getting the good word across to potential employers.

This book will also highlight key phrases and wording techniques that caught the eyes of people whose eyes are usually tough to catch. You will discover a "rhythm" to the words and phrases that have real impact. Then you'll be able to incorporate them into your own original work. By sampling a few phrases from this letter, and a few from that letter, you will be able to create powerful communications that reflect the real you.

In choosing the examples for this book, I was pleased to see that the ones that rose to the top were all businesslike, with no gimmickry or cuteness. Some may even seem a little dry to you, but remember: They worked. This collection of successful job-hunting letters includes the best of the best as determined by line managers, human resource professionals, headhunters, and career management professionals who know a winner when they see one. It is just such people who will be evaluating your efforts, and the drawbridge of opportunity will be raised (or lowered) for you depending on their evaluation.

Now let's learn how to put together the jigsaw puzzle pieces. I suggest that you read this book with a highlighter in hand, so you can flag appropriate sections for later reference. That way you'll have a wealth of good ideas you can use after just one read. Then you'll be ready to create your own unique job-hunting letters that will knock 'em dead.

CONTENTS

Read This First v

1. What Is a Cover Letter?. 1

2. Four Types of Cover Letters 7

3. What Goes In, What Stays Out 17

4. Assembling Your Cover Letter 24

5. The Final Product 34

6. The Plan of Attack. 39

7. Using the Internet and
    Creating Electronic Cover Letters. 58

8. Sample Letters 84

Responses to Online Job Postings

E-Mails

Technical Sales Representative **85** • Investment Banker **86** • Legal Administrator **87** • Manufacturing **88** • Production Supervisor **89**

Responses to Newspaper Advertisements

Letters

Health Care Management **90** • Adjunct Faculty Position **91** • Hydrogeologist **92** • Customer Service Representative **93** • Sales Associate **94** • Medical Biller **95** • Skilled Laborer **96** • Peace Officer **97** • Assessment Coordinator **98** • Office Administrator **99** • Legal Secretary **100** • Accounting Manager **101** • International Sales Manager **102** • Executive Assistant **103**

Power Phrases **104**

"Cold" Responses to Potential Employers

Letters

Entry-Level Network Administrator **108** • Entry-Level Librarian **109** • Manager **110** • Mental Health **112** • Senior Customer Service Specialist **113** • Research Professional **114** • Personal Trainer **115** • Registered Nurse **116** • Entertainment Industry **117** • Management **118** • Physician's Assistant **119** • Radiation Safety Officer **120** • Veterinarian **121** • Internship **122** • Teacher **123** • Production Supervisor **124** • School Board Seat **125** • Sales Professional **126** • Credit Account Specialist **127** • Sales **128** • Rail Industry **129** • Media **130** • Vice President **131** • Pharmaceutical Sales **132** • Recruiter **133** • Project Management **134** • Publishing **135** • International Sales **136**

E-Mails

Banking **137** • Software Development **138** • Internship **139**

Power Phrases **140**

"Cold" Responses to Employment Industry Professionals

Letters

Health Care **143** • Senior Network Control Technician/Administrator **144** • CPA **145** • Quality Assurance **146** • Executive Computer Specialist **147** • Vice President **148** • Senior Manager **149** • International Operations **150**

E-Mails

IT Professional **151** • Computer Professional **152** • Programmer/Analyst **153** • IT Management **154** • Systems Integration **155** • Systems Administrator **156**

Power Phrases **157**

Broadcast

Letters

Faculty Position **160** • Assistant Director of College Housing **162** • Financial Planning Professional **163** • Heavy Equipment Operator **164** • Executive Chef/Hotel/Restaurant Manager **165** • Maintenance Mechanic **166** • Database Engineer **167** • Senior Technical Sales **168** • Telecommunications **169** • Senior R&D Engineer **171** • Multilingual Sales Manager **173** • Management **175** • HR Generalist **177** • Operations Manager **179** • Pharmaceutical Sales **180** • Information Technology Program Manager **181** • Vice President of Operations **182** • Consultant **183** • Project Manager **185**

E-Mails

Senior Buyer/Purchasing Agent/Purchasing Manager **186** • New Product Marketing **187** • Senior Marketing Executive **188** • Logistics **189** • Vice President Asset Liquidation **190**

Power Phrases **191**

Networking

Letters

Managerial/Administrative Position **193** • Administrative Assistant **194** • Internship/Employment **195** • Computer and Information Systems Manager **196** • Management **197** • Chief Financial Officer **198** • General **199** • Accounting **200**

E-Mails

Employee Benefits Administration **201** • Publishing **202**

Power Phrases **203**

Follow-Up (after telephone contact)

Letters

Fundraising Consultant **205** • Adjunct Faculty **206** • Legal Assistant **207** • Purchasing **208** • Manager **209**

E-Mails

General **210** • Arts Management **211**

Power Phrases **212**

Follow-Up (after face-to-face meeting)

Letters

Library System Director **213** • Sales **214** • Loan Processor **215** • Concierge Associate **216** • Merchandise Manager **217** • Manufacturer Representative **218** • General **219** • Librarian **220** • Construction Manager **221** • Executive Assistant **222** • Management Information Systems **223** • Assistant **224** • Sales **225**

E-Mails

General **226** • Sales Manager **227** • Senior Counselor **228** • Management **229** • Corporate Graphic Design **230** • General **231** • Entry-Level **232** • Auditing **233**

Power Phrases **234**

"Resurrection"

Letters

HR Position **238** • Lift Line Driver Position **239** • Community Empowerment
Team Director Position **240** • Stevedore **241** • Social Worker **242** • Wholesale
Market Manager **243** • Construction Manager **244** • Entry-Level **245**

E-Mails

Account Executive **246** • Programmer **247** • Product Manager **248**

Power Phrases **249**

Rejection of Offer

Letters

Public Library Director **250** • Team Supervisor **251** • General **252**

E-Mails

Department Manager **253**

Power Phrases **254**

Acceptance

Letters

Marketing Research Manager **255** • Managing Consultant **256** • Vice President
257

E-Mails

General **258**

Power Phrases **259**

Negotiation

Letters

General **261** • Sales **263** • Senior Lab Specialist **264** • Product Specialist **265**

Resignation

Letters
CCU Nurse **266** • Care Coordinator **267** • Management **268** • Sales Representative **269** • Vice President **270**

E-Mails
General **271**

Power Phrases **272**

Thank-You Letters (after hire)

Letters
General **273**

E-Mails
Software Manager **274**

Power Phrases **275**

Special Reports **276**

Appendix A: Professional Resume Writing Services **282**

Appendix B: Online Resources **292**

Index **298**

WHAT IS A COVER LETTER?

DO YOU EVER receive junk mail? We all do. What do you do with the stuff marked "occupant"?

J unk mail never gets the attention a personal letter does. You junk it—either without reading it, or after a quick glance. Because they are formulaic, most cover letters end up being treated the same way.

Your cover letter is the personalized factor in the presentation of an otherwise essentially impersonal document, your resume. A good cover letter sets the stage for the reader to accept your resume as something special. Only if your cover letter and resume do their job will interviews, and ultimately job offers, result.

When the envelope is opened, your cover letter is the first thing seen. It can make an indelible first impression. Of course, I'm not saying that the letter alone will get you the job, but it does set the tone for your candidacy, and it will get your resume a careful examination. The subsequent follow-up letters you send to advance your candidacy will add to the impact.

The higher up the professional ladder you climb, the more important cover letters and job-hunting letters become. For the candidate who must demonstrate written communication skills in the execution of daily duties (and that's just about all of us), these letters become a valuable vehicle for demonstrating critical job skills. Mess up here and the door to opportunity could well slam shut. Do a good job here and you'll stand out from the competition.

Step One

Grab your reader's ATTENTION. Do this by using quality stationery, and envelopes. Use the same paper your resume is printed on. This way your letter and resume will match and give an impression of balance and continuity. See Chapter 5, "The Final Product," for details on paper choice.

Step Two

Generate INTEREST with the content. Do this by addressing the letter to someone by name and quickly explaining why you are writing, and what you have to offer. The first couple of sentences grab attention, and the rest of the paragraph introduces your candidacy. The rule is: Introduce yourself with conviction. If you don't believe in the professional product that is you, how can you expect anyone else to believe?

Use research to get your letter off to a fast start; anyone can search the Web for articles and visit the employer's own site. For example:

> *"I came across the enclosed article in* Newsweek *magazine and thought it might interest you. It encouraged me to do a little research on your company. I am now convinced of two things: You are the kind of people I want to be associated with, and I have the kind of qualifications you can use."*

On a company's Web site, you will find lots of eye-opening data, including news and press clippings. You can also use search engines to find interesting info about the company by typing in the company name as a keyword.

Of course, not every company you approach will have been mentioned in *Newsweek*, but if there is no mention in the press the chances are still good that their Web site can give you some insight that can be turned to advantage. Here are some more everyday examples.

"I have been following the performance of your fund in Mutual Funds Newsletter. *The record over the last three years shows strong portfolio management. With my experience working for one of your competitors, I know I could make significant contributions . . ."*

"Recently I have been researching the local _____ industry. My search has been for companies that are respected in the field and . . . which prize a commitment to professional development. I am such an individual and you are clearly such a company."

"With the scarcity of qualified and motivated [your desired job title] that exists today, I feel sure that it would be valuable for us to talk."

"Within the next few weeks I will be moving from New York to _____. Having researched the companies in my field in my new home town, I know that you are the people I want to talk to . . ."

"The state of the art in _____ changes so rapidly that it is tough for most professionals to keep up. I am the exception. I am eager to bring my experience to bear for your company."

Step Three

Now turn that INTEREST into DESIRE. First, tie yourself to a specific job category or work area. Use phrases like:

"I am writing because . . ." or *"My reason for contacting you . . ."*

". . . should this be the case, you may be interested to know . . ."

"If you are seeking a _____, you will be interested to know . . ."

"I would like to talk to you about your personnel needs and how I am able to contribute to your department's goals."

"If you have an opening for someone in this area, you will see that my resume demonstrates a person of unusual dedication, efficiency and drive."

Next, call attention to your merits with a short paragraph that highlights one or two of your special contributions or achievements:

"I have an economics background from Columbia and a quantitative analysis approach to market fluctuations. This combination has enabled me consistently to pick the new technology flotations that are the backbone of a growth-oriented technology fund."

Similar statements applicable to your area of expertise will give your letter more personal punch. Include any qualifications, contributions, and attributes that prove you are someone with plenty of talent to offer. If an advertisement (or a conversation with a potential employer) reveals an aspect of a particular job opening that is not addressed in your resume, you can use the cover letter to fill in the gaps.

"I notice from your advertisement that audio- and video-training experience would be a plus. In addition to the qualifications stated in my enclosed resume, I have over five years of experience writing and producing sales and management training materials in both these media."

Step Four

Here's where your letter turns a DESIRE to know more into ACTION. The action you're shooting for is that the reader will dash straight on to your resume, then call you in for an interview. You achieve this with brevity—always leave the reader wanting more. Offer too much information and you may be ruled out of consideration, so whet the reader's appetite but leave them asking questions.

Make it clear to the reader that you want to talk. Explain when, where, and how you can be contacted. You can also be *proactive* by telling the reader that you intend to follow up at a certain point in time if contact has not been established by then. Just as you worked to create a strong opening, make sure your closing carries the same conviction. It is the reader's last impression of you; make it strong, make it tight, and make it obvious that you are serious about entering into meaningful conversation.

Useful phrases include:

"It would be a pleasure to give you more information about my qualifications and experience . . ."

"I look forward to discussing our mutual interests further . . ."

"While I prefer not to use my employer's time taking personal calls at work, with discretion I can be reached at _____."

"I will be in your area around the 20th, and will call you prior to that date. I would like to arrange . . ."

"I hope to speak with you further and will call the week of _____ to follow up."

"The chance to meet with you would be a privilege and a pleasure, so to this end I shall call you on _____."

"I look forward to speaking with you further and will call in the next few days to see when our schedules will permit a face-to-face meeting."

"May I suggest a personal meeting where you can have the opportunity to examine the person behind the resume."

"My credentials and achievements are a matter of record that I hope you will examine in depth when we meet . . . you can reach me at _____."

"I look forward to examining any of the ways you feel my background and skills would benefit [name of organization]. I look forward to hearing from you."

"Resumes help you sort out the probables from the possibles, but they are no way to judge the caliber of an individual. I would like to meet you and demonstrate that I have the personality that makes for a successful _____."

"I expect to be in your area on Tuesday and Wednesday of next week and wonder which day would be best for you. I will call to determine. In the meantime, I would appreciate your treating my application as confidential, since I am currently employed."

"With my training and hands-on experience, I know I can contribute to _____, and want to talk to you about it in person. When may we meet?"

"After reading my resume, you will know something about my background. Yet, you will still need to determine whether I am the one to help you with current problems and challenges. I would like an interview to discuss my ability to contribute."

"You can reach me at [home/alternate#] to arrange an interview. I know that your time investment in meeting with me will be repaid amply."

"Thank you for your time and consideration; I hope to hear from you shortly."

"May I call you for an interview in the next few days?"

"A brief phone call will establish whether or not we have mutual interest. Recognizing the demands of your schedule, I will make that call within the week."

Some people feel it is powerful in the closing to state a date—"I'll call you on Friday if we don't speak before"—or a date and time—"I'll call you on Friday morning at 10 A.M. if we don't speak before," when they will follow-up with a phone call. The logic is that you demonstrate that your intent is serious, that you are organized, and that you plan your time effectively (all desirable behavioral traits).

On the other hand, at least one "authority" has said that an employer would be offended by being "forced" to sit and await your call. Frankly, with thirty years of involvement in the hiring process, I have never met anyone who felt constrained by such statements. What sometimes does get noticed, though, is the person who doesn't follow through on commitments as promised. Therefore, if you use this approach, keep your promises.

FOUR TYPES OF COVER LETTERS

THERE ARE FOUR types of cover letters. The examples that follow will show you which fits your situation.

The General Cover Letter

To show you the nuts and bolts of the *Knock 'em Dead* way to building effective job-hunting letters, we'll start with an example of a general cover letter. It was created using the sample phrases from the last chapter. You, too, can create powerful cover letters with this same technique, taking a sentence from one sample and a phrase from another. Then all you have to do is make the necessary changes to personalize each document.

The following two examples have underlined text to show where I have cut and pasted a phrase from the last chapter. This is the kind of letter you would send with your resume when you do not know of a specific job opening.

James Sharpe
18 Central Park Street • Anytown, NY 14788
(516) 555-1212

October 2, 20—

Jackson Bethell, V.P. Operations
DataLink Products
621 Miller Drive
Anytown, CA 01234

Dear Jackson Bethell,

Recently I have been researching the leading local companies in data communications. My search has been for companies that are respected in the field and who provide ongoing training programs. The name of DataLink Products keeps coming up as a top company.

I am an experienced voice and data communications specialist with a substantial background in IBM environments. If you have an opening for someone in this area, you will see that my resume demonstrates a person of unusual dedication, efficiency, and drive. My experience and achievements include:

- The complete redesign of a data communications network, projected to increase efficiency company-wide some 12 percent.
- The installation and troubleshooting of a Defender II call-back security system for a dial-up network.

I enclose a copy of my resume, and look forward to examining any of the ways you feel my background and skills would benefit DataLink Products. While I prefer not to use my employer's time taking personal calls at work, with discretion I can be reached at (516) 555-1212 to initiate contact. However, I would rather you call me at _____ in the evening. Let's talk!

Yours truly,

James Sharpe

James Sharpe

JANE SWIFT
18 Central Park Street, Anytown, NY 14788
(516) 555-1212

David Doors, Director of Marketing   January 14, 20—
Martin Financial Group
1642 Rhode Island Way
Anytown, NY 01234

Dear David Doors,

I have always followed the performance of your company in *Mutual Funds Newsletter*.

Recently your notice regarding a Market Analyst in *Investor's Business Daily* caught my eye—and your company name caught my attention—your record over the last three years shows exceptional portfolio management. Because of my experience with one of your competitors, I know I could make significant contributions.

I would like to talk to you about your personnel needs and how I am able to contribute to your department's goals.

An experienced market analyst, I have an economics background (M.S. Purdue) and a strong quantitative analysis approach to market fluctuations. This combination has enabled me to consistently pick the new technology flotations that are the backbone of the growth-oriented mutual fund. For example:

I first recommended Targus Fund six years ago. More recently my clients have been strongly invested in Atlantic Horizon Growth (in the high-risk category), and Next Wave Growth and Income (for the cautious investor). Those following my advice over the last six years have consistently outperformed the market.

I know that resumes help you sort out the probables from the possibles, but they are no way to judge the personal caliber of an individual. I would like to meet with you and demonstrate that along with the credentials, I have the professional commitment that makes for a successful team player.

Yours truly,

Jane Swift

Jane Swift

The Executive Briefing

The executive briefing is a different and very effective form of cover letter. You can use it whenever you have some information about a job opening from a help-wanted ad, an online job posting, or a prior conversation. This kind of letter gets right to the point and makes life easy for the corporate recruiter. Why send an executive briefing?

1. The initial resume screener in Human Resources (HR) might not have an in-depth understanding of the job or its requirements, so the executive briefing helps match an open requirement directly to your abilities. This can be a real help to someone working on fifty or more different openings at a time.
2. Your general resume invariably needs customizing for any specific job. (Overly broad resumes are like "one-size-fits-all" clothes—one size usually fits none.) The executive briefing allows you to fill in the gaps in a succinct and helpful manner.
3. Imagine for a moment that a great opportunity comes your way, but your resume is somewhat (or more than somewhat) out of date and you have to send something out immediately to take advantage of the opportunity of a lifetime. The executive briefing allows you to bring that work history right up to date.

The executive briefing can also help you through a screening and multiple interview cycle. Let me explain: Your resume will often be somewhat general in content, and you will also be interviewed by a number of people, not all of whom can be expected to have a thorough understanding of the needs of the job—perhaps surprising but nevertheless true. When this happens, the problems begin.

A manager says, "Spend a few minutes with this candidate and tell me what you think." This means that other interviewers do not have any way to qualify you fairly and specifically for the needs of the job. While the manager will be looking for specific skills relating to projects at hand, the personnel department will be trying to match your skills to the vagaries of the job-description manual.

Also, by taking multiple copies of your resume and the briefing, carefully stapled together, you guarantee that everyone with whom you interview will have the job's specific requirements and your matching skills front and center when they sit down with you.

The executive briefing, which supplements the resume, solves the above problems with its layout. It looks like the following:

James Sharpe
18 Central Park Street • Anytown, NY 14788
(516) 555-1212

October 2, 20—

Dear Sir/Madam:

I have long thought of approaching your company, and hearing that you might have a need for someone with strong closing skills, I knew that now was the time. While my resume will provide you with a general outline of my work history, my problem-solving abilities, and some achievements, I have taken the time to list your current specific requirements and my applicable skills in those areas.

Your Requirements	My Skills
1. Management of public reference, etc.	1. Experience as head reference librarian at University of Smithtown.
2. Supervision of 14 full-time support employees.	2. Supervised support staff of 17.
3. Ability to work with larger supervisory team in planning, budgeting, and policy formation.	3. During my last year I was responsible for budget and reformation of circulation rules.
4. ALA-accredited MLS.	4. ALA-accredited MLS.
5. 3 years' experience.	5. 1 year with public library; 2 with University of Smithtown.

You will see that my attached resume provides further in-depth background. I hope this will enable you to use your time effectively today. I know that I have the skills you need, and the commitment to make a success of this opportunity, please call me at your earliest convenience.

Sincerely,

James Sharpe

James Sharpe

An executive briefing sent with a resume provides a comprehensive picture of a thorough professional, plus a personalized, fast, and easy-to-read synopsis that details exactly how you can help with an employer's current batch of problems.

The executive briefing assures that each resume you send out addresses the job's specific needs and that every interviewer at that company will be interviewing you for the same job.

The use of an executive briefing is naturally restricted to jobs you have discovered through your own efforts or seen advertised. It is obviously not appropriate when the requirements of a specific job are unavailable.

The Broadcast Letter

The broadcast letter is a simple but effective variation on the cover letter. You can use it when:

- You don't have a resume
- Your resume is inappropriate for the position
- Your resume is too dreadful to send out
- You want to try a variation on sending out a resume.

Much of the information will be culled from your resume, because the intent of the broadcast letter is to *replace* the resume. You would be well advised here to conduct an in-depth analysis of your background in much the same way you would for a resume. (You will learn more about this in Chapter 4; such an exercise is also a precursor for composing a resume, as discussed in my book *Resumes That Knock 'em Dead.*) A broadcast letter can get you into a telephone conversation with a potential employer, but that employer may still ask to see a resume. If this happens, always try to schedule the interview and bring the resume with you; the reason for this is that you do not want to further delay getting into a face-to-face conversation with the employer.

If you don't *have* a resume, you might well have to fill out one of those dreadful application forms. This requires putting your background in the format the employer wants—not the package of your choice, and, if you are like me, in some chicken scratch intelligible only to the ancient Egyptians. Consequently, I do not advise using this kind of letter as the spearhead or sole thrust of your campaign. Rather, you should use it as an integral part of the campaign in one of these ways:

- For small, highly targeted mailings to specific high-interest companies, where it works as an effective customizing technique.
- For small, highly targeted mailings to specific high-interest jobs about which you have enough detailed knowledge that such a letter would supersede the effectiveness of your resume.
- As an initial thrust, but with the more traditional cover letter and resume already in place for a back-up second mailing. In practice, the cold-mailed broadcast letter often results in a request for a resume, and other times it results in a telephone interview and subsequent invitation to a face-to-face interview—with the request that you bring a resume.
- As part of a multiple-contact approach where you are approaching a number of people within a company with personalized letters (see Chapter 6).
- As a back-up approach when your cover letter and resume don't generate the response you want from individual target companies.
- To headhunters, who, if you have the skills they're looking for, will help you to package your professional background.

Here is an example of a typical broadcast letter; you can see a whole section of them starting on page 160:

JANE SWIFT
18 Central Park Street, Anytown, NY 14788
(516) 555-1212

October 2, 20—

Dear _____ (name),

For the past seven years I have pursued an increasingly successful career in the sales profession. Among my accomplishments I include:

SALES
As a regional representative, I contributed $1,500,000, or 16 percent, of my company's annual sales. I am driven by achievement.

MARKETING
My marketing skills (based on a B.S. in marketing) enabled me to increase sales 25 percent in my economically stressed territory, at a time when colleagues were striving to maintain flat sales. Repeat business reached an all-time high. I am persistent and pay attention to detail.

PROJECT MANAGEMENT
Following the above successes, my regional model was adopted by the company. I trained and provided project supervision to the entire sales force. The following year, company sales showed a sales increase 12 percent above projections. I am a committed team player, motivated by the group's overall success.

The above was based on my firmly held zero price discounting philosophy, I don't cut margins to make a sale. It is difficult to summarize my work in a letter. The only way I can imagine providing you the opportunity to examine my credentials is for us to talk with each other. I look forward to hearing from you. Please call me at _____.

Yours sincerely,

Jane Swift

Jane Swift

Employment Agencies and Executive Recruiters

You might as well know something about headhunters right from the outset. The best way to get their attention is to give them the respect they deserve. They are, after all, the most sophisticated salespeople in the world—they and they alone sell products that talk back!

A headhunter will be only faintly amused by your exhortations "to accept the challenge" or "test your skills by finding me a job" in the moments before he or she practices hoops with your letter and the trash can. They don't have the time or inclination to indulge such whimsical ideas. So with headhunters—whether they are working for the local employment agency, a contingency, or a retained search firm—bear in mind these two rules and you won't go far wrong:

1. Tell the truth. Answer questions truthfully and you will likely receive help. Get caught in a lie and you will have established a career-long distrust with someone who possesses a very diverse and influential list of contacts.

2. Cut immediately to the chase:

   "I am forwarding my resume, because I understand you specialize in representing clients in the _____ field."

   "Please find the enclosed resume. As a specialist in the _____ field, I felt you might be interested in the skills of a _____."

   "Among your many clients there may be one or two who are seeking a person for a position as a _____."

Remember that in a cover letter sent to executive search firms and employment agencies, you should mention your salary and, if appropriate, your willingness to relocate.

Here is an example of a cover letter you might send to a corporate headhunter:

James Sharpe
18 Central Park Street • Anytown, NY 14788
(516) 555-1212

December 2, 20—

Dear Mr. O'Flynn:

I am forwarding my resume, as I understand that you specialize in the accounting profession. As you may be aware, the management structure at _____ will be reorganized in the near future. While I am enthusiastic about the future of the agency under its new leadership, I have elected to make this an opportunity for change and professional growth.

My many years of experience lend themselves to a finance management position in any medium-sized service firm, but I am open to other opportunities. Although I would prefer to remain in New York, I would entertain other areas of the country, if the opportunity warrants it. I am currently earning $65,000 a year.

I have enclosed my resume for your review. Should you be conducting a search for someone with my background at the present time or in the near future, I would greatly appreciate your consideration. I would be happy to discuss my background more fully with you on the phone or in a personal interview.

Very truly yours,

James Sharpe

James Sharpe

JS
resume attached

WHAT GOES IN, WHAT STAYS OUT

ONCE UPON A time, there were just a few set rules for writing a great job-hunting letter.

The rules of the game have changed; now more than ever, communication is a prerequisite for any job. Saying "I'm a great engineer. Give me a chance and I'll prove it to you" just doesn't cut it any more. It is no longer feasible for employers to take employees on approval, especially in a downsized workplace where employers have so much choice. Today, job skills and your professional behavior profile are under closer scrutiny than ever before. The evaluation process starts the moment you make contact—which means the content and style of your cover letter set the tone for your entire candidacy.

If there is one overriding objective for your initial cover and subsequent follow-up letters it is to grab and hold your reader's attention; the letters must work to keep your candidacy foremost in the employer's mind. You achieve this by demonstrating your awareness and possession of the learned behavioral traits that make for successful professionals and good hires.

How to Develop and Portray a Desirable Professional Profile

There are a handful of universally admired traits that make up a desirable professional profile. They are each something you can learn and apply in your career, and their application will remain a major ingredient of success throughout your work life; they are, in short, your passport to success. When reading your letter, the interviewer will search for clues to determine what kind of person you really are and what you will be like to work with; your cover letter therefore becomes a prime opportunity to set yourself apart from the competition. As you read through the following pages and see the importance of each behavioral trait, you will often recognize that you already possess and apply that particular behavior in your professional life. When this happens, I want you to come up with examples of your using that particular behavior in the execution of your duties. The examples you recall can be used in your letters, and in your answers to interviewer's questions. Then, for example, when you get asked, "So why are you different?" you will have a meaningful reply, replete with the real world illustrations that give a ring of truth to your answers. And, if it happens that you cannot come up with examples of your applying a particular behavior at work, don't worry. You have just identified an area for professional growth, and you should make every effort in the future to turn this weakness into a strength.

Personal Profile

Use these words and phrases to project a successful, healthy personal profile.

Motivation: Enthusiasm and a desire to make a difference for good with your presence, also a willingness to take the rough with the smooth, an eagerness to learn. Employers realize a motivated professional will do a better job on every assignment.

Communication Skills: Verbal, listening and written communication skills, and technological adaptedness. The ability to communicate effectively with people at all levels in a company is key to anyone's success.

Team Chemistry: Someone who takes pride in group achievement over personal aggrandizement. The employer is looking for an employee who does not get rattled, who wears a smile, and who acts with concern for the group good and without self-importance.

Energy: Someone who always gives that extra effort in the little things as well as more important matters. A person should be obviously healthy enough to maintain that energy over the length of the working week. This is a behavior where posture, appearance, and grooming also play a role.

Determination: Someone who does not back off when a problem or situation gets tough.

Confidence: Confident in the skills you have, confident in your ability to learn new skills, and confident enough to ask questions when you aren't sure. It is the confidence to look at challenges calmly, and the commitment to develop the skills and strategies necessary to fully contribute to the team's success. Confidence comes with success, and success comes with the application and interaction of each of these learnable professional behaviors.

Reliability: Showing up is half the battle; the other half is your performance on the job. Reliability means making a personal commitment to your job's success, following up by yourself and not relying on anyone else to ensure the job is done well. It also means keeping management informed.

Honesty/Integrity: Taking responsibility for your actions, both good and bad. An honest person always makes decisions in the best interest of the company, never on a whim or personal preference.

Pride: Pride in yourself as a professional and in a job well done. You always make sure the job is done to the best of your ability and in the best interests of your customer and company. On a day-to-day basis this can mean as little as making the time to pay attention to the details, rather than just getting a job off your desk and onto someone else's. When you exemplify professional pride, your employer offers trust and respect.

Dedication: Dedication to your professional excellence and being the best you can be at what you do.

Analytical Skills: Carefully weighing the pros and cons of every professional decision you make. This includes not jumping to the first or easiest solution to a problem, and being able to weigh the short- and long-term benefits of a solution against all its possible negatives.

Goal Orientation: All employers are interested in goal-oriented people, those who achieve concrete results with their actions and who strive to get the job done, rather than just filling the time allotted.

Profit Orientation: Employers are interested in just three things:

1. *Money saved:* Every penny saved by your thought and efficiency is a penny earned for the company.
2. *Time saved:* Every moment saved by your thought and efficiency enables your company to save money and make more money in the additional time available—a double bonus.
3. *Money earned:* Generating revenue is the goal of every company.

Your sensitivity to the profit goals of your employer makes you vigilant for opportunities to contribute, and your profit orientation also embraces an awareness of efficiency, and procedures.

Efficiency: Always looking for a better way, by keeping an eye open for wasted time, effort, resources, and money. Most problems have two solutions: an expensive one and one that the company would prefer to implement. Ideas of efficiency and economy engage the creative mind in ways other workers might not consider.

Procedures: Follow the chain of command. Do not implement your own "improved" procedures or organize others to do so. Procedures exist to keep the company profitable. Don't work around them. This means keeping your boss informed. Tell your boss about problems or good ideas, don't go over his or her head.

Together, these learnable behaviors spell long-term career success; they are also what you need for any future entrepreneurial success.

As these behaviors are universally admired in all professions and at all levels, it is important that you are able to communicate your awareness of their importance to prospective employers in your written communications and in your conversations. Consequently, your goal is to draw attention to your professional behavioral profile by direct statement, inference, and illustration. *Knock 'em Dead: The Ultimate Job Hunter's Resource*, by the way, will show you how to integrate these behaviors into your answers to hundreds of interview questions.

Writing a job-hunting letter is a bit like baking a cake. In most instances the ingredients are essentially the same—what determines the flavor is the order and quantity in which those ingredients are blended. There are certain ingredients that go into almost every letter, whether it is a cover, broadcast, networking, follow-up, acceptance, rejection, or resignation letter. There are others that rarely or never go in, and there are those special touches (a pinch of this, a smidgen of that) that may be included, depending on your personal accomplishments and the need your letter will satisfy.

Brief Is Beautiful

Ads and job-hunting letters have a great deal in common. The vast majority of ads in any media can be heard, watched, or read in under thirty seconds—the upper limit of the average busy consumer's attention span.

It is no coincidence that cover letters adhere to the same rules, as they too compete for attention from distracted consumers. Your letters are, after all, business communications, and business likes to get to the point.

Before getting started, good advertising copywriters (some of our society's most effective communicators), imagine themselves in the position of their target audience. They understand that their objective is to sell something, so they consider what features their product possesses and what benefits are most likely to appeal to the purchaser. For the next fifteen minutes, imagine yourself in one of your target companies. You are in the HR department on "screening" detail. Fortunately, it is a slow morning and there are only thirty resumes and cover letters that need to be read. Go straight to the example sections of this book now and read thirty examples without a break, then return to this page. You will probably feel disoriented, as if your brain has turned to a rather soggy potato salad.

This is the environment in which your letters and resumes have to function, and now you have some idea of what it feels like. Can you imagine what it would be like to do this every day for a living? Of course you had it easy, the letters you read weren't attached to resumes, which would have made the task even more mind-numbing. The letters you read were demonstrably effective, as they helped land real people real jobs. Even so, you probably felt a little punch-drunk at the end of the exercise, but you learned a very valuable lesson: Brevity, clarity, and punch are beautiful.

The first thing you have to do is understand why some people get hired over others. Every hire is made on a job applicant's ability to satisfy these five concerns of the employer:

1. Ability and suitability.
2. Willingness to go the extra yard, to take the rough with the smooth.
3. Manageability and teamwork: taking direction and constructive input for the good of the team.
4. Problem-solving attitude.
5. A comprehensive and supportive behavioral profile.

An understanding of these five secrets of the hire should always be in mind when writing job-hunting letters.

A Question of Money

Recruitment advertisements sometimes request salary information, either current salary or salary history. With the right letter you will rarely be denied at least a telephone interview, even if you do omit your salary history. Nevertheless, there may be factors that make you feel obliged to include something. I have heard that some personnel people consider the word "negotiable" annoying, though rarely grounds for refusing to talk an applicant.

If you choose to share information about salary, it should go in the cover letter or be attached to the cover letter, never in the resume itself. This is because your resume may be kept in a database for years and thereby typecast you as, say, an entry-level professional in the eyes of that company's computer. When desired salary is requested, don't restrict yourself to one figure; instead, give yourself a range with a spread between the low and the high end. This dramatically increases your chances of "clicking onto" the available salary range that is always determined for every position.

When "salary history" is requested, the prospective employer is usually looking for a consistent progression. Gaps or significant cuts could raise red flags. If you have nothing to hide and have a steadily progressive earnings history, spell it out on a separate sheet. When references get checked, salary and dates of employment always get verified. However, it is usually only for higher level positions (or those handling money) that references prior to your current employer are checked.

Many of us have less than perfect salary histories for any number of perfectly valid reasons. Consequently, we don't want to release these figures unless we are there in person to explain away the seeming anomalies. In these instances the matter is best skirted in the cover letter itself.

Here is one way to address the topic of money in your letters should you feel it is necessary to do so. You will find other examples later in the book.

"Depending on the job and the professional development environment, my salary requirements are in the \$_____ to \$_____ range, with appropriate benefits. I would also be willing to relocate for the right opportunity with your company."

Telephone and E-Mail

Once you have determined a primary contact number for your job hunt, you must ensure that it will be answered at all times. There is no point in mounting a job-hunting campaign if prospective and eager employers can never reach you. Invest in a voice mail system as offered by your telephone company. Keep the message businesslike, and once recorded, listen carefully to the message for diction, tone of voice, and recording quality. Are you impressed? Does it present you as a clear-spoken, confident professional?

Always list your e-mail address immediately beneath your telephone number.

Ingredients: A Basic Checklist

When you examine the sample letters in Chapter 8 you will note that they:

- Address a person, not a title . . . and whenever possible, a person who is in a position to make a hiring decision.
- Are tailored to the reader of the letter as far as is practical, to show that you have done your homework.
- Show concern, interest, and pride for your profession.
- Demonstrate energy and enthusiasm.
- Clearly establish why you are writing and the outcome you hope to achieve.
- Maintain a balance between professionalism and friendliness.
- Whenever possible include information relevant to the job you are seeking.
- Ask for the next step in the process clearly and without apology or arrogance.

Now take another few moments to browse through the sample section to examine the variety of types of letters you have to work with—there are enough examples to help you maximize both the volume of interviews you generate and the value of the offers you receive. With all of these examples, you needn't be restricted to one canned letter of your own. By using that highlighter as you go through the book, it will subsequently be a breeze to customize letters of your own for any circumstance.

ASSEMBLING YOUR COVER LETTER

THERE IS A fine line between pride in achievement and insufferable arrogance when listing experiences and behaviors in your work life that will help advance your candidacy.

You need solid content to put in your cover letters, and that can take a little thought. To make this job easier, complete the questionnaire on the next couple of pages. Do not skip this exercise; it will give you the meat for your letters and will be of real help later, when the time comes to sell yourself at the interview.

Answer every part of every question for every job you have held, starting with the most recent and working backward.

Take some time over this exercise and go back carefully over your past jobs. It isn't going to be necessary to craft *Knock 'em Dead* sentences from scratch;

you'll be able to cut and paste from the samples and then insert your answers to the following questions for the meat—and your end result will be a unique and arresting letter.

The entirely original parts of your letter will be your contributions and achievements. That means you need to spend adequate time in this period of preparation. Do not worry about crafting proper sentences, as whatever you jot down here will be polished later on in the process.

About the Questionnaire

This questionnaire was taken from the comprehensive "Skills Analysis" questionnaire in *Resumes That Knock 'em Dead*. So if you are preparing a resume, you will be working toward that end simultaneously.

Questionnaire
FOR EACH OF YOUR PREVIOUS JOBS:
List three to five major duties. (One example: *Increase sales and margins in perishable goods distribution.*)

_____

_____

_____

FOR EACH OF THESE DUTIES:
What special skills or knowledge did you need to perform each of these tasks? (One example: *Thorough knowledge of entire sales cycle of perishable goods.*)

_____

_____

_____

What were the biggest challenges you faced in each of these five areas? (One example: *Overcoming the traditional way of doing things.*)

_____

_____

_____

What were your solutions, and the result of those solutions in each of the five areas? (One example: *With management approval, implemented approach myself as a test. Once the #'s were in, cost and time savings spoke for themselves.*)

_____

_____

_____

What were your greatest achievements in each of these areas? Think in terms of money made (or saved) or time saved for the employer; think efficiency, economy and procedures. If this is not possible, tie your achievements in other ways to the benefit of the company. (One example: *A telemarketing program saved ten cents on cost per sale on sales volume of two million units.*)

_____

_____

_____

What verbal or written comments, if any, did your peers or managers make about your contributions in each of these areas? (One example: *Boss said, "You really get results when the chips are down."*)

_____

_____

_____

What was your greatest contribution in each area of responsibility you made as a team player? (One example: *We saved time, money and we all had happier customers with fresher produce, and we had fatter paychecks as well.*)

_____

_____

_____

What desirable behavioral traits did you demonstrate in each area to get the job done? (One example: *Analytical skills, determination, motivation, goal orientation, adherence to systems and procedures.* Note how this last one ties everything back to your professional behaviors.)

_____

_____

_____

Once you complete the questionnaire, it's time to put your responses to work for you.

Creating Punchy Sentences

Concise, punchy sentences grab attention.

The most grammatically correct sentences in the world won't get you interviews (except perhaps as a copy editor—and then not always) because such prose can read as though every breath of life has been squeezed out of it.

Sentences gain power with verbs that demonstrate an action. For example, one professional—with a number of years at the same law firm in a clerical position—had written:

> *"I learned to manage a computerized database."*

Pretty ordinary, right? Well, after discussion of the circumstances that surrounded learning how to manage the computerized database, certain exciting facts emerged. By using action verbs and an awareness of employer interests, this sentence was charged up and given more punch. Not only that, but for the first time the writer fully understood the value of her contributions, which greatly enhanced her self-confidence for interviews:

> *"I analyzed and determined the need for automation of an established law office. I was responsible for hardware and software selection, installation, and loading all the data. Within one year, I had achieved a fully automated office. This saved forty hours a week."*

Notice how the verbs show that things happened when she was around the office. These action verbs and phrases add an air of direction, efficiency, and accomplishment to every cover letter. Succinctly, they tell the reader what you did and how well you did it.

Rewrite each of your query answers using action verbs to punch them up. To help you in the process, here are over 175 action verbs you can use. This list is just a beginning. Every word processing program has a thesaurus; type in any one of these words and get more choices for each entry.

accomplished	consolidated	explained	maintained	remodeled
achieved	contained	extracted	managed	repaired
acted	contracted	fabricated	marketed	represented
adapted	contributed	facilitated	mediated	researched
addressed	controlled	familiarized	moderated	restored
administered	coordinated	fashioned	monitored	restructured
advanced	corresponded	focused	motivated	retrieved
advised	counseled	forecast	negotiated	revitalized
allocated	created	formulated	operated	saved
analyzed	critiqued	founded	organized	scheduled
appraised	cut	generated	originated	schooled
approved	decreased	guided	overhauled	screened
arranged	delegated	headed up	oversaw	set
assembled	demonstrated	identified	performed	shaped
assigned	designed	illustrated	persuaded	solidified
assisted	developed	implemented	planned	solved
attained	devised	improved	prepared	specified
audited	diagnosed	increased	presented	stimulated
authored	directed	indoctrinated	prioritized	streamlined
automated	dispatched	influenced	processed	strengthened
balanced	distinguished	informed	produced	summarized
budgeted	diversified	initiated	programmed	supervised
built	drafted	innovated	projected	surveyed
calculated	edited	inspected	promoted	systemized
catalogued	educated	installed	provided	tabulated
chaired	eliminated	instigated	publicized	taught
clarified	enabled	instituted	published	trained
classified	encouraged	instructed	purchased	translated
coached	engineered	integrated	recommended	traveled
collected	enlisted	interpreted	reconciled	trimmed
compiled	established	interviewed	recorded	upgraded
completed	evaluated	introduced	recruited	validated
composed	examined	invented	reduced	worked
computed	executed	launched	referred	wrote
conceptualized	expanded	lectured	regulated	
conducted	expedited	led	rehabilitated	

Varying Sentence Structure

Good writers are at their best when they write short punchy sentences. As a rule, keep your sentences under about 20 words; a good average is around 15. If your sentence is longer than the 20 mark, change it. Either shorten it by restructuring or make two sentences out of one. However, you will want to avoid choppiness, so try to vary the length of sentences when you can.

You can also start with a short phrase ending in a colon:

- Followed by bullets of information.
- Each one supporting the original phrase.

All of these techniques are designed to enliven the reading process, for readers who always have too much to read and too little time. An example follows.

Analyzed and determined need for automation of an established law office:

- *Responsible for hardware and software selection.*
- *Coordinated installation of six workstations.*
- *Trained users.*
- *Full automation achieved in one year.*
- *Savings to company: $25,000.*

K.I.S.S. (Keep It Simple, Stupid)

Just as you use short sentences, use common action words. They communicate quickly and are easy to understand. Stick to short, simple words whenever possible (without sounding infantile).

Persuading your readers to take action is challenging, because many people in different companies will see your letters and make judgments based on them. This means you must keep industry "jargon" to a minimum (especially in the initial contact letters—covers, broadcast, and the like). There will be those who understand the intricacies and technicalities of your profession—but unfortunately, many of the initial screeners do not. You'll need to share your specialist wisdom with the nonspecialists first, before you can expect to reach your professional peers.

Short words for short sentences help make short, gripping paragraphs: good for short attention spans!

Within your short paragraphs and short sentences, beware of name-dropping and acronyms, such as "I worked for Dr. A. Witherspoon in Sys. Gen. SNA 2.31." Such statements are too restricted to have validity outside the small circle of specialists to whom they speak. Unless you work in a highly technical field, avoid doing this. Your letters demand the widest possible appeal, yet they need to remain personal in tone. (Of course, you don't want your letters to sound like they're from Publishers Clearing House, either.)

Voice and Tense

The voice you use for different letters depends on a few important factors:

- Getting a lot said in a small space.
- Packaging yourself in the best way.
- Being factual.
- Using what feels right to you.

The voice you use in your letters should be consistent throughout. There is considerable disagreement among the "experts" about the best voice, and each of the following options has both champions and detractors.

Sentences in all types of cover letters can be truncated (up to a point), by omitting pronouns and articles such as *I, you, he, she, it, they, a,* or *the*:

"Automated office."

In fact, many authorities recommend the dropping of pronouns as a technique that both saves space and allows you to brag about yourself without seeming boastful. It gives the impression of another party writing about you. Others feel that to use the personal pronoun—"I automated the office . . ."—is naive, unprofessional, and smacks of boasting.

At the same time, some recommend that you write in the first person because it makes you sound more human.

"I automated the office."

In short, there are no hard and fast rules—they can all work given the many unique circumstances you will face in any given job hunt. Use whatever style works best for you. If you do use the personal pronoun, try not to use it in every sentence—it gets a little monotonous, and it can make you sound like an egomaniac. The mental focus should not be on "I" but on "you," the person with whom you are communicating.

A nice variation is to use a first-person voice throughout the letter and then a final few words in the third person. Make sure these final words appear in the form of an attributed quote, as an insight to your value:

> *"She managed the automation procedure, and we didn't experience a moment of downtime."*
>
> — *Jane Ross, Department Manager*

Don't mistake the need for professionalism in your job-hunting letters with stiff-necked formality. The most effective tone is one that mixes the conversational and the formal, just the way we do in our offices and on our jobs. The only overriding rule is to make the letter readable, so that the reader can see a human being shining through the pages.

Length

The standard length for a cover letter is usually one page, or the equivalent length for e-mails. Subsequent letters stemming from verbal communications—whether over the telephone or face-to-face—should also adhere to the one-page rule, but can run to two pages if complexity of content demands it. Generally speaking, job-hunting letters should be held to one page, and no job-hunting letter should exceed two pages. Break this rule at your peril; to do so will brand you as a windbag incapable of getting to the point.

Having said this, I should acknowledge that all rules are made to be broken. Occasionally a three-page letter might be required, but only in one of the following instances:

1. You have been contacted directly by an employer about a specific position and have been asked to present data for that particular opportunity.
2. An executive recruiter who is representing you determines that the exigencies of a particular situation warrant a dossier of such length. (Often such a letter and resume will be prepared exclusively—or with considerable input—by the recruiter.)

You'll find that thinking too much about length considerations will hamper the writing process. Think instead of the story you have to tell, then layer fact upon fact until your tale is told. Use your words and the key phrases from this book to craft the message of your choice. When *that* is done you can go back and ruthlessly cut it to the bone.

Ask yourself these questions:

- Can I cut out any paragraphs?
- Can I cut out any sentences?
- Can I cut out any superfluous words?
- Where have I repeated myself?

If in doubt, cut it out—leave nothing but facts and action words! If at the end you find too much has been cut, you'll have the additional pleasure of reinstating your deathless prose.

Your Checklist

There are really two proofing steps in the creation of a polished cover letter. The first happens now. You want to make sure that all the things that should be included are—and that all the things that shouldn't, aren't. The final proofing is done before printing. *Warning:* It is easy, in the heat of the creative moment, to miss crucial components or mistakenly include facts that give the wrong emphasis. Check all your letters against these points:

Contact Information

- The pertinent personal data (name, address, zip code, personal telephone number, and e-mail address) is on every page.
- Your current business number is omitted unless it is absolutely necessary and safe to include it.
- If your letter is more than one page long, each page is numbered "page 1 of 2," etc., and all the pages are stapled together. Remember the accepted way of stapling business communications: one staple in the top left-hand corner.

Objectives

- Does your letter state why you are writing?
- Is the letter tied to the target company and job (if you have details)?
- Does it address points of relevance, such as skills that apply from the ad or agenda items addressed during a conversation?
- Does it include reference to your professional behavioral profile?

- Is your most relevant and qualifying experience prioritized to lend strength to your letter?
- Have you avoided wasting more space than required with employer names and addresses?
- Have you omitted any reference to reasons for leaving a particular job? Reasons for change might be important at the interview, but they are not relevant at this point. Use this precious space to sell, not to justify.
- Unless they have been specifically requested, have you removed all references to past, current, or desired salaries?
- Have you removed reference to your date of availability? If you aren't available at their convenience, why are you wasting their time?
- If your major is mentioned, is it relevant to the advertisement?
- Do you mention your highest educational attainment?
- Have you avoided listing irrelevant responsibilities or job titles?
- Have you given examples of your contributions, your achievements, and the problems you have successfully solved during your career?
- Have you avoided poor focus by eliminating all extraneous information? ("Extraneous" means anything that doesn't relate to your job objective, such as captaining the tiddlywinks team in kindergarten.)
- Is the letter long enough to whet the reader's appetite for more details, yet short enough not to satisfy that hunger?
- Have you let the obvious slip in, like heading your letter "Letter of Application" in big bold letters? If so, cut it out.

Style

- Substitute short words for long words, and one word where previously there were two.
- Keep your average sentence to less than twenty-five words. Break longer sentences into two, if they cannot be shortened.
- Keep every paragraph under five lines, with most paragraphs shorter.
- Make sure your sentences begin with or contain, wherever possible, powerful action verbs and phrases.

THE FINAL PRODUCT

CHAPTER · CHAPTER · CHAPTER · CHAPTER · CHAPTER · CHAPTER

5

STYLE—so easy to see but so difficult to define—usually has a distinct look and feel. Here are some of the basics you should keep in mind when creating your own stylish and professional job-hunting letters.

Layout

The average cover letter arrives on a desk along with many others, all of which require reading. You can expect your letter to get a maximum of thirty seconds of attention, and that's only if it's accessible to the reader's eye.

The biggest complaints about job-hunting letters that nosedive into the trashcan in record time are:

- They have too much information crammed into the space and are therefore hard on the eyes.

- The layout is unorganized, illogical, and uneven. (In other words, it looks shoddy and slapdash—and who wants an employee like that?)
- In the age of spell checkers, there are no excuses for misspellings, and none are acceptable.

Fonts

Choose businesslike fonts; stay away from scriptlike fonts. They may sometimes look more visually exciting, but the goal is to be kind to the tired eyes of the reader who is plowing through stacks of resumes when he or she gets your message. Capitalized copy is also harder to read and causes eyestrain.

How to Brighten the Page

Once you decide on a font, stick with it. More than one font on a page can look confusing. You can do plenty to liven up the visual impact of the page within the variations of the font you have chosen. You can, of course, use a different font for the contact information as you create the letterhead.

Most fonts come in a selection of regular, bold, italic, and bold italic. Good job-hunting letters will take judicious advantage of this: You can vary the impact of key words with italics, underlined phrases, and boldface or capitalized titles for additional emphasis. There are a lot of options, but these options won't work with e-mail, as the e-mail won't retain your formatting. There is a good lesson here: you can brighten the page, but the words alone must be able to carry your message!

You will notice from the occasional example in this book that letters will use more than one typographical variation of the same font. For example, a writer who wants to emphasize personality traits might italicize only those words or phrases that describe these aspects. That way the message gets a double fixing in the reader's mind. You will also notice powerful letters that employ no typographic pyrotechnics and still knock 'em dead! In the end, it's your judgment call.

If you are crafting letters that are general in content, you will need to use the mail merge feature of the word-processing program. What this does is fill in the blanks: "Dear _____" becomes "Dear Fred Jones."

Dear *Fred Jones*:
Your *January 11, 2004* ad in the *Chicago Tribune* described a need for an accountant.

All this does is state loud and clear that this is a form letter sent, in all likelihood, to hundreds. Why needlessly detract from your chances of being taken seriously?

Another no-no is the use of "clip art" to brighten the page. Those little quill pens and scrolls may look nifty to you, but they look amateurish to the rest of the business world.

Proofing and Printing

It simply isn't possible for even the most accomplished professional writer to go from draft to print, so don't try it. Your pride of authorship will blind you to blemishes you can't afford to miss.

You need some distance from your creative efforts to give yourself detachment and objectivity. There is no hard and fast rule about how long it should take to come up with the finished product. Nevertheless, if you think you have finished, leave it alone at least overnight. Then come back to it fresh. You'll read it almost as if it were meeting your eyes for the first time.

Before you print your letters make sure that your writing is as clear as possible. Three things guaranteed to annoy cover letter readers are incorrect spelling, poor grammar, and improper syntax. Go back and check all these areas. If you think syntax has something to do with the IRS, you'd better get a third party involved. Here's a practical solution that one job seeker found: She visited the library, waited for a quiet moment, and got into a conversation with the librarian, who subsequently agreed to give her letter the old once-over. (Everyone loves to show off special knowledge!)

The quality of paper always makes an impression on the person holding the page. The folks receiving your letter see dozens of others every day, and you need every trick available to make your point. Compared to printer paper, good quality paper sends an almost subliminal message about attention to detail. By the way, if an emergency demands you send a letter by fax, remember to follow it up with a copy on regular paper. This is because everything you send is likely to end up in your "candidate dossier." A fax can obliterate important parts of any communication.

Although you should not skimp on paper costs, neither should you buy or be talked into the most expensive available. Indeed, in some fields (health care and education come to mind), too ostentatious a paper can cause a negative impression. The idea is to create a feeling of understated quality. You can get 500 sheets of excellent paper for about $20.

As for color, white is considered the prime choice. Cream is also acceptable, and I'm assured that some of the pale pastel shades can be both attractive and effective. These pastel shades were originally used to make letters and resumes stand out. But now everyone is so busy standing out of the crowd in Magenta and Passionate Puce that you just might find it more original to stand out in white or cream. White and cream are straightforward, no-nonsense colors. They say BUSINESS.

It is a given that cover letter stationery should always match the color and weight of your envelopes and resume. To send a white cover letter—even if it is your personal stationery—with a cream resume detracts from the statement you are trying to make. In fact, when you print the finished letter, you should print some letterhead sheets at the same time and in the same quantity. You don't need to get too fancy; base your design on other stationery you've been impressed with.

All subsequent letters should be on the same paper. Your written communication will be filed. Then, prior to the hiring decision, the hiring manager will review all the data on all the short-list candidates. Your coordinated written campaign will paint the picture of a thorough professional. The sum of your letters will be more powerful as a whole simply because they exist as a coordinated package.

Envelopes Send Messages, Too

What goes on the envelope affects the power of the message inside. Over the last six months, I've asked a number of line managers and human resources professionals about the appearance of the envelopes they receive. Did it affect the likelihood of the letter being read and if so, with what kind of anticipation? Here's what I heard:

> *"I never open letters with printed pressure-sensitive labels; I regard them as junk mail, and I simply don't have the time in my life for ill-targeted marketing attempts."*

> *"I never open anything addressed to me by title but not by name."*

> *"I will open envelopes addressed to me by misspelled name, but I am looking with a jaundiced eye already; and that eye is keen for other examples of sloppiness."*

"I always open correctly typed envelopes that say personal and/or confidential, but if they're not, I feel conned. I don't hire con artists."

"I always open neatly handwritten envelopes. What's more, I open them first, unless there's another letter that is obviously a check."

There are those who recommend enclosing a stamped self-addressed envelope to increase the chances of response. You can do this, but don't expect many people in the corporate world to take advantage of your munificence. I have never known this tactic to yield much in the way of results. On the whole, I think you are better advised to save the stamp money and spend it on a follow-up telephone call. Only conversations lead to interviews. I have never heard of a single interview being set up exclusively through the mail.

(*Neat trick department*: I recently received an intriguing resume and cover letter; both had attached to the top right-hand corner a circular red sticker. It worked as a major exclamation point; I was impressed. I was even more impressed when I realized that once this left my hands, no other reader would know exactly who attached the sticker, but they *would* pay special attention to the content because of it. Nice technique—don't let the whole world in on it, though.)

Appearance

Remember that the first glance and feel of your letter can make a powerful impression. Go through this checklist before you seal the envelope:

- Does the paper measure 8½" by 11", and is it of good quality, between 16 and 25 pounds in weight?
- Have you used white, off-white, or cream-colored paper?
- Did you make sure to use only one side of the page?
- Are your name, address, and telephone number on every page?
- If more than one page, have you paginated your cover letter: "1 of 2" at the bottom of the page and so on?
- Are the pages stapled together? Remember, one staple in the top left-hand corner is the accepted protocol.

THE PLAN
OF ATTACK

GREAT COVER, broadcast, and follow-up letters won't get you a job by sitting on your desk like rare manuscripts. You have to do something with them.

Even a company that isn't officially hiring can still be expected (based on national averages) to experience a 14 percent turnover in staff in the course of a year. In other words, every company has openings *sometimes*, and any one of those openings could have your name on it.

The problem is, you won't have the chance to pick the very best opportunity unless you check them all out. Every intelligent job hunter will use a six-tiered approach to cover all the bases, including:

- Internet job postings
- Newspaper advertisements
- Personal and professional networking
- Direct-researched opportunities
- Employment agencies and recruiters
- Business and trade publications

Online Job Postings

Here is where the Internet can play an especially useful role. There are thousands of job sites that carry help-wanted advertising, called "job postings" in Internet speak; almost every one of these sites has a resume bank. When you place your resume in a resume bank, it is available for view by any employer or headhunter. So long as there is a privacy feature to protect your identity, this is a very viable marketing tool.

Here's how to use them to greatest effect.

Visit the job sites—there's a good selection in Appendix B at the end of this book—and search for appropriate job openings. Most of these job sites have a feature called an "e-mail alert." The alert allows you to identify the type of work you are seeking and receive an e-mail from the site every time a suitable job is advertised by one of their clients. You don't want these e-mails to come to you indiscriminately at work, so be sure to use your personal e-mail address.

The on-site resume banks will work well for you too. From an employer's point of view, these resume banks are like big fish tanks. The fishing analogy works for you too; your resume in resume banks is like having a baited hook in the water while you go about your business. Resume banks often trash your resume after 90 days, so if you are looking longer than this you will need to go back and reload. It is not a bad idea to keep your resume posted online as an ongoing career management tool; it will keep you aware of who is looking for what and how much they are paying and will keep your finger on the pulse of the job market. At the very least you will always know what skills are in demand; beyond that you don't have to interview for those jobs, and if you do, you don't have to accept the offers, but overall you will be in far greater control of your professional destiny. If you are writing as a result of an online job posting, you should mention both the Web site and the date you found it on:

"I read your job posting on your company's Web site on January 5th and felt I had to respond . . ."

"Your online job posting regarding a _____ on _____.com caught my eye, and your company name caught my attention."

"This e-mail, and my attached resume, are in response to your job posting on _____."

Help-Wanted Advertisements

A first step for many is to go to the want ads and do a mass mailing. Bear in mind, there should be a method to your madness when you do this. Remember, if it is the first idea that comes to *your* mind, hitting the want ads will be at the front of everyone else's thoughts, too.

A single help-wanted advertisement can draw hundreds of responses. The following ideas might be helpful:

- Most newspapers have an employment edition every week (usually Sunday, although sometimes midweek), when, in addition to their regular advertising, they have a major drive for help-wanted ads. Make sure you always read this edition of your local paper.
- So-called authorities on the topic will tell you not to rely on the want ads—that they don't work. Rockinghorse droppings! Want ads don't work only if you are too dumb to know how to use them. Look for back issues. Just because a company is no longer advertising does not necessarily mean that the slot has been filled. The employer may well have become disillusioned—and is now using a professional recruiter to work on the position. They may have filled the position; perhaps the person never started work or simply did not work out in the first few months. Maybe they hired someone who did work out well and now they want another person for a similar position. When you go back into the want ads you'll find untold opportunities awaiting you, and instead of competition from 150 other job hunters responding to this Sunday's want ad there may be just one or two people vying for the slot.

I had a letter from a *Knock 'em Dead* reader recently who told me he had landed a $90,000 job from a seven-month-old want ad he came across in a pile of newspapers in his father-in-law's garage! (You see? There is a use for in-laws, after all.)

- In many instances jobs are available but just aren't being advertised. It's what the press refers to as the hidden job market. Likewise, in some high-demand occupations where want ads aren't famous for drawing the right caliber of professional, the employer may only run one or two major "institutional" ads a year for that type of position.
- Cross-check the categories. Don't rely solely on those ads seeking your specific job title. For example, let's say you are a graphic artist looking for a job in advertising. You should flag all advertising or public relations agencies with any kind of need. If they are actively hiring at the moment, logic will tell you that their employment needs are not restricted to that particular title.

If you are writing as the result of a newspaper advertisement, you should mention both the publication and the date. Do not abbreviate advertisement to "ad" unless space demands, and remember to underline or italicize the publication's title:

> *"I read your advertisement in the* Daily Gotham *on October 6th for a _____ and, after researching your company, felt I had to write . . ."*

> *": Ref: Your advertisement in the* Columbus Dispatch *on Sunday the 8th of November."*

> *"Dear _____:*
> *As you compare your requirements for the above mentioned position with my attached resume, you will see that my entire background matches your requirements."*

> *"Your notice regarding a _____ in _____ caught my eye, and your company name caught my attention."*

> *"This letter and attached resume are in response to your advertisement in _____."*

Networking

Networking is one of those dreadful words from the 1970s that unfortunately is so entrenched we might as well learn to live with it. I'd prefer however, that you think of it as professional connectedness, as you'll see over the coming paragraphs.

The danger with the traditional concept of networks is that once you are comfortably networking among friends and acquaintances, you might unconsciously derail your job hunt by ignoring other and possibly more fruitful avenues of exploration for job opportunities. An effective job hunt is more than writing to and shooting the breeze with old cronies on the telephone. Besides, you will often discover that your network is not as comprehensive as you might have wished.

The important thing for any professional to grasp is that to have a friend you must be a friend. Just because you worked with someone five years ago, and haven't spoken to them since doesn't mean they still regard you as a friend. From personal experience and surveys through my own professional networks, I can confirm that my following conclusions on connectivity are shared by just about everyone else.

- To those requests from people I didn't know, I asked for a resume (of course, if they had an introduction or were fellow members of an association, things would be different). If I received it in good time with a thoughtfully prepared accompanying letter, I would give that person help if I could.
- To those requests from people with an introduction from someone I liked and respected, I gave time and consideration and, wherever possible, assistance.
- To those requests from friends, people I had worked with at one time and *who had kept in touch* since we had worked together, I stopped everything and went through my Rolodex. I provided leads, made calls on their behalf, and I insisted they keep in touch. I also initiated follow-up calls myself on behalf of these people.
- To those requests from people who regarded themselves as friends but who had not maintained contact, or who had only reestablished contact when they wanted something, I looked through the Rolodex once but for some reason was unable to find anything. I wished them the best of luck. "Sorry I couldn't help you. If something comes to mind, I'll be sure to call."

Nothing works like a personal recommendation from a fellow professional—and you get that best by *being* a fellow professional—by being connected to your profession and the professionals within it. It is no accident that successful people in all fields know each other—they helped each other get that way, because they stayed in touch.

If you are going to use business colleagues and personal friends in your job hunt, don't mess up and do it half-heartedly. We live in a very mobile society, so you shouldn't restrict yourself to family, friends, and colleagues just where you are looking. Everyone can help—even Aunt Matilda in Manila: Maybe she just happens to have had her cousin's wife's brother, who is a senior scientist at IBM, as her house guest for a month last summer and he is now forever in her debt for the vacation of a lifetime. Maybe not, but still, people know people, and they know people not just here but all over. Sit and think for a few minutes; you will be amazed at the people *you* know all over the country. Every one of them has a similar network.

Here are some tips for writing letters (and making calls) asking for assistance. If you feel awkward writing a letter to certain contacts, use these guidelines as a basis for the telephone conversation you'll have instead.

1. Establish connectivity. Recall the last memorable contact you had or someone in common that you have both spoken to recently.

2. Tell them why you are writing: "It's time for me to make a move; I just got laid off with a thousand others and I'm taking a couple of days to catch up with old friends."

3. Ask for advice and guidance: "Who do you think are the growing companies in the area today?" "Could you take a look at my resume for me? I really need an objective opinion and I've always respected your viewpoint." Don't ask specifically, "Can you hire me?" or "Can your company hire me?"

4. Don't rely on a contact with a particular company to get you into that company. Mount and execute your own plan of attack. No one has the same interest as you in putting bread on your table.

5. Let them know what you are open for. They will invariably want to help, but you have to give them a framework within which to target their efforts.

6. Say you hope you'll get to see each other again soon—and do it.

7. When you do get help, say thank you. And if you get it verbally, follow it up in writing. The impression is indelible, and it just might get you another lead.

8. You never know who your friends are. You will be surprised at how someone you always regarded as a real pal won't give you the time of day and how someone you never thought of as a friend will go above and beyond the call of duty for you.

9. Whether they help you or not, let them know when you get situated, and maintain contact in one form or another at least once a year. A career is for a long time. It might be next week or a decade from now when a

group of managers (including one of your personal network) are talking about filling a new position and the first thing they will do is say "Who do we know?" That could be you . . . if you establish "top-of-the-mind awareness" now and maintain it.

If you are writing as the result of a referral, say so and quote the person's name if appropriate:

"Our mutual colleague, John Stanovich, felt my skills and abilities would be valuable to your company . . ."

"The manager of your San Francisco branch, Pamela Bronson, has suggested I contact you regarding the opening for a _____."

"I received your name from Henry Charles, the branch manager of the Savannah Bank last week, and he suggested I contact you. In case the resume he forwarded is caught up in the mail, I enclose another."

"Arthur Gold, your office manager and my neighbor, thought I should contact you about the upcoming opening in your accounting department."

Direct-Research Contacts

The Internet is a most comprehensive job-hunting resource, although by no means a resource that you can rely on exclusively. There are job sites that provide a wide array of services. Careerbuilder.com is an excellent example of such a site. This site, like many others, features a job-search tool that allows you to search other job sites' job banks simultaneously, provides descriptions and links to thousands of U.S. companies, has comprehensive salary surveys in all fields, provides free resume posting, and has many other useful tools. Chapter 6 on using the Internet and Appendix B on job-hunting resources will give you plenty of information for making the most of online options.

Most companies are also listed in one of the reference sources in your library. Take the time to do library research and you will discover job opportunities that 90 percent of your professional competitors never dreamed existed. The business reference section can give you access to numerous research books that can help:

- Standard and Poor's
- The Directory of Directories

- State Directory of Manufacturers
- Contacts Influential

Again, the reference librarian will be pleased to help you make good use of the library's resources, and may also lead you to other productive reference works. Search each of the appropriate reference works for every company within the scope of your search that also falls within your geographic boundaries. Not every library has every book, so you may not find all of the reference books relevant to your search. However, almost all libraries belong to inter-library lending systems, so be sure to ask the reference librarian for help if you cannot find the book you need.

Your goal is to identify and build personalized dossiers on the companies in your chosen geographic area. Do not be judgmental about what and who they might appear to be: You are fishing for possible job openings, so cast your net wide and list them all. To this end you should also check out local Yellow Pages, which list smaller local companies. Don't turn your nose up at this, because the majority of all job growth in America is in companies with 100 employees or less. Only if you present yourself as a candidate for all available opportunities in your geographic area of search will you maximize your chances of landing the best possible opportunity.

If you are 50 plus and experiencing age discrimination, the smaller companies (where most of the job growth is anyway) are far more likely to feel the need for an experienced hand.

Unfortunately, no single reference work is ever complete. Their very size and scope mean that most are at least a little out of date at publication time. Also, no single reference work lists every company. Because you don't know what company has the very best job for you, you need to research as many businesses in your area as possible, and therefore you will have to look through numerous reference books.

Copy all the relevant information for each company. You'll want to include the names of the company's president and all other management names and titles, a description of the complete lines of company services and/or products, the size of the company, and the locations of its various branches. Of course, if you find other interesting information, copy it down, by all means. For instance, you might come across information on growth or shrinkage in a particular area of a company; or you might read about recent acquisitions the company has made. Write it all down.

All this information will help you target potential employers and stand out in different way: Your knowledge will create a favorable impression when you first contact the company; that you made an effort is noticed and sets you apart from other applicants who don't bother. The combination says that you respect the company, the opportunity, and the interviewer; combined, these perceptions help say that you are a different quality of job candidate.

All your efforts have an obvious short-term value in helping you with job interviews and offers. Who would *you* interview and subsequently hire? The person who knows nothing about your company, or the person who knows everything and shows enthusiasm with that knowledge?

Your efforts also have long-term value, because you are building a personalized reference work of your industry/specialty/profession that will get you off to a running start the next time you wish to make a job change.

Purchasing Mailing Lists

Posting your resume online is a useful technique, although the blasting of your resume across the Internet has far from lived up to its hype. And nowadays when everyone is delivering everything by e-mail it might just be the time to think about a serious traditional mail campaign to support (but not as the sole or main thrust of your job-hunting campaign) your other job-hunting activities. You can put together your own lists of people to pitch your resume to, or you can purchase mailing lists from mailing list companies; the lists themselves aren't expensive, and with a little research you may be able to find one appropriate to your needs. A good list would be the one for membership of your professional association (more on this in a minute). These lists can be broken down for you by title, geography, zip code—all sorts of ways. They are affordable, too; usually about $100 for 1,000 addresses. To contact a broker, just look in your Yellow Pages under "mailing list brokers/compilers."

If you want the most comprehensive source catalog, call the Direct Marketing Association at (212) 768-7277. Ask for the publications department; for $30 you can get the List Brokerage Directory. This is the single most comprehensive source of mailing lists available, but it might be way more than your situation demands, so check it out at the library first. With compilations of specialists in every conceivable area, this directory can certainly lead you toward the right list.

As we have noted, even the most up-to-date lists and directories are out of date by the time they get to you, so if you don't have Internet access, it is a good investment of time to call and verify that Joe Schmoe, VP of Engineering, is still there. Apart from the obvious goal of sending any type of mail to the right person, if Joe is no longer there you may be able to find out where he went. If so, you'll have uncovered another opportunity for yourself.

A serious direct mail campaign might have a place in some campaigns, if the message is good and if the list you build or buy is accurate, and, just as importantly, if you address the envelopes by hand rather than use preprinted labels.

Associations

You're a member of an appropriate professional association, aren't you? If not, you will want to invest in membership just as soon as humanly possible. The professional connectedness you achieve through membership, the skills you will learn, and the contacts you make will pay dividends throughout your career. Not to mention the networking directory you get to use immediately. You don't know of an appropriate association? Your local research librarian will gladly lead you to an enormous blue and yellow tome published by Bowker called *The Encyclopedia of Associations*. Your gang will be listed there.

Alumni/ae Associations

Most schools from the Ivy leagues to vocational schools have an active alumni/ae association. These associations have alumni who post jobs and most members will offer assistance to someone from their old alma mater. You can usually get mail and e-mailing lists from them which vary from just names to names and occupations and employers. Every working alumni is worthy of a networking letter (just check through the networking letter section for examples) and a follow-up call. Never, ever, underestimate the power of "the old school tie."

Employment Agencies and Executive Recruiters

There are essentially three categories: state employment agencies, private employment agencies, and executive recruiters.

State Employment Agencies

These are funded by the state labor department and typically carry names like State Employment Security, State Job Service, or Manpower Services. The names may vary, but the services remain the same; they will make efforts to line you up with appropriate jobs and mail resumes out on your behalf to interested employers and will often initiate calls of introduction. It is not mandatory for employers to list jobs with state agencies, but more and more are taking advantage of these free services. Once the bastion of minimum-wage jobs, these public agencies now list positions with salaries reaching $100,000 a year. In fact the job bank that connects them all together—America's Job Bank at *www.ajb.dni. us*—is our country's largest.

If you are moving across the state or across the country, your local employment office can plug you into this national job bank, if you don't have Internet access at home. The most effective way to use this service is to visit your local office and ask for an introduction to the office in your destination area. Then send them a cover letter (via e-mail and regular mail) with your resume, and follow up with a phone call.

Private Employment Agency Sources

The following are a few sources for employment service listings, from temporary help through local employment agency, contingency, and retained headhunters. Depending on who you are and what you are looking for, any or all of these categories could be of interest to you. Here is some contact data for the most comprehensive lists and directories available.

National Association of Personnel Consultants
10905 Ft. Washington Road, Suite 400
Fort Washington, MD 20744
(301) 203-6700
National Directory of Personnel Consultants, $30.00 (includes shipping and handling). Identifies companies by occupational specialization and geographical coverage. Includes employment agencies, contingency, and retained search companies in membership. The industry's premier organization, with thousands of reputable contacts.

Directory of Executive Recruiters
Kennedy & Kennedy Inc.
Kennedy Place, Rte. 12 South
Fitzwilliam, NH 03447
(603) 585-2200
Directory of Executive Recruiters, $47.95 (pb). Details on 2,000 retained and contingency firms throughout North America.

USA Jobs
(478) 757-3000 (Available 24 hours a day)
www.usajobs.opm.com
The official United States of America Federal Government job resource directory. Nearly 16,000 government jobs are listed in the free online database (updated daily). There is also a link for government jobs geared toward students, as well as general employment information.

Job Finders Online
Planning/Communications
7215 Oak Avenue
River Forest, IL 60305-1935
(708) 366-5200
(888) 366-5200 (Orders only)
www.jobfindersonline.com
A large online job-hunting directory. Job Finders publishes the *Job Quest Catalog* (both online and in print). The catalog lists hundreds of books and resource guides covering all facets of the job search. Prices vary.

American Staffing Association
277 South Washington Street, Suite 200
Alexandria, VA 22314
(703) 253-2020
A full industry-wide listing of more than 13,000 firms is available for $705.80 for members, and $950.00 for nonmembers.

Don't restrict yourself to any single category in this area. Executives, especially, should not turn their nose up at local employment agencies. Often a local agency has better rapport and contacts with the local business community than the big-name search firms. I have also known more than one "employment agency" that regularly placed job candidates earning in excess of $250,000 a year. Don't get hung up on agency versus search firm labels without researching the firms in question; you could miss some great opportunities.

Business Magazines

There are a number of uses here. The articles about interesting companies can alert you to growth opportunities, and the articles themselves can provide a neat little entry in your cover letter. Most professional trade and professional association magazines rely more or less on the contributions of industry professionals. So articles bylined by Bill Edwards, VP of Openings at Sesame Furnaces, could go into a little dossier for strictly targeted mailings. It's also a neat idea to enclose the clipping with your letter. These mailings to sometime authors can be tremendously rewarding. Writing is hard, and writers have egos of mythical proportions (just ask my editor). A little flattery can go a long way.

By the same token, you can write to people who are quoted in articles. It's great to see your name in print; in fact there is only one thing better, and that is hearing that someone *else* saw your name in print and now thinks you're a genius. (You should bear in mind that most of these magazines also carry a help-wanted section.)

These ideas are just some of the many unusual and effective ways to introduce yourself to companies, you'll find more in the *Knock 'em Dead: The Ultimate Job Hunter's Guide.*

Sending Out Your Cover Letters

Your first effort with a cover letter is to find an individual to whom you can address it. As noted earlier, "Sir/Madam" or "To whom it may concern" says you don't care enough about the company to find out a name—they will pay more attention to the candidates who do. A name shows you have focus and guarantees that a specific individual will open and read your letter. You also have someone to ask for by name when you do your follow-up telephone call—it's important to take the initiative when you are interview hunting.

Must you send out hundreds or even thousands of letters in the coming weeks? I spoke to a woman on a call-in TV show recently who had "done everything and still not gotten a job." She explained how she had sent out almost 300 letters and still wasn't employed. I asked her several questions that elicited some revealing facts: She had been job-hunting for almost two years (that equals two or three letters a week), and there were, conservatively, 3,000 companies she could work for. (That equals a single approach with no follow-up to only one in ten potential employers.) Two employer contacts a week will not get you back to work—or even on the track with the kind of job that can help you advance toward your chosen worklife goals. Only if you approach and establish communication with every possible employer and follow up properly will you create the maximum opportunity for yourself.

In the world of headhunters, the statistical average is 700 contacts between offers and acceptances. These are averages of professionals representing only the most desirable jobs and job candidates to each other. When I hear the oft-quoted statements that it takes a white-collar worker about eight months to get a job nowadays, I have a feeling those 700 or so contacts are being spread out needlessly. If you approach the job hunt in a professional manner, the way executive search professionals and employment agents approach their work, you can be happily installed on the next rung of your career ladder much sooner than the national average—that is, if you really put the advice of the *Knock 'em Dead* books to work for yourself. Just look at the reader endorsements at the front of the book to see what you can achieve if you follow this advice in letter and in spirit.

I am not recommending that you immediately make up a list of 700 companies and mail letters to them today. That isn't the answer. Your campaign needs strategy. While every job-hunting campaign is unique, you will want to maintain a balance between the *number* of letters you send out on a daily and weekly basis and the *kinds* of letters you send out. This needs to all be integrated into an intelligent overall campaign that includes other job-search activities; just mailing resumes with none of the other job-hunting approaches is a sad excuse for a job hunt.

The key is to send out a balanced mailing representing all the different types of leads, and to send them out regularly and in a volume that will allow you to make follow-up calls. There are many headhunters who manage their time so well that they average over fifty calls a day, year in and year out. While you may aim at building your call volume up to this number, I recommend that you start out with more modest goals.

To start the campaign:

Source	Number of Letters Per Day
Internet job postings	10
Newspaper ads	10
Networking	10 (5 to friends, 5 to professional colleagues)
Direct-research contacts (online searches, reference works, magazines, etc.)	10
Headhunters	10

Do You Need to Compose More Than One Letter?

Almost certainly. There is a case for all of us having a number of letters and resumes targeted for different specific needs. The key is to do each variation once and do it right. Your computer makes this job 100 times easier than it used to be, and you can use these letters again and again over the years as your circumstances demand. You may find it valuable to send upward of half a dozen contact letters to a desirable target company, just to assure that they know you are available. To illustrate, let's say you are a young engineer crazy for a job with Last Chance Electronics. It is well within the bounds of reason that you would submit a cover letter and resume to any or all of the following people, with each letter addressed by name to minimize its chances of going straight into the trash:

- Company President
- Vice President of Engineering
- Chief Engineer
- Engineering Design Manager
- Vice President of Human Resources
- Technical Engineering Recruitment Manager
- Technical Recruiter

Each of these letters would require a slightly different introductory sentence, while the body of the letter could remain the same.

The Plan

A professionally organized and conducted campaign should include both an e-mail and a traditional mail dimension. So when I talk about "mail" and "mail campaign," understand it to embrace both communication mediums.

Approach #1

A carefully targeted rifle approach of a select group of companies. You will have first identified these "super-desirable" places to work as you researched your long list of potential employers. You will continue to add to this primary target list as you unearth fresh opportunities in your day-to-day research efforts. In this instance you have two choices:

1. Mail to everyone at once, remembering that the letters have to be personalized and followed up appropriately.

2. Start your mailings off with one to a line manager and one to a contact in human resources. Follow up in a few days and repeat the process to other names on your hit list.

With the e-mail dimension of your campaign, you can bookmark target companies and check in on their openings on an ongoing basis. As employers cannot be relied on to keep your resume front and center, you should hit your target companies on a regular basis, say every six weeks. The worst that can happen is that someone finally pays attention!

Approach #2

A carpet-bombing strategy designed to reach every possible employer, on the basis that you won't know what opportunities there are unless you go find out. (Here, too, you must personalize and follow up appropriately.)

Begin with a mailing to one or two contacts within the company and then repeat the mailings to other contacts when your initial follow-up calls result in referrals or dead ends. Remember, just because Harry in engineering says there are no openings in the company, that's not necessarily the case; always find out for yourself. Even if he doesn't have a need himself, another contact in the same company (see the chapter "Getting Live Leads from Dead Ends" in my book *Knock 'em Dead: The Ultimate Job Hunter's Resource*) could know the person who is just dying to meet you.

Once you have received some responses to your mailings and scheduled interviews, your emphasis will change. Those contacts and interviews will require follow-up letters and conversation. You will be preparing for interviews.

This is exactly the point where most job hunts stall. We get so excited about the interview activity we convince ourselves that "This will be the offer." The headhunters have a saying, "The offer that can't fail always will." What happens is that the offer doesn't materialize, and you are left with absolutely no interview activity.

The more resumes you send out, the more follow-up calls you can make to schedule interviews. The more interviews you get, the better you feel and the better you get at interviewing. The better you get at interviewing, the more offers you get.

So no matter how good things look, continue the campaign—maintain activity with those companies with whom you are in negotiation, and continue to make fresh submissions every week. You must maintain your marketing schedule. Your daily plan now looks like this:

Source	Number of Letters Per Day
Internet job postings	5
Newspaper ads	5
Networking (associations, alumni, colleagues)	5
Direct-research contacts (online searches, reference work, magazines, etc.)	5
Headhunters	5
Follow-up letters and calls	15–20

Small but consistent mailings have many benefits. The balance you maintain is important, because most job hunters are tempted simply to send the easy letters and make the easy calls (i.e., network with old friends), but only doing this will knock your job hunt out of balance.

Even when an offer is pending, keep plugging—and by "pending" I include all variations on "Harry, you've got the job and you can start Monday; the offer letter is in the mail." Yeah, just like the check in the old saying. Never accept the "yes" until you have it in writing, have started work, and the first paycheck has cleared at the bank! Until then, keep your momentum building.

Following Up: A Cautionary Tale

In theory, your perfect letter will generate a 100 percent response. But there is no perfect letter, and this is a less-than-perfect world. Although you will get calls from your mailing, if you sit there like Buddha waiting for the world to beat a path to your door, you may wait a long time.

Not long ago a pal of mine put a two-line ad in the local paper for a programmer analyst. By Wednesday of the following week he had received over 100 responses. Ten days later he was still plowing through them when he received a follow-up call (the only one he did receive) from one of the ad respondents. The job hunter was in the office within two hours, returned the following morning, and was hired by lunchtime.

The candidate's paperwork was simply languishing there in the pile waiting to be discovered. The follow-up phone call got it discovered. The call made the interviewer sort through the enormous pile of paper, pull out the letter and resume, and act on it.

Follow-Up Calls Work

You'll notice that many examples in the letter section mention that they will follow up with a phone call. This allows the writer to explain to any inquisitive receptionist that Joe Schmoe is "expecting my call" or that it is "personal," Or, "it's accounting/engineering/customer service business."

I find it surprising that so many people are nervous about calling a fellow professional on the phone and talking about what they do for a living. To help reduce any nervousness, understand that there is an unwritten professional credo shared by the vast majority of successful professional people: You should always help another if it isn't going to hurt you in the process. Because of this, almost everyone you speak to will recognize and be sympathetic to your cause.

If you are not already successful in management, you need to know the principle outlined in my management books *Hiring the Best* and *Knock 'em Dead Management:* "The first tenet of management is getting work done through others." A manager's success is based on this single idea. Managers are always on the lookout for competent professionals in their field for today and tomorrow. In fact, the best managers maintain a private file of great professionals they can't use today but want to keep available. I know of someone who got a job as a result of a letter retained in these files. She got the interview (and the job) from the letter and resume she'd sent months earlier.

No manager will take offense at a call from a competent fellow professional. To know exactly how to make the call and what to say, look at the chapter entitled "Painting the Perfect Picture on the Phone" in *Knock 'em Dead: The Ultimate Job Seeker's Resource.*

Using a Contact Tracker

To ensure that you keep track of the contacts you have sent and the results of the follow-up phone calls, I recommend that you create a Contact Tracker on a spreadsheet program like Microsoft Excel. Create columns for the company name, telephone number, e-mail address, and contact name. A mailing loaded in your contact tracker today will allow you to have a follow-up call plan set and ready to go for a few days later. As a rule of thumb, a mailing sent today is ripe for follow-up four to eight days from now. Any sooner and you can't be sure the mail has arrived; much later and it may already have gotten lost or been passed on. In addition to your Contact Tracker, it may be helpful to use your computer address book to keep track of who you contact.

You will know that your job hunt is on track when you are filling in more contacts every day as a result of a mailing, and creating a second Contact Tracker as a result of your follow-up calls.

If you follow the advice in this book, you will get interviews. If you follow the advice in *Resumes That Knock 'em Dead* and *Knock 'em Dead: The Ultimate Job Seeker's Resource*, you will get multiple job offers—people do all the time. When you get your first job offer, you will want to read the section on generating multiple offers in *Knock 'em Dead*, which will show you how to turn many of these contacts into additional interviews and competitive offers.

Recently I spoke to a gentleman on a radio call-in show who had been out of work for some months. He had bought the books and followed my advice to the letter and had generated four job offers in only five weeks. I have lost count of the number of similar encounters I've had over the years. Follow my advice in letter and spirit and the same good fortune can be yours. After all, good fortune is really only the intersection of opportunity, preparation, and effort.

Using the Internet and Creating Electronic Cover Letters

THE INTERNET has established itself as a useful and vital job search tool. Here's the lowdown on everything you need to know to get online effectively and with results!

How the Internet Can Help in Your Job Hunt

This chapter focuses on giving you the facts and the most effective techniques in online job-hunting. Knowing these facts, you can decide on the merits of Internet searches for yourself.

The Internet offers you an array of opportunities and chances to get your resume on the desks of thousands of companies and recruiters. It will not, however, effectively replace your other job-hunting activities. You need to utilize it as another one of the many useful weapons already in your job-hunting arsenal.

A job search becomes more effective when you widen its geographic scope, and the Internet easily allows you to access numerous job openings in major metropolitan areas. The usefulness of an Internet search diminishes when you are only looking for jobs in your immediate area. Nevertheless, online searches can still provide valuable information about local opportunities as well.

Most companies are now using their Web sites as recruiting portals. From the corporate perspective, Internet recruitment serves a dual purpose: their personnel openings are posted on the Web to attract candidates, and the technologically challenged are screened out by virtue of default. How can the Internet benefit your job search? It allows you to:

- Create customized electronic documents and communicate with potential employers and recruiters pretty much instantly.
- Find job openings through job banks and employers' job sites.
- Have potential employers find you, whether you are currently looking for a position or just managing your career growth opportunities.
- Do research on companies, potential employers, and your industry.

The Internet offers you access to millions of job openings, and tens of thousands of companies and recruiters. Of course, they are not all going to be in your town, so once the first blush of excitement wears off you'll realize that this is *just* another useful weapon in your arsenal. You can post your resume on the Internet so that companies and recruiters can find you; you can surf for job openings and you'll have access to more information about prospective employers, making you a better-informed candidate.

What You Need to Start an Online Job Search

You need computer access from outside the workplace. Using your office computer for writing your resume, sending out e-mails, or surfing the net for job listings is the Internet equivalent of stealing company stationery and postage stamps. Studies show that 50 percent of all companies either read their employees' e-mail and/or track their Internet usage. Some companies have assigned IT staff members whose job it is to track inappropriate Internet usage, and they have software packages to help with that tracking. Originating primarily in the high-tech industries, this practice seems to be on the rise in industries across the board. Don't ignore this warning because you feel your boss is computer illiterate, too stupid to catch you, or too trusting to snoop. Almost all companies are using the Internet for recruitment purposes; someone in Human Resources could accidentally stumble across your online resume, which lists the company for whom you're currently working.

Online Privacy and Organization

Personal privacy and confidentiality become serious issues when you use the Internet for job-hunting and resume distribution. It's a good news/bad news situation—with the ease of electronic document distribution comes the fear of prying eyes. So take precautions to protect your privacy.

If you have Internet access at home, it is probably through a local ISP (Internet service provider) such as MSN, AOL, or Earthlink. These accounts typically come with more than one e-mail address, so you can utilize one of the additional addresses for career management activities. It is a good idea to set up a separate online identity and maintain it exclusively for your job search.

As your experience broadens, your education and professional experience will allow you to pursue a number of different jobs. Therefore, you have the option of creating multiple professional identities online. Setting up separate e-mail accounts for each of these career-specific identities will allow you to keep things organized by job classifications, giving more focus to your search and allowing you to effectively manage your job-hunting activities.

Privacy Is a Concern for Everyone

Don't include too much personal information in an online resume. It could allow unscrupulous people to use your personal or professional identity for their own purposes. Posting your home phone number or address on the Internet attracts junk mail and telemarketing calls.

Anyone who has an e-mail account is familiar with junk e-mail, commonly referred to as spam. Reverse spamming is when an electronic "spider" grabs your personal information, e-mail address, or resume, then redistributes it to other sites or a third party. An electronic spider is a programmed tool that searches the Internet for certain types of information the "spider owner" specifies. Don't be afraid to use the Internet in your job search, but be aware that the information that you post is readily available to other users. Be careful about the type of information and the amount of personal data you make electronically available.

If you use a free e-mail account, handling junk mail is an expected inconvenience you must tolerate for the service. Identity fraud, however, is a far more serious complication that can potentially arise in free e-mail usage. You put your professional identity at risk when listing professional license or certificate numbers on your resume—so don't do it, ever! In addition, dates of birth, driver's license numbers, and social security numbers should never be included on electronic resumes. With that information alone, someone could steal your identity and ruin your personal or professional credibility.

Rules to Protect Your Online Privacy

Here are some general guidelines for making online job sites and resume banks work *for* you rather than *against* you:

- Look at the site's privacy statement. Read it carefully to understand the extent of protection afforded personal information. Even without guarantees, this is a security starting point.
- Only post your resume to sites that protect their resume bank with a password (this is the best prevention against those pesky spiders). Password protection means that the site electronically screens all visitors. This helps to ensure that only credible employers and recruiters have access to your resume.
- Know who owns and operates the site. The owner's contact information should be available. If they are unwilling to share their identity with you, don't share yours either.
- You must be able to update, edit, and remove your posted resume, along with any other personal information whenever you choose.
- Blocked resume bank services supposedly allow you to block access to your information from specifically unwanted viewers, such as a current employer. Do not trust these services to actually do so. These sites are not foolproof, so only post items that you don't need blocked.
- If you decide to build and create your own Web site to post your resume and work samples, password-protect it.
- Never put your social security number, driver's license number, or professional license number on your resume in any format.
- Do not use your company e-mail address, computer, or Internet lines to search for jobs or to access your private e-mail account.

Free E-Mail Accounts

There are dozens of sites that offer free e-mail accounts that take only minutes to set up. While many personal interest sites offering free accounts exist, remember that your career e-mail address shouldn't contain any personal information.

For example *Martin@match.com* reveals altogether too much personal information, and obviously isn't appropriate for professional use. You want to create a professional, eye-catching image right from the start; take time in selecting your professional e-mail service and user names.

As an example of the process, let's create a new identity for a fictional job search candidate, Susan O'Malley. Go to *www.hotmail.com*, and then select the "New Account Sign Up" icon on the front page of the site. That will link you to a page requesting a user profile. When you complete the profile, you will be directed to the site user agreement. This explains user rules and the site's privacy policy. Read this information carefully; you have to accept the terms of the agreement before your address becomes active. Stick with the larger, more public firms, because they tend to be more reliable and honorable about such terms. Typically, public sites offer paid upgrades to your new account that allow you more control over your e-mail address. Upgrades are unnecessary if you limit the number of messages stored in your mailbox at any given time, or if you don't care to pay to limit spam.

Account signup

You will notice that I chose a professional user name for Susan: SOMALLEYHRPRO—this gives her the e-mail address *somalleyhrpro@hotmail.com*. Remember: this account is set up strictly for job-search purposes.

An appropriately named professional e-mail like this acts as an arresting headline for prospective employers.

Should you run into a situation where the user name you want is not available, choose your alternatives wisely. Most sites will make suggestions, usually by adding numbers to the end of the user name. This is not appropriate for job-hunting and career management needs. You do not want to be confused with *jsmith118@hotmail.com* when you are assigned the name *jsmith119@hotmail.com*, nor do you want to choose a number that could easily be mistaken for your year of birth. Instead, make it a career-related screen name as I did for Susan.

How to Organize Your Job-Hunting E-Mail Account

For those of you planning to use public or shared computers, free accounts such as this one offer a nice security feature at the front door—provided you utilize it. Susan activated the highest level of security by clicking on the "Public/shared computer" button. At this increased level of security, Susan will be asked for her user name and password whenever she attempts to enter her account from any computer. If Susan always uses her home or private computer, the "Neither" or the "Keep me signed in" option assumes that every time her Web browser links to Hotmail, she is identified as the user and is automatically logged in. This also allows her to keep her job hunt secure on her family computer. For your own safety, emulate Susan and set up your account at the highest security level possible.

Whether you use Hotmail, Yahoo!, Outlook, or some other major e-mail program, all of them allow you to create and manage folders. (Do you see the buttons for "Create Folder" and "Manage Folders" in the figures on the following page?)

Think of these as the electronic equivalent of paper folders and filing cabinets. What folders do you need? Let's start with the two major sites where Susan will be posting her resume and searching for jobs: Monster.com and SHRM.org (the Society for Human Resource Management Web site). Both of these sites offer job delivery service, so when she signs up at either of these sites using her new e-mail account, she is quickly able to review jobs and file those she wants to save.

Susan will also create a folder for leads. As the leads mature into communication and contact with specific companies and recruiters, she can create specific folders for them. To get started, Susan's new e-mail account looks like this:

The new e-mail account

Organization does not end there. It is crucial to your long-term ability to manage your career that you are constantly and consistently building a contact manager for job prospects. This applies both to companies you might want to work for, and for contacts within recruiting firms. Follow Susan's example and you will be ten steps ahead of the game when you next need to make a strategic career move. Most of these companies will still be there and still looking for the same types of people.

Take another look at the previous screen shot, only this time look up to the right, above the messages. Locate the tab in the middle of the screen labeled "Address Book." This tab sends you to another screen, where you are given additional options. These options allow you to send e-mail, view and edit messages, delete e-mail, and, most importantly for your organizational efforts: create a new address book.

In creating new address books, you want to organize groups of addresses, and not just add individual ones. Each "group" will contain a separate set or group of addresses, tailored to specific audiences for current or future job searches. Typically, these groups fall into three categories: companies, recruiters, and networking prospects/professional colleagues. By creating an address book group for each of these categories, you create a database for your work life.

Address book groups

Additions to these groups needn't be based on direct contact, interviews, or job offers. If you see a recruiter within an industry of interest, put that address in the recruiter book. If you find a company in your geographic area or professional field, put that address in the company book. By doing this regularly, you create a vehicle for launching a massive career blitz whenever the need arises. Organize yourself now, and the information you collect along the way can be used throughout your entire work life. You'll have an enormous database loaded and ready to go!

Cover Letters and Online Job-Hunting

A great resume is critical to job search success, but it will remain unread without a dynamite cover letter to go with it. In the electronic world, your cover letter is embedded in the e-mail message preceding your resume, and it should include an attention-grabbing e-mail subject line.

The Internet and subsequent growth of the electronic recruitment process have been both a blessing and a curse for corporate recruiters. Although electronic recruitment can be much more efficient for them in many ways, it tends to yield more responses from a wider range of candidates. This creates a time management challenge for corporations and recruiters who must review the avalanche of resumes the medium generates. This has resulted in a dramatic growth in resume software capable of scanning resume databases by keywords.

These programs allow companies to scan and digitally input resumes into their databases, saving them for later access using keywords and other criteria to rank their usefulness. Initially, only large companies could afford these services, but with competition and the growth of the Internet, resume scanning and searching capabilities are now available to virtually all companies and recruiters.

With traditionally mailed resumes, a powerful cover letter separates a job hunter from the crowd. This is equally applicable with an electronic version. As is the case for your electronic resume, your electronic cover letter must:

1. Have the right keywords.
2. Be scannable if delivered in print form.
3. Be transmittable over the Web via e-mail.

Think of your cover letter as an electronic talent agent, the opening act for your resume. The two must complement each other. Both play crucial roles in the successful electronic job search. No matter how well written cover letters are, or how sophisticated your electronic approaches become, an ineffectively presented resume (either from keyword or compatibility failures) will result in a job-hunting dead end.

Differences Between Electronic and Print Cover Letters

Modern workplaces tend to demand 60+ hours weekly from busy, multitasking employees. I've spoken to corporate executives who base their decisions on listening to voice mail messages depending on the first ten words recorded. Your cover letter competes for the attention of this same audience.

E-mail communications are treated in a similar fashion. Daily, the amount of e-mail traffic grows exponentially. Most professionals receive dozens, sometimes hundreds, of messages per day. Hit your main points quickly, or lose the reader's attention. A good e-mail subject line determines what attention your resume and cover letter receives. If the first two sentences don't succinctly state your purpose and grab their attention, they'll have little reason for wasting any more precious time on the rest of your message.

Cover letters usually consist of three to five carefully constructed paragraphs. Very rarely should they exceed one full page, in most cases, a second page simply won't get read. They should strategically emphasize, or re-emphasize, points made in your resume. They can also be used to customize applications for specific positions, or to address issues not covered in your resume.

Just as you would limit a paper cover letter to one page, you should try to keep an electronic cover letter to one screen view where possible. This can sometimes be less than the length of your original script, so edit as strongly as you can. If you cannot get your entire letter in one screen view, at least make an effort to get the meat of your pitch onto that first full screen.

Before discussing formatting, let's take a minute to focus on cover letter content issues. We've established the fact that electronic cover letters need to be concise, giving the reasons why the message is being sent and why the reader should move onto your resume. Review the samples below. Look for the ways in which these letters build bridges between writers and readers, use keywords, make points about the writers' suitability for the positions, and then request next step information.

Sample #1

I was excited to see your opening for a Financial Analyst vacancy (job #1854) on the NationJob.com Web site. As my attached resume demonstrates, the open position is a perfect match for my payroll, general ledger, and accounts receivable experience. I welcome the opportunity to discuss my skills and your job requirements in greater detail. Please respond with a time of day I might call you.

Sample #2

While browsing the jobs database on careerbuilder.com, I was intrigued by your Regional Sales Manager job posting (MZ - wj25508). Although I am currently employed by one of your competitors, I have kept my eye open for an opportunity to join your organization. Over the past year I have:

- *Built a sales force of 7 reps*
- *Exceeded my quota—growing revenue to $2.3 million*
- *Implemented a customer service plan that successfully reduced client turnover*

Please review my attached resume and contact me to schedule a time for us to meet.

Sample #3

It was great meeting you Monday for lunch. I enjoyed sharing ideas with a fellow association member, and, as you suggested, I have attached a copy of my current resume. Since our meeting I have given more thought to your company goals and believe they are closely related to my skill set and career objectives. I will call you next week to schedule a time when we can continue our conversation.

Sample #4

Your colleague, Bill Jacobson, suggested that I send you my resume. He mentioned that your department is looking for a Database Administrator with experience in Intranet implementation and management. As my attached resume demonstrates, I have done that type of work for six years with a regional organization on a platform of 15,000 users. I welcome the opportunity to discuss your specific projects and explore the possibility of joining your team.

Sample #5

Although I am currently employed by one of your major competitors, I must admit that I was captivated by your company's mission statement when I visited your Web site. Your dedication of resources within assisted care facilities not only piqued my interest but is also, as my attached resume indicates, precisely my area of expertise. With significant experience in an area of such importance to your firm, I look forward to the opportunity to discuss available positions.

Sample #6

A former colleague of mine, Diane Johnson, recommended your recruiting firm to me as you recently assisted her in a strategic career move. I understand that your firm specializes in the consumer products industry. As a Marketing Director with 12 years of experience in consumer products, I have:

- *Doubled revenues in just 18 months*
- *Introduced a new product which captured a 78% market share*
- *Successfully managed a $5 million ad budget*

I have pasted and attached my resume for your review and will call you next week to discuss any openings for which your firm is currently conducting searches.

The content of each of these cover letter samples follows a similar format. They all accomplish three things:

- They identify why you are sending your resume.
- They identify why the reader should read the resume.
- They ask for the interview or next contact.

Let's examine each of these points more closely:

Identify why you made contact: You probably initiated contact because of a job posting, a colleague, or because your research identified them as a potential employer or suitable recruiting firm. Just state the reason and tell the reader you see a match. When submitting because of a job posting, always indicate the job title or job number if there is one. Likewise, if a friend, associate, or colleague initiated the contact, clearly state their name and your connection. If you found the opening through Internet research, state that as well.

Give them a reason to read your resume: Quickly and concisely, identify why you believe you are a match. Read the job posting again and then repeat the keywords that you share with it. If appropriate, explain the reason why your mutual acquaintance or colleague referred you, as a segue into stating your credentials. This is your chance to whet the reader's appetite. If you are currently employed by, or have worked for a competitor, say it here—many companies seek the expertise of their competitors, and love to lure employees away from them.

Ask for the next step: Wrap up this brief but powerful communication by suggesting a meeting, phone call, or interview. Go ahead and state that you will follow-up with them, especially if you are currently employed and confidentiality could be an issue. But if you say you are going to follow-up, you must make time to do it.

The Need for Multiple Cover Letters

You will be sending your resume and cover letter in response to many different situations (as well as in several different mediums). To maximize effectiveness, you will have to tailor your cover letters to specific audiences. Addressees may include:

1. Companies and recruiters in response to online job postings.
2. Companies you've found from research, newspapers, trade publications, and the Internet.
3. Recruiters and the all-important headhunters.
4. Friends and professional colleagues as a means of networking and staying in touch professionally.

When sending resumes to each of these types of contacts, slightly different cover letters will be required, and you'll find lots of examples to emulate and customize later in this book. First let's look at how we store and send electronic communications in a job hunt, and in the process learn an effective way to organize your campaign. My suggestion is to compose letters in a word processing program, not in your e-mail folder. Even though you are most likely to send the cover letter via e-mail, it is best to compose them elsewhere and move them into e-mail when you're satisfied with the content.

Creating and saving them in a word processing program allows you to use each letter type you create as a template that can be pasted into an e-mail and customized to the unique needs of that particular situation. In the long run, templates make you more time-efficient in your job-hunting campaign, because you will always have a base from which to start.

You need to organize your job-search documents. If you get organized at the start, you will stay organized throughout the job hunt. You also have the beginnings of a lifelong career management database, allowing you to adapt your templates to specific future needs. Time spent organizing your own database now saves time and makes future searches easier and more effective.

Go to your "My Documents" or "My Briefcase" folders, then create a series of new folders for the various documents and relationships you will be building. This is what Susan's initial folder system looks like:

Job search folders

As you can see, she's created a separate section in the "My Documents" folder, then created a series of subfolders for "Resumes," "Cover Letters," "Job Descriptions," "Follow-up Letters," and "Interview Research." She also reserves space for "Job Offers" and "Employment Contracts" folders to handle such responses when her job search gains momentum.

Remember, in each of these folders, you need to name documents appropriately; create additional subfolders like Susan's "Text Cover Letters" subfolder, which is embedded in the "Cover Letters" folder. Get organized in advance, then you'll never worry about it again.

A Scannable Cover Letter

When a letter and resume are delivered electronically they are stored in a database, sometimes without first being read. Likewise, it is increasingly likely that your print resume will be scanned, digitized, and stored in the same manner. Be careful about formatting and font issues in the organization process; you don't want your documents in an unreadable state when received. In all word processing programs you can save the document as "Text," which will allow it to retain its formatting when pasted into an e-mail.

Don't use dark stationery, page borders, columns, excessive bolding, underlining, italics, or fonts smaller than 12-point in e-mail documents. I know most experts say 10-point, in order to allow you to get more on the page, but making life difficult for the reader is self-defeating. Use 12-point where you can, as it makes life much easier on the tired eyes of a harried reader. They may look good on hard copy, but they may not be scannable in that format; and it'll all most likely get lost in e-mail formatting anyway.

Focus on the creation of effective e-mail cover letters and attention-grabbing subject lines (more on that in a few paragraphs). They can be based on any of your templates; just be sure to make every word count, and send them to yourself first so you can see that most, if not all, of the message is on a single screen.

Make Sure Your Cover Letters Are in the Correct Electronic Format

Let's revisit Susan O'Malley in the process of editing her cover letter template, and converting it to an ASCII or text-based document for e-mail distribution.

Susan's cover letter is nicely formatted, matching the layout of her resume. At this point, the letter is one full page in length listing a dozen bullet points regarding her skill set. It can certainly be shortened for a specific opening where she has some idea of the requirements.

Unlike regular business letters, e-mail letters do not always follow typical letter-writing protocols. For example, you do not include your address, because your contact information and the date and time of your communication is entered automatically. Begin your business e-mail messages with a simple salutation, "Dear Tiffany Carstairs," for example. Basic professional courtesies still apply, so don't address the recipient on a first-name basis unless you are already familiar with them; use the same courtesy and respect you would in a hard-copy version.

Always end your business e-mails stating your name and a brief summary of your contact information (confidential phone or fax number, and mailing address). Remove the traditional enclosure indication if you used it, and state instead that it is pasted into the body of the e-mail and also *attached* (the correct term for e-mail communication, as you have just seen in the examples), You would obviously prefer to have your nicely formatted resume in the attachment viewed, but you should always paste in it into the body of your e-mail because many people simply do not open attachments from people they don't know personally.

The first edit of Susan's resume looks like this:

The first edit of the cover letter

Although this letter is still too long, it allows flexibility for specific tailoring. She can edit the bulleted list according to the requirements of any individual position she seeks. At this point, Susan's letter can be altered as needed, so let's ignore the length issue to focus on format. If placed into the body of an e-mail message, this text would develop character and spacing problems. To avoid such problems, convert your cover letters to ASCII or text-based document before pasting it into or attaching it to your e-mail. This is accomplished by following these simple steps.

Copy the entire document by choosing "select all" from the "edit" pull-down menu. Then, choose "copy" from the "edit" pull-down menu or Ctrl+C for Windows. With a Macintosh you simply choose "save" from the pull down file menu, click "save" and then, when the dialog box opens up, click on "format" and scroll to "text."

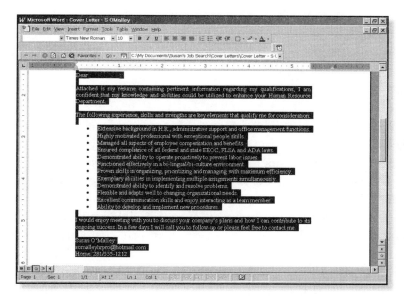

Selecting all text

You want to avoid all chances of character and spacing problems in your e-mail cover letter; sticking to a straight text-based document allows all readers to receive your message in the style you wish it viewed.

Sometimes the document will lose many of its features and the spacing can change dramatically, even when saved in "text," so you need to spend time proofreading your new document before sending. Any tabs, tables, or columns used in a formatted version wreak havoc on new text-based versions. In order to prevent wrapping or flowing issues, you need to remove empty spaces and tabs to make the document flush left.

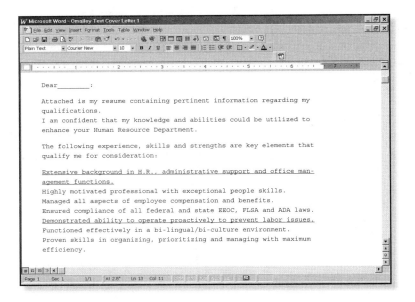

A cover letter with formatting removed

Since the bullets have disappeared in the translation, either adjust the spacing to create a new type of emphasis, or use characters on your keyboard such as "*" to replace the bullets. Additionally, the bullet statements need to be shorter and more concise. If you allow statements to wrap to the next line, your electronic cover letters will be unappealing, less effective, and too long. Save your document to protect all these changes. Keep in mind that this is a template. Once an actual contact or job opening has been identified, customization will be the next step.

How to Use the All-Important Subject Line of E-Mail Effectively

The use of a powerful subject line can mean the difference between getting your resume read by human eyes or relegated to the HR resume database. When sending e-mail—not just job related e-mails—but all e-mails, it is only professional to provide a clear, concise and professional subject line. It allows the receiver to immediately know who you are and what you want.

The subject line of an e-mail containing your resume needs to be factual, professional, and intriguing. The subject line you use is like the headline for a newspaper article, and can have the same effect on the audience—it will attract the reader or turn them off. The intent of your e-mail subject line must be to grab the reader and draw him or her into the body of the e-mail message and your resume. Do not use the subject line to state the obvious, like "Resume" or "Jim Smith's Resume." If you are responding to a job posting, the job title and job posting number are necessary, but just a start. Combine this factual information with a little intrigue such as:

> Job #6745 - Top Sales Professional Here
> IT Manager - 7 yrs IT Consulting
> Financial Analyst #MB450 - CPA/MBA/8 yrs exp
> Benefits Consultant - Nonprofit Exp in NY
> Posting 2314 - MIT Grad is interested
> Referral from Tony Banks - Product Management Job

Remember, although you want to grab someone's attention, this is still a professional and serious topic—your career. Do not go overboard and use an overly aggressive subject line. Do not think you can trick someone into reading your resume by claiming to be a Harvard graduate when you are not. Besides the fact that because everyone gets so much junk mail, a whimsical subject line might land your resume right in the delete bin.

How to Customize and Send Your Electronic Cover Letter and Resume

Let's pull it all together and watch Susan, an HR professional, customize her electronic cover letter, pick an effective subject line, and send her resume to a potential employer.

Susan has been using the Society for Human Resource Management career site (*www.shrm.org*) and has found an appealing position in sunny California. A specialty food distributor is seeking a Regional HR Manager.

Job posting

The job posting has requested that correspondence be sent in the following manner:

> Qualified candidates send resume, salary history and cover letter to: *jadariav@gourmetaward.com* or fax 555-555-1234.

Susan is going to e-mail and regular mail her customized cover letter and resume to this employer. Since the employer did not provide any additional direction, it is best if Susan attaches the resume to her e-mail message as well as pastes it into the body of the e-mail. Let's start by customizing her electronic cover letter template and then choose a strong subject line.

Since Susan was smart enough to get herself organized, she can quickly find her electronic cover letter template. By comparing this longer template to the actual job description, she can easily spot the "hot points." This position requires 10 years of experience and the job description indicates that knowledge of employment laws such as EEOC, FLSA, and ADA are important. Additionally, Susan is interested in moving to California, so this is a good match.

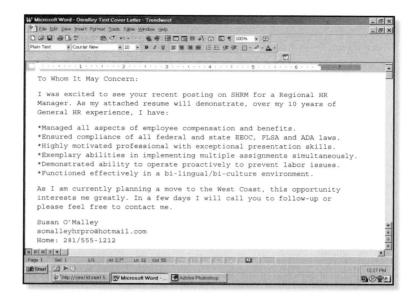

Electronic cover letter for job opening

Susan has customized her cover letter template well: She stated why she is sending the e-mail, hit her "hot points" to get the reader's attention, and asked for the follow-up. In fact, she even renamed the document to reflect the company she will be sending it to and saved it in her cover letter folder.

The next step is to create the e-mail, insert the cover letter, and attach the resume. Susan will go back to her newly established Hotmail account, enter her user name and password, and create a new message by choosing "Compose" from the tabs along the top of the page. By placing her cursor within the message of the newly created e-mail, Susan can then paste the contents of her custom electronic cover letter in the message box. Simply choose "Paste" from the "edit" pull-down menu or Ctrl+V for Windows (or Cmd+V for Macintosh).

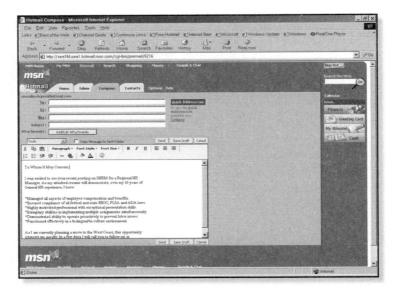

Sending e-mail to employers

With the letter safely pasted in the body of the e-mail, turn your attention to addressing the e-mail to the proper recipient and drafting your subject line. The subject line needs to be factual, professional, yet intriguing: for example, "Your next Reg HR Manager—EEOC, FLSA, & ADA exp" or "EEOC, FLSA, & ADA candidate."

Many people do not realize that the subject line can hold many characters. While a message in your inbox will reveal a maximum of 60 characters, an opened message will show up to 150 characters. To be safe, you should, get your headline in the first 30 characters, but do feel free to use all this extra headline space for a subhead; for example,

"Your next Reg HR Manager—EEOC, FLSA, & ADA. 10 years experience in all facets of HR including arbitration, campus and executive recruitment selection, compensation, training and development." This will only be seen when someone opens the document, but it *will* be seen and noticed. This technique is most effective when you have detailed knowledge of the job and your skills are a good match. This way, the receiver will see your entire subject at all times.

Adding the e-mail address and subject line

It's a smart strategy to keep a copy of all correspondence. You can do this by selecting that option from virtually any e-mail program. With Hotmail (the example we are using in the illustrations) there is a small box that can be clicked directly above the message box that reads "Copy Message to Sent Folder." This means that a copy of every e-mail you send will be saved in the "sent" folder. This way, you can always refer back to specifically see what was sent, to whom, and when. Additionally, you can always move messages from one folder to another once you have started a communication stream with a particular company, and need to isolate and follow the flow of ongoing communication.

Finally, we need to talk a little about your resume. In Hotmail, under the subject of the new e-mail Susan created, there is a button for "Add/Edit Attachments." In other programs, such as Microsoft Outlook, there is a button that looks like a paper; regardless of the program, all the attachment devices work pretty much the same way. Once selected, you will then need to find the document you want to attach. Follow the instructions on the screen. Once you have "browsed" to locate the file, select "open." In Hotmail, once you've browsed and found the file you must then select "attach." The name of your file will appear in the attachment box. Continue to follow the instructions and select "OK."

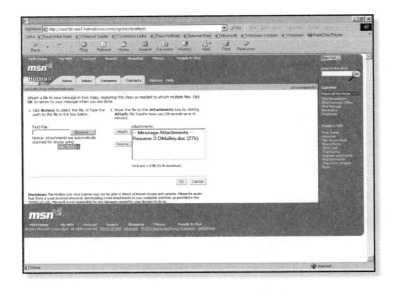

Attaching your resume

Before you send this message, recall two points we addressed earlier when Susan initially found this job posting. First, the employer did not suggest a format in which to send the resume. The most popular is what we have done, but it is not 100 percent effective if the employer does not have Microsoft Word or cannot, for some reason, open the attachment.

Here's a quick solution: Just as you copy and paste your text/ASCII cover letter into the e-mail message box, do the same with your resume. You already have it created—simply go to your "Text Resumes" folder, select the text, copy it, and then return to the e-mail message you just created.

Scroll down through your electronic cover letter. Below your name and contact information insert the word "Resume" (but please not in quotation marks) and then paste in your "Text" saved resume. If the employer has trouble with the attachment, you have sensibly provided a backup solution, which speaks well to your general professional skill sets. Now all that is left to do is hit the "send" button.

Reaching the Right Person

One challenge with the electronic part of your job hunt is to reach human eyes. When the job posting does not list a person's name to contact, you may need to do a little sleuthing to find it. From the contact information, we have an e-mail address and a physical address. Often with company e-mail addresses, the Web site of the company is part of the address that comes after the person's username and the "@" symbol. In this case it is safe to assume that if we break up the e-mail address of *jadariav@gourmetaward.com*, we can probably find the company's home page at *www.gourmetaward.com*.

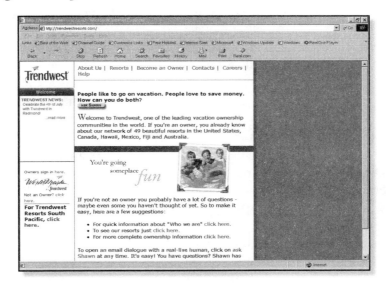

www.gourmetaward.com

Surf the company site and look for a job board, the bios and contacts of company executives, and press releases. Your mission is to find another doorway into this company, perhaps another name to whom you can also send your submission with a slightly different cover letter. With a little extra effort, you could establish a direct connection to your next boss and avoid the corporate resume database altogether. You might also gather other useful information about the company that will help you stand out at the interview.

Electronic Signatures and "Fake" Real Stationery

Although they are not terribly difficult, I group these tools with Web and HTML resumes—if you are in a creative or Web design profession, then you probably need them to show your technical expertise. The rest of us can make better use of our time. However, if you are determined to use these tools, or if the majority of professionals you know use them, then go ahead and try it.

While most of the free e-mail programs will not support these fancy features, they are available in both Microsoft Outlook and Outlook Express, and in the other deluxe programs. By going to your e-mail program and choosing the "Tools" menu button and then selecting "Options," you will find a box full of many options to customize your e-mail. Under "Options," if you select "Mail Format," you will find both the stationery and signature capabilities.

Although I advise against the use of e-mail stationary or any unusual fonts therein, I will propose a middle ground on the signature—use the many fonts available in your word processing program. When you receive an e-mail that contains what appears to be a real signature, someone has actually signed, scanned, and digitized their signature, imbedding it into the body of the message. However, you should never use your real signature—with the littlest bit of technical expertise, anyone could copy it and electronic signatures can have the same legal validity as a written signature. Don't risk your online security.

Do not think for a moment that you see my signature in the following message. My handwriting has never been that legible, nor would I compromise my identity in this way. It is really just a font. Much less effort than scanning in your true signature and risking your credit line.

E-mail with fake signature

Accuracy Is Essential

Maybe your family doesn't mind the jokes with misspelled words. Perhaps your colleagues forgive typos, understanding that you are busy. But this is your job hunt, and you need to put your best professional foot forward. Under "Options" choose "Spelling" as seen below.

Spell-checking options

Now this is a truly useful little tool. Here you can set your e-mail to check spelling before each and every message is sent. Set this feature to always check before sending, but never forget that automatic spell check is not perfect.

Before you send any online communication, take a deep breath and remember to proof your resumes, cover letters, or any career communication. Practice using your e-mail and send your electronic cover letters and resume attachments to yourself, and friends, family members, and colleagues. Have friends print your practice e-mail messages and resumes—make sure that what you think you are sending is received in the way you intended.

You now know what it takes to put together a *Knock 'em Dead* cover letter. Now it is time to read through all the examples with your highlighter to get a feel for the many different styles that can work for your campaign. Flag the phrases you like and then go to work creating templates for your own *Knock 'em Dead* job-hunting letters.

SAMPLE LETTERS

HERE'S THE REAL meat and potatoes of the book—the sample letters you can use as models for your own.

Now we come to the letters. Apart from the sender's name and address (the personal stationery aspect), all letters adhere to Houghton Mifflin's *Best Writer's Guide* specifications. To those who might notice these things, it is important that we present an impeccable attention to detail.

E-Mail Response to Online Job Posting
(Technical Sales Representative)

From: Joan Carter [jcartersalespro@hotmail.com]
To: mbroome@palmettonetworksecurity.com
Cc:
Subject: Tech sales/key acct/new territory dev/negotiation/customer service

Dear Ms. _____:

Please accept this letter as application for the Technical Sales Representative position currently available with your company, as listed on Monster.com. My confidential resume is attached for your review and consideration, and I believe you will find me well qualified.

Detailed on my resume you will find a solid background in Sales and Marketing, with over two years in technical sales. In this capacity, I have developed an expertise in new and key account acquisition, new territory development and management, contract negotiation, and customer service. I am confident that my experience in these areas will prove to be an asset to ABC Corporation.

Additionally, I am familiar with blueprints, part number breakdowns, and the bidding process of our major accounts, which include _____, _____, _____ and _____ Corp. I have doubled my sales from $40,000/month to $80,000/month in just two years, and I am known for effectively identifying and resolving problems before they affect related areas, personnel, or customers.

I would welcome the opportunity to discuss with you how I might make similar contributions to the success of ABC Corporation. I look forward to hearing from you to schedule a personal interview at your convenience.

Sincere regards,

Joan Carter
(516) 555-1212
jcartersalespro@hotmail.com

E-Mail Response to Online Job Posting (Investment Banker)

From: James Stratton [jsinvest@aol.com]
To: lwilliam@teweles.com
Cc:
Subject: "Can do" administrator

Dear Mr. _____:

In response to your job posting for a _____ on your company's Web site, I have attached my resume for your consideration.

My experience as an administrative investment banker and assistant to a Vice Chairman is, I believe, readily adaptable to your needs. I have spent five years in a position best described as "doing whatever needs to be done" and have capitalized on my ability to undertake a large and widely varied array of projects, learn quickly, find effective solutions to problems, and maintain a sense of humor throughout.

My years as a line and administrative professional have also provided me with an unusual sensitivity to the needs of senior professionals. I have substantial computer experience and am fully computer literate. I have been told my verbal and written communication skills are exceptional.

I believe your firm would provide a working atmosphere to which I would be well suited, as well as one where my diverse experience would be valuable.

My salary requirements are reasonable and negotiable based on the responsibilities and opportunities presented.

Sincerely,

James Stratton
(516) 555-1212
jsinvest@aol.com

E-Mail Response to Online Job Posting (Legal Administrator)

From: Helen Darvik [darviklegalpro@earthlink.net]
To: ggoodfellow@budownoble.com
Cc:
Subject: Administrator/mgmnt/mktg/cmptr/acctg/planning/personnel

Dear Ms. _____:

I am responding to your job posting on Hotjobs.com for a legal administrator of a law firm. I wrote to you on (date) about law administrator positions in the metropolitan _____ area. I have attached another resume of my educational background and employment history. I am very interested in this position.

I have been a legal administrator for two 21-attorney law firms during the past six years. In addition, I have been a law firm consultant for over a year. Besides my law firm experience, I have been a medical administrator for over ten years. I believe that all of this experience will enable me to manage the law firm for this position very successfully. I possess the management, marketing, computer, accounting/budgeting, financial planning, personnel, and people-oriented skills that will have a very positive impact on this law firm.

I will be in the _____ area later in the month, so hopefully, we can meet at that time to discuss this position. I look forward to hearing from you, Ms. _____, concerning this position. Thank you for your time and consideration.

Very truly yours,

Helen Darvik
(516) 555-1212
darviklegalpro@earthlink.net

E-Mail Response to Online Job Posting (Manufacturing)

Shows loyalty, depth of experience in several positions, reliability,
and accomplishments, as well as his well-earned reputation.

From: Murray Danton [manufacturerMD@mindspring.com]
To: resumes@NexPress.com
Cc:
Subject: Warehouse pro committed to productivity

Dear Sir/Madam:

Please accept the attached resume in application for a position with your company that will utilize my extensive background in material handling, shipping, receiving and warehousing. Throughout my career, I have demonstrated my loyalty, commitment to excellence and solid work ethic. I am confident that I will make an immediate and long-term contribution to your company.

For the past 26 years, I have been successfully working in manufacturing and warehouse settings. I am a hard-working employee who always looks for ways to improve productivity, efficiency and accuracy. In past positions, I have identified ways to reduce downtime and waste, as well as methods to increase production.

I am dedicated to the principles of quality, continuous improvement and customer satisfaction. My supervisor has noted my record of "excellent attendance and dependability" and praised me as "reliable and highly motivated."

I would like to meet with you to discuss my qualifications. Please call me at the following phone number, or leave a message, to arrange an interview. Thank you for your consideration.

Sincerely,

Murray Danton
(516) 555-1212
manufacturerMD@mindspring.com

E-Mail Response to Online Job Posting (Production Supervisor)

From: Edwin Pastore [productionpro@yahoo.com]
To: hr@TimesGKielLabs.com
Cc:
Subject: Production Super matches your exact requirements

Dear Ms. _____:

In response to the job posting on your company's Web site, please consider my resume in your search for a Production Supervisor.

With a hi-tech background in *Fortune* 500 companies, I feel well qualified for the position you described. I am presently responsible for the coordination of production in three assembly and test areas which employ 35 union personnel. Maintaining control of work of this magnitude and complexity requires my ability to function independently, and a willingness to make decisions quickly and effectively.

I am accustomed to a fast-paced environment where deadlines are a priority and handling multiple jobs simultaneously is the norm. I enjoy a challenge and work hard to attain my goals. Constant negotiations with all levels of management and union employees have strengthened my interpersonal skills. I would like very much to discuss with you how I could contribute to your organization.

I am seeking an opportunity to excel in a more dynamic company and am looking forward to relocating to the _____ area.

Please contact me at your earliest convenience so that I may share with you my background and enthusiasm for the job. Thank you for your time and consideration.

Sincerely,

Edwin Pastore
(516) 555-1212
productionpro@yahoo.com

Response to Newspaper Advertisement (Health Care Management)

This applicant desires to transition to an administrative position in the field of health care; thus we highlighted her leadership and administrative skills.

REBA WOODWARD

9999 Oracal Ave. • Sunny, Texas 79000
(999) 999-9999 (H) • (999) 777-7777 (C)
r w o o d 5 8 6 @ h o t m a i l . c o m

February 15, 20–

Human Resources Coordinator
Sunny Home Nursing Service
9999 Hospital Ave.
Sunny, Texas 79000

We make a living by what we get,
but we make a life by what we give.
—Winston Churchill

Re: ADMINISTRATOR OF HEALTH CARE SERVICES

Dear Human Resources Coordinator:

Your recent classified ad in the *City-Wide Journal* caught my eye. As an experienced registered nurse, I am currently investigating career opportunities in the field of management in the health care industry where my highly developed skills will nicely transcend. The enclosed résumé reflects an exceptionally viable candidate for the above-named position.

I am a well-established native of this area with a background as program director, school nurse, operating room circulator, and charge nurse in clinic, ER, OR, and hospital floor environments. The following skills and characteristics are reason to take a closer look at my credentials. I am:

- **strong in handling multiple tasks and multifaceted situations while maintaining satisfactory interpersonal relationships with staff, physicians, patients, students, and families.**

- **an expert at ensuring compliance with regulations while keeping costs within budget.**

- **talented in prioritizing issues and tasks and visualizing the "big" picture when considering the long-term effects of my decisions.**

- **an outcome-oriented self-starter with superior organizational and administrative skills.**

After reviewing my résumé, you will discover that my qualifications are a good match for this position. The opportunity for a personal interview to further discuss employment possibilities would be mutually beneficial. You may reach me at (999) 999-9999 to schedule an appointment at your convenience. In the meantime, thank you for your time and consideration.

Sincerely,

Reba Woodward

Reba Woodward

Enclosure: Résumé

Response to Newspaper Advertisement (Adjunct Faculty Position)

A speech therapist in a local school district, this candidate is looking for
an adjunct faculty position with a community college.

Harriette L. Christophorous

585-398-6194   27 Crystal Valley Overlook   harrichris@aol.com
                            Batavia, New York 14020

January 12, 20–

Ms. Alexandra Kinkead
Director of Human Resources
Monroe Community College
1000 East Henrietta Road
Rochester, New York 14623

Dear Ms. Kinkead:

Your recent advertisement for adjunct faculty positions has captured my serious interest. I am confident that my 25 years' experience as a Speech Therapist in the Batavia Central School provides me with the capabilities to fulfill the **Voice & Articulation** position mentioned in the ad. Accordingly, I have enclosed a résumé that briefly outlines my professional history.

Some key points you may find relevant to this opportunity include:

✓ *Experience assessing needs of and providing instruction to the disabled. In my current position, I work one-on-one with students having hearing loss, emotional disorders, ADHD, autism, and other physical disabilities impacting their ability to acquire speech. I also develop IEPs and participate in the CSE process to define students' needs and implement instruction plans.*

✓ *Excellent leadership skills, with experience mentoring co-workers. Currently, I mentor speech therapists and teachers working with hearing-impaired students, as well as direct the activities of two other speech therapists.*

✓ *A master's degree in Speech Pathology, plus NYS Certification as a Speech & Hearing Handicapped Teacher. In addition, I have attended workshops in Phonemic Awareness, Autism, and Pervasive Developmental Disorders.*

In my current role, I am accountable for addressing the needs of approximately 300 elementary and secondary school students with various speech deficiencies. I believe that my knowledge and expertise would allow me to effectively serve your students in this Voice & Articulation instructional role. I would enjoy speaking with you in person to discuss in fuller detail how my qualifications can fulfill your needs. Please contact me via phone or e-mail to arrange a mutually convenient date and time for us to meet.

Thank you for your time and consideration. I look forward to talking with you soon.

Sincerely,

Harriette L. Christophorous

Harriette L. Christophorous

Enclosure

Response to Newspaper Advertisement (Hydrogeologist)

Applying for positions in a newly emerging scientific discipline; her resume requires a heavy emphasis on educational background information.

Aileen Renfro
545 Appleton Street ▪ Houston, TX 77068
(713) 888-9900 ▪ aileenrenfro@msw.com

June 30, 20–

Human Resources Department
CRPH
155 Garner Avenue, Suite 1000
Los Angeles, CA 95496

RE: Position of Hydrogeologist/Groundwater Modeler, Company Job ID: ACHZ4121-234059, AJB Reference Number: 4950495, Job ID #0000BZ/BBBB

Dear Human Resources Representative:

I learned about your position description for a Hydrogeologist/Groundwater Modeler with great interest, as my qualifications match your requirements for this position. Therefore, please accept my resume for your review and allow me to explain briefly how I can contribute to the future success of CRPH.

With an MS Degree in Hydrologic Sciences and over 7 years of research experience, I have developed a strong background in advanced theories of solute transport modeling; consequently, I have developed effective quantitative skills and a practical understanding of the fundamental principles and concepts associated with hydrogeology.

My resume will provide additional details regarding my educational background and professional experience. Beyond these qualifications, it may be helpful for you to know that I have worked successfully in both independent and team project environments, adapt readily to rapidly changing work conditions, and enjoy the prospect of contributing to CRPH's "80-year reputation as a water industry leader" in the advancement of hydrogeologic and groundwater projects.

I would welcome the opportunity to interview for this position and discuss the results you can expect from me as a member of your team. Thank you for your time and consideration.

Sincerely,

Aileen Renfro

Aileen Renfro

Enclosure

Response to Newspaper Advertisement
(Customer Service Representative)

An ad response with requested salary history.

Cassidy Stratton

444 Marks Street • Brentwood, NY 11717 • (631) 435-1879 • cassidy123@custsrv.net

---

February 4, 20–

Mr. Josh Williams
Personnel Director
LI Financial Group
777 Alexander Road
Huntington Station, NY 11746

Dear Mr. Williams:

In response to your open position announcement in *Newsday* for a customer service representative, I am forwarding my resume for your review and consideration. Ideally, this position will make optimal use of my experience working in capacities that require strong interpersonal communication and customer needs assessment skills, an ability to interface effectively with internal/external contacts, and a skill for ensuring the accurate, timely processing of electronic, verbal, and written information.

Since 1990, I have held longstanding positions of increased responsibility for leading financial services organizations, in charge of tracking, monitoring, reviewing, and processing of account and market-related data. In these positions, I have proved and continue to prove myself as a capable, take-charge team player with an ability to coordinate diversified departmental and customer support functions. Combined with my ability to proficiently manage and train others on the complexities of comprehensive databases and improve workflow efficiencies, I am confident that I would be an asset to your customer service organization.

I would welcome the opportunity to meet with you for an in-depth interview. Thank you for your review and consideration. I look forward to hearing from you soon.

Sincerely,

Cassidy Stratton

Cassidy Stratton

Salary Requirement:
$34,000 – $42,000

Salary History:
LI Financial Group. Starting $27,000; Ending $38,000
Credit Checkers: Starting $18,000; Ending $24,000

Response to Newspaper Advertisement (Sales Associate)

An entry-level cover letter to convince the employer that he can tackle a full-time job even though he is still in school.

.... MARC LOMBARDI

September 3, 20–

Mr. John Relka
Sales Manager
A-Jay Sports Outfitters
226 First Avenue
Ocean City, NJ 99999

Re: Sales Associate Position

Dear Mr. Relka:

If you are searching for a success-driven Sales Associate who is a hard worker and an innovator, look no further. Highlights of my achievements include the following:

- Awarded with 3 plaques and nominated to President's Club for exemplary sales performance.
- Started a business from scratch and grew customer base using multiple marketing methods.
- Earned most of college expenses since 2002.

Although I will not graduate until December, I am eager to start work as soon as possible—either full- or part-time. I am certain that I can balance the responsibilities of a Sales Associate position with my studies, because I have successfully handled full-time employment with a full course load in the past.

My résumé is enclosed for your consideration. I believe that I can make a positive contribution to A-Jay Sports Outfitters and look forward to discussing my qualifications in detail.

I will call you next week to arrange for a meeting at a mutually convenient time. Thank you for your consideration.

Sincerely,

Marc Lombardi

Marc Lombardi

Enclosure

....
111 Park Place • Ocean City, NJ 99999 • (555) 555-5555 • mlombardi@dotresume.com

Response to Newspaper Advertisement (Medical Biller)

Emphasizes people skills, which are as important as
technical abilities in a busy medical office.

Doreen Canfield
703 West Pike Street
Valley Forge, PA 00000
(555) 555-5555
doreen&george@dotcom.com

February 27, 20–

Healthcare Associates
P.O. Box 000
Philadelphia, PA 00000

Dear Hiring Manager:

I am very interested in the medical biller position you advertised in Sunday's *Inquirer* and believe I have the qualifications to successfully fulfill your requirements.

As you review my enclosed resume, you will see that I have a solid administrative background, combined with intensive training in medical billing policies and procedures received at Franklin Institute for Allied Health Professionals. My coursework heavily emphasized the international classification of diseases (ICD-9) and complex CPT coding for insurance purposes, and also included instruction in standard billing procedures to produce invoices or superbills within the office, utilization of outside billing services, and electronic billing.

From my prior experience, I had many occasions when I had to deal with confused and difficult clients, not unlike the patients at a doctor's office who do not understand the provisions of their healthcare plans. With my personable manner of interaction and skill in tactfully communicating or clarifying information, I was able to quickly resolve disagreements, answer questions, and retain their confidence. I am equally comfortable in close working relationships with physicians and other professional staff, learning quickly, and adapting easily to any office environment.

I feel confident that I could be a valuable asset to your practice and look forward to an interview to discuss how I may be able to contribute to your profitability and efficiency. May I hear from you soon?

Sincerely,

Doreen Canfield

Doreen Canfield

Enclosure: Resume

Response to Newspaper Advertisement (Skilled Laborer)

This cover letter had to overcome an obvious "overqualification" barrier.

JACK LEVAN

1121 MAILER AVENUE ◆ KNOXVILLE, TENNESSEE 37901 ◆ JLEVAN555@YAHOO.COM ◆ 865.555.5555

Tuesday, 11 November, 20–

Mr. Drake Norris
Lockheed Martin Corporation
1122 Cortland Avenue
Suite 210
Miami, Florida 33101

Dear Mr. Norris:

When I saw your announcement for a skilled laborer at Cudjoe Key, I made writing this letter my first priority. Of course, I've already applied online. But, the more I thought about this opportunity, the more it seemed a perfect match for both of us. And so I wanted you to have a good deal more than the usual, impersonal, application.

I think you deserve to see the contributions I can make to the Lockheed Martin team at once. That's why you'll find my résumé different from others you may have run across. In place of the usual "objective statement," you'll read about four, productivity-building capabilities I can bring to the job. And, right below them, are seven examples of the kinds of contributions I've made to my employers.

But I am concerned that you may think I am "overqualified." To put that in plain language, you may feel I will be bored by the job. In fact, your position fits in nicely with my goal of getting my degree in Aerospace Engineering. I can't think of a better opportunity to see the OT&E process at work that being "in the trenches" on a project like yours.

I do best when I can learn about my employer's special needs. May I call in a few days to explore how I might fit best onto your team?

Sincerely,

Jack Levan

Jack Levan

Encl.: Résumé

Response to Newspaper Advertisement (Peace Officer)

As a recent graduate, his education section needed to come first
and have the primary focus; however, he also wanted to emphasize
his experience as a trainer and team leader.

JAMES BURLINGTON
9803 Clinton Avenue
Lubbock, TX 79424

(806) 783-9900
jamesb@door.net

September 13, 20–

Lubbock Police Department
320 9th Street
Lubbock, TX 79416

Dear Hiring Representative:

I am submitting my résumé in application for the position of Peace Officer. I have recently completed necessary educational requirements, and I am enthusiastic about the possibility of interviewing for this position.

My studies at Texas Tech University provided me the opportunity to study and analyze key concepts, principles, and practices associated with human behavior and criminal justice. Subsequently, I demonstrated in-depth knowledge of law enforcement and social science issues through excellent work in class assignments and projects. Of course, I realize that there is a significant difference between academic studies and practical field experience, but I am confident that my strong knowledge in criminal justice will increase my ability to perform effectively within your department.

Additionally, I earned recognition from my managers in my employment positions for my leadership and organizational skills. As a Certified Trainer at Orlando's, I trained a staff of eight bussers and contributed to improved team performance by building great relationships with team members and guests. As a Garden Shop Associate at Sutherland's, I organized the garden area in such a way that made it easy for both employees and customers to find items readily. The additional skills I gained from these positions could transfer readily to your department, as well.

My résumé is enclosed to provide you with additional details concerning my background and achievements. Thank you for your time and consideration.

Sincerely,

James Burlington

James Burlington

Enclosure

Response to Newspaper Advertisement (Assessment Coordinator)

Anna M. Sanchez

· ·

123 Fort Avenue • Huntington, NY 12752 • (631) 555-2222 • Cellular (631) 555-3333

2 PAGES VIA FAX   June 11, 2004
DEPT. HD 212-555-9999

Your advertisement in the *New York Times*, on June 9, 20–, for an **Assessment Coordinator** seems to perfectly match my background and experience. As the International Brand Coordinator for Kahlúa, I coordinated meetings, prepared presentations and materials, organized a major off-site conference, and supervised an assistant. I believe that I am an excellent candidate for this position as I have illustrated below:

YOUR REQUIREMENTS	MY QUALIFICATIONS
A highly motivated, diplomatic, flexible, quality-driven professional on every project.	Successfully managed project teams involving different business units. The defined end results were achieved.
Exceptional organizational skills and attention to detail	Planned the development and launch of the Kahlúa Heritage Edition bottle series. My former manager enjoyed leaving the "details" and follow-through to me. Coverdale project management training.
College degree and minimum 3 years relevant business experience	B.A. from Vassar College (1994). 5+ years business experience in productive, professional environments.
Computer literacy	Extensive knowledge of Windows & Macintosh applications.

I'm interested in this position because it fits well with my new career focus in the human resources field. Currently, I am enrolled in NYU's adult career planning and development certificate program and working at Lee Hecht Harrison.

I have enclosed my resume to provide more information on my strengths and career achievements. If after reviewing my material you believe that there is a match, please call me. Thank you for your consideration.

Sincere regards,

Anna M. Sanchez

Anna M. Sanchez

AS
enclosure

Response to Newspaper Advertisement (Office Administrator)

Mark Stevenson

May 5, 2004
Philip _____
(title)
ABC Firm
1 Industry Plaza
Lansing, MI 48180

Dear Mr. _____:

Your notice for an **Office Administrator** caught my attention because my background appears to parallel your needs. Please refer to the enclosed resume for a summary of my qualifications. I am sure you have been flooded with hundreds of qualified applicants; please allow me to explain why you would want to call me first.

I am very **self sufficient** and able to **work independently with little supervision**. With little formal training, I have taken the initiative to learn about and remain current with my company's products, processes, and expectations. I am looked at as **an information resource** and enjoy sharing my knowledge with others. I also enjoy **managing projects** and **planning meetings, trips, and special events**.

I am always looking for ways to **streamline processes** and become more efficient. I have **developed systems and processes** using available software to automate production reporting, notify customers of changes, and inform the field staff of corporate changes or initiatives. When supervising clerical staff, I always try to **plan ahead** to make the best use of their time.

I **work well with executives, sales representatives, customers, vendors, *and* coworkers, and demonstrate strong interpersonal communication and good judgment**. I always try to listen closely and understand what others need. Then, I look for ways to help solve the problem. I have particularly found that listening, without interrupting, can diffuse a tense situation and allow the issue to be resolved more quickly with a positive outcome.

I am confident that I can deliver similar results for ABC Firm. I would appreciate the opportunity to speak with you to schedule an appointment and provide you with more information. Thank you for your time and consideration; I look forward to speaking with you soon.

Sincerely,

Mark Stevenson

Mark Stevenson
MS
enclosure

---

200 Westwood Drive • Trenton, MI 48183 • (313) 555-9020 • officeadministrator@hotmail.com

Response to Newspaper Advertisement (Legal Secretary)

Marianne Johnston

293 Hunter's Pointe / Berea, Ohio 44110
216-248-1699 / 440-737-1725 (Cellular)
legalsecretary@earthlink.com

(Date)

Emily _____
(Title)
ABC Bar Association
1 Industry Plaza
Columbus, OH 44119

RE: OBA OFFICE OF BAR COUNSEL LEGAL SECRETARY

Dear Ms. _____:

It is with continued interest and enthusiasm that I respond to your advertisement for Legal Secretary to the ABC Bar Association's Office of Bar Counsel. I believe that my education and experience combine to create a perfect match for the position, and would appreciate careful consideration of my credentials as presented below and within my resume, enclosed.

It has long been my dream to pursue a career in the legal arena, and my goal to associate with the top professionals in the field. Where better to continue my professional development than within the heart of the organization as a provider of administrative support to members of the Ohio Bar Association itself!

Although a relative newcomer to the field, I have earned my degree in Paralegal studies, graduating in 1999 with Magna Cum Laude distinction. With more than two years of experience after graduation providing administrative and clerical support in private practice, I am confident that I possess the expertise and dedication that will make an immediate and significant contribution to the efficiency and organization of the Office of Bar Counsel.

If you are looking for a legal support professional who is committed to the highest standards of performance, relates well with others, is self-directing and highly motivated, and is looking for a long-term employment relationship, please contact me to arrange an interview. I will make myself available at your first convenience.

Thank you for your consideration; I will look forward to the opportunity to speak with you soon.

Sincerely yours,

Marianne Johnston

Marianne Johnston

MJ
enclosure (Resume and Professional References)

Response to Newspaper Advertisement (Accounting Manager)

Paul Anthony

516.555.4844 | 169 Laure Road | accountingpro@bellsouth.net
Hunt Town, New York 11553

(Date)

Phillip _____
(Title)
ABC Corporation
1 Industry Plaza
Long Island, NY 11551

Dear Mr. _____:

Re: File No. 213

I have nine years of accounting experience and am responding to your recent advertisement for an Accounting Manager. Please allow me to highlight my skills as they relate to your stated requirements.

Your Requirements	**My Experience**
• A recognized accounting degree plus several years of practical experience	• Obtained a C.A. degree in 1995 and have over four years' experience as an Accounting Manager.
• Excellent people skills and demonstrated ability to motivate staff	• Effectively managed a staff of 24 including two supervisors.
• Strong administrative and analytical skills.	• Assisted in the development of a base reference library with Microsoft Excel for 400 clients.
• Good oral and written communication skills	• Trained four new supervisors via daily coaching sessions, communication meetings, and technical skill sessions.

I believe this background provides the management skills you require for this position. I would welcome the opportunity for a personal interview to further discuss my qualifications.

Yours truly,

Paul Anthony

Paul Anthony

PA
enclosure

Response to Newspaper Advertisement (International Sales Manager)

Suzanne A. Kennedy
2490 Sierra Ridge Overlook
Colorado Springs, Colorado 80922
719-265-1109

(Date)

Phillip _____
(Title)
ABC Corporation
1 Industry Plaza
Denver, CO 80911

Dear Mr. _____:

Re: International Sales Manager, *Globe & Mail*, September –, 20–

I was recently speaking with Mr. _____ from your firm and he strongly recommended that I send you a copy of my resume. Knowing the requirements for the position, he felt that I would be an ideal candidate. For more than eleven years, I have been involved in international sales management, with seven years directly in the aerospace industry. My qualifications for the position include:

- establishing sales offices in France, Great Britain and Germany;
- recruiting and managing a group of 24 international sales representatives;
- providing training programs for all of the European staff, which included full briefing on our own products as well as competitor lines;
- obtaining 42%, 33% and 31% of the French, German, and British markets, respectively, dealing with all local engine and airframe manufacturers; and
- generating more than $32 million in sales with excellent margins.

My Bachelor of Science degree in electrical engineering was obtained from the University of _____ and my languages include French and German.

I feel confident that an interview would demonstrate that my expertise in setting up rep organizations and training and managing an international sales department would be an excellent addition to your growing aerospace corporation.

I look forward to meeting with you, Mr. _____, and will give you a call to follow up on this letter the week of (date) _____.

Yours truly,

Suzanne A. Kennedy

Suzanne A. Kennedy

SK
enclosure

Response to Newspaper Advertisement (Executive Assistant)

Andrew F. Petersen

387 Rockingham Place • Rochester, New York 14613
585-287-6981 • executiveassistant@localnet.com

(Date)

Box 9412
New York, NY 01234

Dear _____:

I was very pleased to learn of the need for an Executive Assistant in your company from your recent advertisement in _____. I believe the qualities you seek are well matched by my track record:

Your Needs	My Qualifications
Independent Self-Starter	• Served as company liaison between sales representatives, controlling commissions and products.
	• Controlled cash flow, budget planning and bank reconciliation for three companies.
	• Assisted in the promotion of a restaurant within a private placement sales effort, creating sales materials and communicating with investors.
Computer Experience	• Utilized Lotus in preparing financial spreadsheet used in private placement memoranda and Macintosh to design brochures and flyers.
	• Have vast experience with both computer programming and the current software packages.
Compatible Background	• Spent 5 years overseas and speak French.
	• Served as an executive assistant to four corporate heads.

A resume is enclosed that covers my experience and qualifications in greater detail. I would appreciate the opportunity to discuss my credentials in a personal interview.

Sincerely,

Andrew Petersen

Andrew Petersen

AP
enclosure

POWER PHRASES

Consider using adaptations of these key phrases in your responses to newspaper advertisements.

I believe that I am particularly well qualified for your position and would like to have the opportunity to meet with you to explore how I may be of value to your organization.

Your advertisement #5188 in the March 25th edition of The _____ *has piqued my interest. This position has strong appeal to me.*

I am confident that with my abilities I can make an immediate and valuable contribution to _____.

I would be pleased if you contacted me for an interview.

I was recently speaking with Mr. _____ from your firm and he strongly recommended that I send you a copy of my resume. Knowing the requirements for the position, he felt that I would be an ideal candidate.

I've had both large and small company experience and it is my preference to work in a smaller operation where goals are measurable, results are noticeable and contributions really make a difference!

I feel confident that an interview would demonstrate that my expertise in setting up rep organizations, and training and managing an international sales department, would be an excellent addition to your growing _____ company.

I look forward to meeting with you, Mr. _____, and will give you a call to follow up on this letter the week of September –th.

The opportunity to work with your client is appealing to me, and I would appreciate an opportunity to discuss the position further. I look forward to hearing from you soon.

I believe this background provides the management skills you require for this position. I would welcome the opportunity for a personal interview to further discuss my qualifications.

In response to your ad, please consider my resume in your search for a Sales Service Coordinator.

I look forward to hearing from you in the near future to schedule an interview at your convenience, during which I hope to learn more about your company's plans and goals and how I might contribute to the success of its service team.

I am accustomed to a fast-paced environment where deadlines are priority and handling multiple jobs simultaneously is the norm. I enjoy a challenge and work hard to attain my goals. Constant negotiations with all levels of management and union employees have strengthened my interpersonal skills. I would like very much to discuss with you how I could contribute to your organization.

I am seeking an opportunity to excel in a dynamic company and am looking forward to relocating to _____.

Please contact me at your earliest convenience so that I may share with you my background and enthusiasm for the job.

Your ad captured my attention.

My personal goal is simple: I wish to be a part of an organization that wants to excel in both _____ and _____. I believe that if I had the opportunity to interview with you it would be apparent that my skills are far-reaching.

Although I'm far more interested in a fine company and an intriguing challenge than merely in money, you should know that in recent years my compensation has been in the range of $45,000 to $60,000.

May we set up a time to talk?

What you need and what I can do sound like a match!

Please find enclosed a copy of my resume for your review. I believe the combination of my _____ education and my business experience offers me the unique opportunity to make a positive contribution to your firm.

As you will note in my resume I have not only "grown up" in and with the Operations and Warehousing area of a major (apparel) (consumer products) company,

I have also established my expertise and my value to a discriminating and brilliant employer who depended upon me—on a daily basis—to represent and protect his interests and contribute significantly to his profitability.... I am seeking an opportunity to replicate this situation and again utilize my considerable abilities to dedicate myself to the profitability of my employer.

I am available to meet with you to discuss my qualifications at your convenience. I can be reached at _____. I would like to thank you in advance for your time and any consideration you may give me. I look forward to hearing from you.

Having been born and raised in the _____ area and wishing to return to this area to work as a _____, I have been researching _____ firms that offer the type of experience for which my previous education and work experience will be of mutual benefit. Highlights of my attached resume include: _____.

Please consider my qualifications for the position of _____ which you advertised.

As you will note on the enclosed resume, the breadth of my expertise covers a wide area of responsibilities, thereby providing me with insights into the total operation.

Recently, I saw an advertisement in the _____ for a position as a Technical Trainer. My candidacy for this position is advanced by my experience in three areas: training, support, and a technological background.

I thrive on challenge and feel that my skills and experience are easily transferable.

I would appreciate an opportunity to discuss my abilities in more depth, and am available for an interview at your earliest convenience.

Is the ideal candidate for the position of _____ highly motivated, professional, and knowledgeable in all functions concerning _____? Well, you may be interested to know that a person possessing these qualities, and much more, is responding to your ad in the _____ for this position.

I very much enjoy working in a team environment and the rewards associated with group contribution.

The skills you require seem to match my professional strengths.

I have a strong background in telemarketing small and medium-sized businesses in the _____ District and outlying areas.

I look forward to hearing from you soon to set up an appointment at your convenience. Please feel free to give me a call at my office at _____ or leave a message at my home number, _____.

As a recent MBA graduate, my professional job experience is necessarily limited. However, I believe that you will find, and previous employers will verify, that I exhibit intelligence, common sense, initiative, maturity, and stability, and I am eager to make a positive contribution to your organization.

I read, with a great deal of interest, your advertisement in the October 20 _____, issue of _____.

Please allow me to highlight some of my achievements which relate to your requirements: _____.

I would greatly appreciate the opportunity to discuss this position in a personal interview. I may be contacted at _____ to arrange a meeting.

I would appreciate an opportunity to meet with you. At present I am working as a temp but am available to meet with you at your convenience. I look forward to meeting you.

Thank you for taking the time recently to respond to my questions concerning a _____ position with _____.

I will be in your area Friday, December -th, and will call you early next week to see if we might schedule a meeting at that time.

This experience has provided me with a keen appreciation for the general practice of _____.

A salary of $30,000 would be acceptable; however, my main concern is to find employment where there is potential for growth.

"Cold" Cover Letter to a Potential Employer (Entry-Level Network Admin.)

Network administrator seeking entry-level opportunity; highlights his certifications to emphasize recent professional development. Good idea when attempting ground-floor position.

ANDREW J. STELLS

P. O. Box 2146 ◆ Buffalo, New York 27893 ◆ (505) 554-9021 ◆ ajs@hotmail.com

Dear Sir or Madam:

I have received my **MCP Certification**, and I am currently working on my **A++ Network Certification**. I am seeking an opportunity that will enable me to utilize my training and hands-on technical exposure within an **entry-level Network Administrator** position. A brief highlight of the skills and values I would bring to your organization include:

- Knowledge of installation, configuration, troubleshooting and repair of sophisticated, state-of-the-art software and hardware developed through recent computer operations training.

- Acquired analytical, research, troubleshooting, interpersonal and organizational skills developed through on-the-job training within an IT environment.

- Proven success in prioritizing time, completing projects and meeting deadlines under time-sensitive circumstances, achieving stellar results.

- An energetic, enthusiastic, and "people-driven" communication style.

Since a résumé can neither fully detail all my skills and accomplishments, nor predict my potential to your organization, I would welcome a personal interview to further explore the merging of my training and knowledge with your **IT** needs.

Very truly yours,

ANDREW J. STELLS

Enclosure

"Cold" Cover Letter to a Potential Employer (Entry-Level Librarian)

Helena, who emigrated from Poland, has completed her master's in library science and is looking for her first full-time position in her career field.

Helena Swenka

(410) 997-5555	555 Chestnut Street Columbia, MD 21044	helenaswen@nsn.com

November 15, 20–

Mr. Jeffery Devine, Library Division Director
Columbia Public Library
2774 Swan Point Road
Columbia, MD 21046

Dear Mr. Devine,

Does your library anticipate the need for an **Entry-Level Research or Reference Librarian or Cataloguer?** With my recent MLIS degree from an ALA-accredited program, as well as internship experience in the reference department of academic and state government libraries, perhaps I can be of service.

My résumé is enclosed for your review. You will find evidence of my librarianship training, library database and computer skills, and work history. What you will not immediately see on my résumé are my character traits and achievements—allow me to list some of them for you that I believe are relevant:

✓ *Hard-working, determined achiever* – *I set my sights high, whether attaining a* **3.95 GPA** *at University of Maryland in a demanding* **MLIS Degree** *program, empowering foreign nationals to achieve their goals of US citizenship by teaching them English and Civics (pass rate of 100% over 8-year period with more than 2000 individuals), or responding to reference requests with a high-level of customer service and promptness (within 1–3 hours).*

✓ *Information technology savvy and fast learner* – *My references will attest to how quickly I assimilated knowledge of library databases, computer software, and integrated library automation systems. With hands-on experience using* **Voyager Module, AACR2r, LC classification scheme, MARC format, and OCLC,** *as well as* **Lexis-Nexis, Dow-Jones, Dialog Web and Classic,** *I have worked with diverse reference materials such as legal, Maryland State and Federal, genealogy documents, as well as periodicals.*

✓ *Proactive problem-solver and team player* – *Utilizing my broad foreign language skills (Polish, Russian, Slovak, German, Latin) allowed me to problem-solve with confidence and correctly catalog foreign language materials while serving a* **reference library internship** *with* **The Baltimore County Library.** *As an* **intern cataloger,** *I worked cooperatively with others in serial publication cataloguing and serial control, achieving high rates of daily production.*

Providing high-level customer service and efficiency is my goal in library services and support. My knowledge and practical use of Internet resources and navigational tools, combined with my experience with library databases, affords you the opportunity to hire an entry-level library professional with proven librarianship success. May we meet soon to discuss your needs? I will call your office next week to schedule a mutually convenient appointment, if that is agreeable with you. Thank you for your time and consideration.

Sincerely,

Helena Swenka

Helena Swenka

Enclosure

"Cold" Cover Letter to a Potential Employer (Manager)

Concerned that his company is not doing well financially, William has decided to "test the waters" for another position similar to those he has done in the past.

WILLIAM C. KITE

7271 Foxhill Drive
Livingston, NJ 07039

(973) 740-5555
Wmckite@hotmail.com

December 12, 20–

Mr. Jacob Abernathy
Warehouse and Assembly Services
17 Industrial Way
Livingston, NJ 07039

Dear Mr. Abernathy,

More than ever, good companies need proven performers who can get results in competitive industries and a tough economy, whether working independently or leading teams. If you are in need of a Warehouse Manager, Inventory Control Specialist, Production Manager, or Assembly Order Fulfillment Supervisor, consider my track record:

✓ Efficiently scheduled assembly, material handlers, and warehouse personnel, and closely monitored interplant transfers of raw materials from 20 warehouses. Assembly production and distribution procedures yielded high levels of productivity: 90% on-time delivery, including emergency orders, of up to $1 million in SKUs per week. (Expediter/ Production Dept. Scheduler, Mony-Schaffer Corp.)

✓ Developed cooperative relationships with field sales reps of major corporations, such as PricewaterhouseCoopers, U.S. Healthcare, and UPS, and served as liaison with in-house account executives and customer service reps at The Hibbert Group, to streamline receiving and shipping operations and upgrade quality control. (Warehouse Manager, The Devaney Group)

✓ As final assembly and inspection member of 4-person team, met heavy production schedule (35 to 60 complex, fabricated units per day) with 6% or less error rate. (Order Fulfillment Clerk, Mony-Schaffer)

✓ Working as part of a team, created, tested, packaged, and directed to shipping custom ship sets of complex hose assemblies, meeting deadlines 99-plus% of the time. Utilized quality assurance testing methods, including pressure testing of assembled units, to ensure highest level of customer satisfaction. (Hose Fabrication Technician, Mony-Schaffer Corp.)

I am confident I can deliver similar results for your company.

With well-rounded experience in assembly, expediting and scheduling, shipping and receiving, order fulfillment, customer service, sales, supervision and training, and a 15-year track record of meeting deadlines in demanding (even emergency) situations, I believe I have the proven skills that can benefit your company.

Page 1 of 2

In addition, I realize it is hard-working and cooperative people who deliver results. My focus on teamwork and productivity has proven successful in my past assignments. I am confident I can convince you that I have the technical experience and knowledge that you need, as well as the intangible qualifies—enthusiasm, strong work ethic, dedication and dependability—to get the job done right.

May we meet soon to discuss your needs? I will contact your office next week to schedule a mutually convenient appointment, if that is agreeable with you. Thank you for your consideration.

Sincerely,

William C. Kite
Enclosure

"Cold" Cover Letter to a Potential Employer (Mental Health)

An applicant with a MSW seeking to advance his career.

.... **PETER A. EDGEWATERS**

Dear Sir or Madam:

Throughout my career, I have held increasingly complex positions within the Mental Health Care industry, gaining extensive experience in working both with patients and in administrative functions. My particular areas of expertise are:

- Physical Medicine and Rehabilitation
- Adult Intervention
- Family Counseling
- Legal Issues
- Government Regulations
- Child Evaluation

My greatest strength lies in my ability to communicate with all types of people and different levels of professionals. Being able to work with patients, physicians, legal officers, and family members has enabled me to be a highly effective therapist and an advocate for the patient and the patient's family. As a Veteran's Administration official, I have been inducted into the intricacies of the federal government and have been able to gain a thorough understanding of the workings of various government agencies as they relate to mental health, including the Social Security Administration, Department of Veteran's Affairs, Department of Defense, and other entities.

I feel my knowledge and strengths would be best applied as a consultant or private Mental Rehabilitation Therapy. Further, I desire to return to a more focused health care organization such as yours and would welcome an opportunity to interview with you in person.

I look forward to speaking with you at your earliest convenience and appreciate your time in reviewing my credentials and qualifications. I am confident that my professional knowledge and strengths, combined with my dedication, work ethic, and energy, will add measurable value to your organization. Thank you for your consideration.

Sincerely,

Peter A. Edgewaters
PETER A. EDGEWATERS

Enclosure

....
40 Land Avenue • Plain, New Jersey 05050 • (555) 555-5555 • xxxxxxxxx@msn.com

"Cold" Cover Letter to a Potential Employer
(Senior Customer Service Specialist)

This candidate's most impressive qualifications are summarized in an eye-catching bulleted list.

Maria H. Berretta
111 Creamery Road
Skippack, PA 99999
Home: (555) 555-5555
Cell: (999) 999-9999
berretta@dotresume.com

March 3, 20–

Ms. Jayne Longnecker
Customer Service Manager
Whittier Insurance Company
111 State Road
Blue Bell, PA 99999

Re: Senior Customer Service Specialist

Dear Ms. Longnecker:

Are you looking for a Senior Customer Service Specialist who is:

- A consistent top performer with a strong desire to get the job done.
- A team player, able to achieve results through coordination with employees in all functional areas.
- An effective communicator with excellent writing, training, and telephone skills.
- Able to learn quickly, analyze complex information, and find solutions to problems.
- Organized, thorough, and precise.

If so, you will be interested in my qualifications. I have a bachelor's degree in business administration and seven years of experience in the insurance/financial industry, serving in diverse roles as customer relations advisor and calculations processor. For more than a year and a half, I have consistently received the highest ratings in my unit despite the fact that the difficult cases frequently find their way to my desk. I have also contributed to my team by putting in extra time to clear backlogs and analyzing existing procedures to devise more efficient methods of operation.

My résumé is enclosed for your review. I believe that I can make a positive contribution to Whittier Insurance Company and look forward to meeting with you to discuss my qualifications in detail. Thank you for your time and consideration.

Sincerely,

Maria H. Berretta

Maria H. Berretta

Enclosure

"Cold" Cover Letter to a Potential Employer (Research Professional)

Darrin is a data specialist working for the state, compiling birth/death and census statistics. He wants to enter the private sector to do more consumer/product research projects.

Darrin Wilson

MARKET RESEARCH ANALYST

Dear Sir/Madam:

As a research professional, I understand that success depends on a strong commitment to **customer satisfaction**. Executing the basics and using logic and reasoning to identify the strengths and weaknesses of alternative solutions, conclusions or approaches to problems are key to increasing performance and market share. I believe that my background and education reflect a commitment and ability to find solutions to these challenges. I developed excellent skills in **project coordination and the design and development of research projects** that increased the effectiveness of my organization.

I am considered an energetic, aggressive and innovative leader who is extremely client-oriented.

My position encompasses multiple tasks and responsibilities that include:

♦ Examining and analyzing statistical data to forecast future trends and to identify potential markets.

♦ Designing and implementing new formats for logging and transferring information while working as part of a team researching data and statistics.

Thank you for your consideration. I approach my work with a strong sense of urgency, working well under pressure and change. I look forward to meeting with you personally so that we may discuss how I may make a positive contribution to your organization.

Sincerely yours,

Darrin Wilson

Darrin Wilson

Enclosure

1124 Liberty Street, 3rd Floor • Chester, PA 18940 • 267.757.5462 • dWilson53@excite.com

"Cold" Cover Letter to a Potential Employer (Personal Trainer)

Transitioning into fitness training after a long and successful career in general management, sales, and customer relationship management.

JAMES J. HUTCHISEN
P.O. Box 901 ▪ Montrose, New Hampshire 58723
(303) 527-9501 ▪ jjhutch@hotmail.com

Dear Sir or Madam:

Reflecting on my professional sales and management experience within the marine industry, it is at this point in my career I am seeking to pursue a long-term personal and professional goal of a challenging opportunity as a **Personal Trainer/Strength Coach** within a health club, physical therapy and/or fitness facility. Let me briefly highlight the skills, values and contributions I will bring to your organization:

- **Certified Personal Trainer/Health Fitness Instructor at leading training facility.**
- Possess over 25 years health club experience with most types of cardiovascular, plate and free-weight systems.
- Proven ability to plan and implement training programs through experience as a Personal Trainer for a health club.
- Strong general management, sales, marketing and customer relationship management expertise developed through 16 years as an Owner/Operator of a marine business.
- Comprehensive experience in human relations, within the retail/service arena, has characterized me as considerate, dependable, honest, straightforward, hard-working, and personable.

Since a résumé can neither fully detail all my skills and accomplishments, nor predict my potential to your organization, I would welcome the opportunity to meet and discuss the possible merging of my talent and experience with your **personal trainer** needs.

Very truly yours,

James J. Hutchisen
JAMES J. HUTCHISEN

Enclosure

"Cold" Cover Letter to a Potential Employer (Registered Nurse)

An applicant transitioning out of the Navy, where he gained a great deal of experience with trauma treatment and crisis management.

RICHARD P. ISAACS, RN, BSN

529 Springdale Road • Springwater, New York 14560 • 585-624-6184 • richi@cs.com

January 12, 20–

Ms. Florence Blackwell, RN
Director of Nursing
Long Island Medical Center
1234 Hospital Row
Levittown, New York 11799

Dear Ms. Blackwell:

In anticipation of completing my military service in April, 2004, I am seeking a civilian position that will capitalize on my experience and training as a US Navy Registered Nurse. I believe that my clinical background and specialized training in emergency response and crisis management would make me an asset to your nursing staff. With this in mind, I have enclosed a résumé for your review that outlines my credentials.

Some key points you may find relevant to a nursing position with your facility include:

- **Caring for a broad array of patients, ranging from infants to senior citizens, and including post-operative, medical, infectious disease, oncology, and end-of-life scenarios.**

- **Developing rapport with diverse cultural groups, both in clinical and social settings. The patients I have dealt with cut across the full spectrum of ethnic and socioeconomic strata, from enlisted personnel to flag officers and their dependents. In my current assignment in Tokyo, I have had the opportunity to experience the local culture and interact with the local population.**

- **Completing training and engaging in field exercises that have prepared me for deployment to combat zones. This is relevant to a civilian setting because it encompasses mass casualty treatment, nuclear and biohazard treatment, and field hospital training, all of which relate to disaster response in a civilian community.**

I am confident that my dedication to caring for patients and capacity to function as an integral part of a treatment team would allow me to make a significant contribution to the health and well being of your patients. I would enjoy discussing with you how I can fulfill your needs in a clinical nursing role. Please contact me via phone or e-mail to arrange a mutually convenient date and time for an initial interview.

Thank you for your time and consideration. I look forward to speaking with you soon.

Sincerely,

Richard P. Isaacs, RN, BSN

Enclosure

"Cold" Cover Letter to a Potential Employer (Entertainment Industry)

This letter begins with an attention-grabbing opening followed by statements indicating that she understands the high-energy demands and realities of the entertainment industry. She ends the letter with a call to action.

MARY MANSON

1234 Hillside Drive / Los Angeles, CA 90049
Home (310) 555-5554 / Cell (310) 555-5555
mm@email.com

[Date]

[Name]
[Address]
[City, State Zip]

Dear [Salutation]:

Perhaps your company is in search of a highly motivated recent college graduate who is passionate about the Entertainment Industry and has the energy and drive to "pay my dues," acquire knowledge and advance professionally. If so, then we should talk!!

I offer a combination of creative talents and a strong work ethic as well as the following qualifications:

- BA in Communications from the University of California, Santa Barbara...
- Hands-on experience directing, acting in and producing short independent and student films...
- Realistic understanding of the demands of the entertainment industry, gained through internships for TV production company...
- Operating knowledge of a variety of audio and video equipment...

While my enclosed résumé provides a brief overview of my background, I look forward to a personal meeting at which time we can discuss your needs and my qualifications in detail.
I will call you next week to schedule a meeting; in the meantime, you can contact me at the above numbers. Thank you in advance for your time and consideration.

Sincerely,

Mary Manson

Mary Manson

Enclosure

"Cold" Cover Letter to a Potential Employer (Management)

Scott's recent experience with his last employer focused on IT implementation and project management. He seeks to gain a project management position with an IT consulting firm where he can make use of both his technical expertise and his management skills.

SCOTT A. McFADDEN

72 WOODBRIDGE TRAIL • FAIRPORT, NEW YORK 14450
585-223-9899 • SAM@EARTHLINK.COM

January 12, 20–

Mr. Addison Elgar
Director of Client Engagement
Computer Consultants, LLC
1234 Technology Terrace
Rochester, New York 14692

Dear Mr. Elgar:

Capitalizing on a career that encompasses substantial IT project management experience and extensive sales/marketing experience, I am seeking a new professional challenge that will combine these skills in a senior account management, project management, or technical leadership role. With this goal in mind, I have enclosed for your review a résumé that outlines my qualifications.

Some key points that you may find relevant to a position with your firm include:

- *Managing the technical deployment of six different releases of Cannon's SalesTeamXpert sales force automation tool over the past three years. This has involved ensuring that hardware platforms in the field are prepared to receive the latest release and resolving technical issues impacting end-user training for 6,000 users at 34 sites across the US.*

- *Building relationships with key decision-makers at Fortune 500 firms while serving as Marketing Manager for two different firms providing end-to-end transportation solutions for firms importing and exporting materials and products.*

- *Hands-on experience providing desk-side support to end-users; configuring hardware and installing software in the field; and delivering training to end-users and IT specialists.*

I am confident that my knowledge and expertise would allow me to make a meaningful contribution to the success of your firm and its clients. I would enjoy discussing with you in person how my capabilities can match your needs, and will contact you soon to arrange an appropriate time for an initial meeting.

Thank you for your time and consideration. I look forward to speaking with you soon.

Sincerely,

Scott A. McFadden

Scott A. McFadden

Enclosure

"Cold" Cover Letter to a Potential Employer (Physician's Assistant)

This individual has worked as a paramedic and recently finished her Physician's Assistant degree. She is looking to combine her education and extensive practical experience in an emergency medicine position with a large hospital.

Tiffany A. Mitchell
1299 Horseshoe Lane
Henrietta, New York 14467
585-334-1207
tam@frontiernet.net

January 12, 20–

Lara Angleton, R.N., Ph.D.
Director of Medical Human Resources
Clara Barton Memorial Hospital
One Nightingale Parkway
Rochester, New York 14692

Dear Dr. Angleton:

As a Physician's Assistant with nearly two years of clinical experience in an emergency department setting, I hope to utilize my skills in an emergency medicine position at your hospital. With this in mind, I am writing to you regarding potential opportunities, and have enclosed for your reference a résumé that outlines my education and other qualifications.

In addition to a B.S. from Rochester Institute of Technology, I have extensive training and experience in emergency medicine. Some of the highlights of my background include:

➢ Over twenty years' experience as a volunteer and as paid staff for the Henrietta Volunteer Ambulance Corps in suburban Rochester. In addition to logging over 7,600 active duty hours, I served as Vice President/General Manager for this busy service that answers over 4,700 calls each year. In this position, I was responsible for all operational aspects of the services provided.

➢ Three years' experience as a Flight Paramedic for Mercy Flight. I provided critical care to patients being transported by this air medical service that covers an 11-county region, transporting patients to critical care facilities.

➢ Nearly two year's experience in Rochester General Hospital's Emergency Department, treating a wide array of patients from infants to senior citizens, with cases ranging from acute injuries and medical conditions to routine, non-acute cases.

I am convinced that my education, training, and extensive experience have prepared me to effectively contribute to the care of your patients. I would enjoy speaking with you in person about the opportunities that exist and how I can best serve your needs. Please call me at 585-334-1207 to arrange a convenient day and time for us to meet. I look forward to talking with you soon.

Thank you.

Sincerely,

Tiffany A. Mitchell

Tiffany A. Mitchell, R.N., P.A.

Enclosure

"Cold" Cover Letter to a Potential Employer (Radiation Safety Officer)

This highly skilled and highly educated physicist is applying for the post of Radiation Safety Officer, which is his boss' job, as the boss leaves for another opportunity. He is competing with highly qualified external candidates, and his best asset is his familiarity with the institution, based on existing experience.

Michael Z. Ostrowski

2491 Goodman Street, Apartment 12 / Rochester, New York 14620 / (585) 258-6911

michaelzo@earthlink.com

January 12, 20–

Mr. Zachary P. Emerson
University of Buffalo
601 Transit Road, Box 2345
Williamsville, New York 14221

Dear Mr. Emerson:

Please accept this letter and the enclosed résumé as an expression of my interest in the Radiation Safety Officer position you are currently seeking to fill. I am confident that my education, experience, and familiarity with the University of Buffalo Research Center facilities provide me with the necessary skills to meet or exceed your expectations in this role.

For the past year, I have been a Health Physicist with UB, with responsibility for a variety of functions, including:

- Testing & Monitoring Equipment
- Training Medical Staff
- Ensuring Compliance with NYS Regulations
- Monitoring Staff Exposure
- Achieving CRESO Certification
- Supervising Four Technicians
- Serving on Various Committees
- Consulting with Physicians
- Maintaining Updated Technical Knowledge

Earlier, I held a similar position at University of Wisconsin's School of Medicine and Hospital. There I trained and supervised the work of a six-person technical team. I ensured that all equipment, materials, and supplies were in compliance with state regulations. State inspection results were always outstanding. Throughout my career, I have built a reputation for quality, flexibility, and professionalism in all areas. My commitment to health and safety has resulted in a perfect safety record.

I hold two master's degrees, one in Nuclear Engineering from Oklahoma State University, the other in Nuclear Physics from Sao Paulo University in Brazil. I have taught Biophysics at the university level. In addition, I speak three languages (English, Portuguese and Russian). Having lived and worked in other countries has given me a sensitivity and understanding of diverse cultures and customs.

I have thoroughly enjoyed working at UB, and would welcome this opportunity to make an even more significant contribution to the success of its mission. I would enjoy discussing my qualifications with you in person and invite you to contact me to arrange an initial interview.

Thank you for your time and consideration. I look forward to speaking with you soon.

Sincerely,

Michael Z. Ostrowski

Michael Z. Ostrowski

Enclosure

"Cold" Cover Letter to a Potential Employer (Veterinarian)

This veterinarian practices in an elite niche, treating only competitive horses at racetracks. His goal is to split his time between a track in the Southeast during winter months and one in the Northeast during the summer, allowing him to follow the horses throughout the racing year.

PARKER DOUGLASS, DVM
27 SANTA ANITA CIRCLE ◆ PORT ST. LUCIE, FLORIDA 38291 ◆ 305-934-8816

January 12, 20–

Dr. Amber Morgenstern, DVM
Gainesville Equine Hospital
1218 Shoreline Highway
Gainesville, Florida 34489

FAX: 352-129-6630
E-mail: dramber@juno.com

Dear Dr. Morgenstern:

My extensive experience addressing the health and performance needs of elite race horses at major tracks makes me a strong candidate for the opening you recently advertised at the AAEP website. Accordingly, I have attached my résumé for your consideration and review.

Some key points you may find relevant include:

- **Strong capacity to function independently and make critical decisions without direct supervision. My knowledge of horses and experience at several major tracks means that I will need minimal orientation to "hit the ground running."**

- **An excellent track record of maintaining the health of elite thoroughbreds and quarter horses, as well as assisting trainers in enhancing the performance of horses by improving their respiratory and general health as well as dealing with lameness issues (references can be provided).**

- **The ability to effectively evaluate young horses prior to purchase, through observation and diagnostic testing. I routinely produce quality repository radiographs and review radiographs in a repository setting. I also accompany buyers to auctions (Keeneland, etc.) to assess horses being considered.**

- **Experience assisting trainers setting up effective farm-based training programs, as well as helping breeders address reproductive health issues.**

I believe that I can be an asset to your organization and would enjoy discussing further how my knowledge, expertise, and professional dedication can address your needs. Please feel free to contact me to arrange either a phone or in-person interview at a mutually convenient date and time.

Thank you for your time and consideration. I look forward to speaking with you soon.

Sincerely,

Parker Douglass, DVM

Parker Douglass, DVM

Enclosure

"Cold" Cover Letter to a Potential Employer (Internship)

A cover letter to apply for a competitive college internship in the financial services industry.

Carlos M. Nunez

Current Address
Boston University
45 Bay State Road
Miles Standish Hall Box 1356
Boston, MA 02215-9105

Telephone: (617) 353-0698
Email: nunezc@bu.edu

Permanent Address
3948 Amsterdam Ave.
Apt. 4
Bronx, N.Y. 10453-6613

Telephone: (718) 901-4544

January 13, 20–

Karen Carmichael
Morgan Stanley, Inc.
1690 Broadway
New York, NY 10036
Re: Finance Intern

Dear Ms. Carmichael:

Are you looking for a driven, overachieving intern committed to excelling in business and finance?

As a junior at Boston University, I am pursuing a BSBA with a major in Finance. My passion for financial markets and economics has steadily increased over the last five years and I am committed to developing my career path as a business leader within a major corporation.

I approach all of my work with discipline and focus; as an intern with your organization, I would look forward to effectively contributing to your program goals. Boston University, Cushing Academy, and The Boys Club of New York have acknowledged my academic and leadership achievements for excellence in academic studies, volunteerism, and peer mentoring.

Please feel free to contact me at my campus number in Boston, (617) 353-0698. Thank you for your consideration. I am enthusiastic about working at Morgan Stanley Group. My background, professionalism, and enthusiasm will make me an effective member of your team.

Sincerely,

Carlos M. Nunez

Enclosure

"Cold" Cover Letter to a Potential Employer (Teacher)

A cover letter sent with the resume hard copy as a follow-up to the resume submission via e-mail.

JONATHAN YOUNG

November 14, 20–

Ms. Jennifer Jones
Personnel Coordinator
ABC Language Corporation
555 First Street, Suite 555
Vancouver, BC V9J 5G9
Canada

Dear Ms. Jones:

Although I recently submitted my résumé to your office via e-mail, I am submitting the enclosed hard copy as a follow-up. I welcome any questions you might have.

With this letter, I would like to reiterate my sincere motivation to teach in Japan. My experience as a substitute middle school teacher has helped me to understand methods of student interaction and reach a level of comfort in the classroom. I strive to build relationships with students—as much as a substitute teacher can—to facilitate classroom activities and inspire the learners. It is something I really enjoy.

The ABC web site encourages "all outgoing, dynamic, and flexible people to apply." In my current position as a flight attendant for Hawaii Wings Airlines, I am required to demonstrate these characteristics daily. Communication and quick-thinking skills are a must onboard an aircraft full of passengers. Flexibility is essential in the areas of customer service, in interaction with colleagues, and in work scheduling.

My motivation is indeed genuine, and I look forward to the possibility of discussing the opportunity with you. I will gladly make myself available for a telephone or videoconference interview.

Respectfully,

Jonathan Young

Jonathan Young

Enclosure: One-page résumé

555 King Street • Honolulu, Hawaii 95555 • (808) 555-5555 • jon@jonyoung.com

"Cold" Cover Letter to a Potential Employer (Production Supervisor)

Two problems to overcome: transitioning from automotive service manager to production supervisor and a break in employment of more than a year.

FERGUS McLEAN
4040 Wisteria Way
Kalamazoo, Michigan 49001

313.358.7470
FML5505@bellsouth.net

Tuesday, October 28, 20–

Mr. Charles W. Worth
Vice President for Operations
TopLine, Inc.
500 Northridge Parkway
Suite 400
Montgomery, Alabama 36100

Dear Mr. Worth:

How big is that gap between what the TopLine leadership wants from its skilled, semi-skilled and unskilled employees and what the TopLine bottom line gets? If you'd like to shrink that costly mismatch, we should explore adding me to your team as your transportation manager.

On the next pages, you'll see more than a half-dozen contributions I have made in this area. They illustrate the five, profit-building capabilities I've listed right at the top of the next page. I'd like to put those advantages to work for you right away.

Over the last year, the health of a family member made the most demands upon me and guided my relocation from Knoxville to Montgomery. Now that problem is resolved and I am ready to return to my first love: helping teams want to do well.

If my approach and philosophy appeal to you, please let me suggest a next step. I would like to hear about your special needs in your own words. May I call in a few days to arrange a time to do that?

Sincerely,

Fergus McLean

Fergus McLean

Encl.: Résumé

"Cold" Cover Letter to a Potential Employer (School Board Seat)

Having retired after thirty years of public service, this applicant decided to target a vacated seat on the Board of Education as a preparation for future political moves.

THOMAS DAVIS
743 Red Fox Road
Dayton, OH 45439
937.423.1258
tdavis@ci.dayton.oh.us

January 13, 20–

Ms. Jillian Laurent, Treasurer
Dayton City Schools Administrative Offices
227 West Florence Avenue
Dayton, OH 45439

Dear Ms. Laurent:

Please let this letter serve as my intent to seek the vacated seat on the Dayton City School Board. My motivation for seeking this position is that of public service. Because I have a deep commitment to community service and an in-depth knowledge of how a community works, I recognize that a public education system is critical to overall community success.

After retiring from law enforcement with thirty years of service, I returned to public service two years ago. I currently work as the Substance Abuse Prevention Coordinator for the City of Dayton Health Department. My expertise in the areas of substance abuse and public health would be beneficial to the school board.

My community involvement is outlined in the enclosed résumé. Since moving to Dayton in 1978, I have continued my life in community service with various organizations. In addition, leadership skills have been honed by coordinating police in-service training sessions, serving as Detective Sergeant for the Dayton Police Department, speaking to students and civic groups as a law enforcement representative, and holding offices in professional associations.

In today's world, we fear for the security of our homeland. Our students and teachers need to be in a safe environment. Parents need to be confident that their children are secure at school and school-sponsored events. From my life experiences and training, I also bring expertise to the school board in this area.

Public service has always been my calling. An appointment to the Dayton City School Board would allow me to use the skills gained from a 32-year career in public service to make a difference in people's lives. Though my children are grown, I look forward to a strong school system for my grandchildren. I have the time to devote to the task and the drive, energy, experience, and vision to make a positive contribution as a board member. I ask you to consider not only my qualifications, but also my desire to serve.

Sincerely,

Thomas Davis

Thomas Davis

Enclosure

"Cold" Cover Letter to a Potential Employer (Sales Professional)

George has two special needs: to show the sales aspect of his previous career as an accountant, and to convince a new employer that his desire to leave his current company was based solely upon having to work in an oversold market.

George Williams

1212 Currie Lane — Montgomery, Alabama 36100
334.555.5555 — 334.555.6666 (cellular) — gwilliams102@charter.net

Thursday, July 20, 20–

Ms. Laura Worth
Sales Manager
TopLine, Inc.
500 Northridge Parkway
Suite 400
Montgomery, Alabama 36100

Dear Ms. Worth:

I want you to get the credit for adding ROI to the TopLine sales team. Specifically, I'd like to become your newest sales professional. And, perhaps the best way to link those two ideas is with this graph that shows how I'm performing right now.

What I do isn't magic. I just work harder and smarter than my competition by finding some profitable way to say "yes" to every customer and potential customer.

My focus on your sales needs starts on the next pages. I wanted you to see a résumé that offers more than the usual recitations of job titles and responsibilities. That's why you'll find six capabilities I want to put at TopLine's disposal at once. Backing them up are a dozen examples of sales that show those capabilities in action.

My company values what I do. And, if I thought our market was growing as fast as yours, I would stay with them. While I cannot control market conditions, I am interested in making even greater contributions to my employer. That's why I'm "testing the waters" with this confidential application.

I do best using the consultative approach to sales. So, as a first step, I'd like to hear about TopLine's sales needs in your own words. May I call in a few days to arrange time to do that?

Sincerely,

George Williams
George Williams

Encl.: Résumé

"Cold" Cover Letter to a Potential Employer (Credit Account Specialist)

Kim wants to affiliate herself with a larger company that offers a more challenging role in analyzing and managing financial accounts; she also seeks to take on more responsibility to allow her to grow professionally.

KIMBERLY A. CARTER

888 West Road ▪ Anywhere, Michigan 55555 ▪ 555.222.2222

December 8, 20–

Marcy Johnson
ABC Accounting Company
333 Capital Avenue
Anywhere, Michigan 55555

Dear Ms. Johnson,

As a well-qualified credit account specialist, I demonstrate my ability to effectively communicate with clients, resolve payment issues, and collect on past due payments. I bring over 18 years of accounts receivable experience in addition to being involved in all processing stages of collections. The scope of my experience includes, but is not limited to, commercial, automotive, and manufacturing environments.

My focus is to deliver results and provide superior service by quickly identifying problem areas in accounts receivable and developing a solution strategy to ensure issues are resolved. My expertise lies in my strong ability to build rapport with clients, analyze accounts, and manage all aspects related to my appointed position and areas of responsibilities. I find these qualities to be my greatest assets to offer employers.

Due to an unforeseen circumstance, I was unable to continue my employment as a cash applications analyst with a well-known automotive industry leader. Since my employment with A-1 Corporation, I have accepted a temporary position as a billing assistant with a local company. My objective is to secure a position in accounts receivable and credit collections with an established company. As you will note, my résumé exhibits a brief review of contributions I have made to my employers and I enjoy challenges.

A complete picture of my expertise and experience is very important. Therefore, I will follow up with you next week. I look forward to speaking with you soon to answer any questions you may have regarding my background.

Regards,

Kimberly Carter

Kimberly Carter

Enclosure

"Cold" Cover Letter to a Potential Employer (Sales)

After "playing around" with part-time and seasonal positions for six years after college, John was ready to combine his variety of sales and customer service achievements into a bid for a serious, high-paying sales career.

JOHN MICHAEL ANDERSON

29 Davison Street • Asheville, NC 28800
(828) 555-0000 (H) • (828) 555-0001 (Cell) • gatehous@aol.com

Dear Hiring Professional:

My competitors were like pesky flies—they kept popping up everywhere, opening with lots of glitz, taking all the customers, and then crashing and burning after six months. But during those six months they were trying to take all <u>my</u> customers! As a newly graduated college student in his first real management position, these were serious challenges to which I responded with all the advertising ideas and new gimmicks I could muster—free pool playing, fruity drinks for girls, I even gave away free beer one night using three kegs we couldn't get rid of.

Today I am the same aggressive, ambitious sales professional I was then. OK . . . these days I wouldn't give away free beer (it might even have been illegal), but I <u>do</u> respond to sales challenges with all the competitiveness, creativity, and customer concern in my heart. In my last sales position, I was quite successful selling vacation packages by telephone for several reasons:

- I qualified my targets well.
- I was very knowledgeable about the product and painted a good picture of the product in the customer's mind.
- I think well and profitably on my feet.
- I'm honest and a natural rapport-builder.

The point of my enclosed résumé is that I would like to talk with you about bringing all the sales, problem-solving, and customer service skills to which it refers to work for your organization. When can we meet?

Sincerely,

John Michael Anderson

John Michael Anderson

enc.

"Cold" Cover Letter to a Potential Employer (Rail Industry)

Bruce wants to pursue his boyhood passion to become a train engineer.

BRUCE PETRELLI

55 Birch Crest Road • Brockport, New York 14420 • (585) 637-1037

January 12, 20–

Mr. Casey Jones
Director of Personnel
Atcheson, Topeka, and Santa Fe Railroad
1234 Railroad Boulevard
Topeka, Kansas 56789

Dear Mr. Jones:

As a mature individual with a life-long interest in railroads, I am seeking a job opportunity that will lead to a fulfilling career in the rail industry.

Enclosed for your review is a resume that briefly outlines my relevant qualifications. Some of the key skills that I believe make me a strong candidate for a position with your rail line include:

➢ **Significant experience as an Equipment Operator and Truck Driver.**

➢ **Experience dispatching for the New York State Dept. of Transportation.**

➢ **An excellent aptitude and desire to learn new tasks.**

➢ **An enjoyment of and willingness to work outdoors—in all weather conditions.**

➢ **Exceptional attention to detail and accuracy in my work.**

➢ **Responsible worker who is dedicated to consistently exceeding expectations.**

I understand the structure of the rail industry and am more than willing to accept an entry-level position (and all the challenges that go with it) in order for the opportunity to break-in with a railroad line. I would enjoy speaking with you in person about how I could fill a need for your company. Please call me at (585) 637-1037 to arrange a meeting at your convenience. I look forward to talking with you soon.

Thank you.

Sincerely,

Bruce Petrelli

Bruce Petrelli

Enclosure

"Cold" Cover Letter to a Potential Employer (Media)

Letting her professors speak for her and then confirming their words with her own words of commitment is a very effective strategy. The strength of the text is enhanced by the brevity of the letter.

BROOKE M. WELLINGTON   BROOKEWELLI@AOL.COM

6600 BELLESTONE STREET ◆ COLUMBUS, OHIO 43229 ◆ PHONE: (614) 374-6636

"I would rank Ms. Wellington's work in the top 10% of students I have taught; she is not afraid to tackle tough projects; I believe she has the ability to quickly make positive contributions..."

—John Weiss, Ph.D., Chairperson, Department of Communications, Albian College

"Brooke was an exemplary Journalism major. She took charge of the tasks given to her and performed them in a superior manner. I admire her strong enthusiasm and her attention to detail..."

—Stephen M. Ross, Assistant Director of Television Technical Operations, Albian College

---

Dear Selection Committee:

Tenacious and driven are terms my colleagues have used to describe my work habits. It is with a strong sense of career commitment that I submit my résumé for your review.

Having completed classes in August, I will be granted a B.A. in Journalism from Albian College in December 20–. Sometimes holding two jobs while attending school, I will have completed my degree in three years. It is with the same passion, integrity and energy that I intend to pursue my career.

Like so many, I possess the talent and understanding of how demanding a career in media can be. But unlike most, I am willing to "pay the price" of hard work, rough work schedules and total availability that the industry requires.

Thanks so much for your consideration. I am eager to learn more about the challenges facing your organization and to discuss how I can make a difference.

Best Regards:

Brooke M. Wellington

Brooke M. Wellington

"Cold" Cover Letter to a Potential Employer (Vice President)

Richard T. Carpenter

6 College Drive • San Francisco, California • (921) 784-6306

carpenter_vp@aol.com

(Date)

Emily _____
Title
ABC Corporation
1 Industry Plaza
San Francisco, CA 94162

Dear Ms. _____,

As a Chief Financial Officer, I have built a reputation for my strong ability to provide decisive leadership. For the past several years, my career as a senior-level executive has provided me with opportunities to promote high-level strategic business and financial planning goals for worldwide multimillion dollar corporations. My ability to identify challenges to and capitalize upon opportunities to expand revenue growth, reduce operating costs and improve overall productivity has been one of my strongest assets to my employers.

My strengths in financial and accounting management as well as my thorough understanding of finance operations have vastly contributed to my career and success as a leader. I maintain self-confidence, credibility and stature to make things happen with colleagues inside and outside the company. Just as significant are my abilities to develop rapport among coworkers and management, build effective teams and promote team effort.

My objective is to secure a position as a CFO or Vice President and to pursue new opportunities with an organization providing new and exciting challenges. Having a complete picture of my expertise and experience is very important. As you will note in my resume, I have made significant contributions to my employers and take my job very seriously.

I appreciate your time and consideration and will be in contact next week to see if we are able to schedule a meeting date for an interview. I look forward to speaking with you soon.

Regards,

Richard Carpenter

Richard Carpenter

RC
enclosure

"Cold" Cover Letter to a Potential Employer
(Pharmaceutical Sales)

Elana M. Carter

1267 Campton Drive • Northville, Michigan 48167

Emily _____   (Date)
(Title)
ABC Corporation
1 Industry Plaza
Dearborn, MI 48120

Dear Ms. _____:

    I currently hold a sales management position for a very successful retail company. My talents to achieve high sales volume, work cooperatively with diverse personalities, and focus on providing exceptional customer service has allowed me to excel in customer relations and succeed in sales and marketing.

    I have always enjoyed a challenge and have made the decision to extend my experience to the pharmaceutical sales field. Pharmaceutical sales has been an interest of mine for some time and I am confident that my background and skills in customer service, human relations, and product distribution would transition well into pursuing this change. What I may lack in specific experience in your business, I more than make up for with my dedication, energy, and determination.

    I thoroughly understand the importance of developing customer relations, generating revenue from sales potential within a designated territory, and maintaining accurate customer information. I have the aptitude and willingness to learn the necessary technical medical materials to promote your products. I am fully capable of projecting a positive and professional image of an organization and its products, and I strongly believe I possess the necessary skills and qualifications your organization seeks to be successful in this field of work.

    Your time in reviewing my confidential resume is greatly appreciated. I will follow up next week to answer any questions you may have regarding my qualifications. At that time, I would like to discuss the possibility of setting up a personal interview at your convenience. Please contact me if you would like to speak sooner.

Very truly yours,

Elana Carter

Elana Carter
enclosure

"Cold" Cover Letter to a Potential Employer (Recruiter)

Interested in fast-track career progression, but has reached her peak with her current employer. She is seeking a position in a high-growth global corporation.

BETSY McGILL

256 East 73rd Street – Apt. 7M • New York, New York 10021 • (212) 895-9045

(Date)

Alice _____
(Title)
Krieger, Skvetney, Howell
Executive Search Consultants
2426 Foundation Road
New York, NY 10025

Dear Ms. _____:

Having spent several years as an executive recruiter, I realize the number of resumes you receive on a daily basis. However, I remember how valuable a few always turned out to be.

The purpose of this communication is to introduce myself and then to meet with you about joining your organization.

When asked which business situations have been the most challenging and rewarding, my answer is the time spent in the search profession.

My background, skills and talents are in all aspects of sales and sales management. My research indicates that your expertise is in this area.

I have enclosed a resume which will highlight and support my objectives. I would appreciate the opportunity to meet and exchange ideas. I will call you over the next several days to make an appointment. If you prefer, you may reach me in the evening or leave a message at (212) 895-9045.

Thank you and I look forward to our meeting.

Sincerely,

Betsy McGill

Betsy McGill

BM
enclosure

"Cold" Cover Letter to a Potential Employer
(Project Management)

Matthew A. Sims
4545 Oakland
Chicago, Illinois 60671
(224) 555-3513

(Date)
Mr. _____
ABC Company
1 Industry Plaza
Chicago, IL 60675

Dear Mr._____:

Information technology expertise, combined with visionary leadership, the ability to motivate cross-functional teams, and develop cost-effective solutions, are key to creating long-term customer satisfaction and loyalty.

As a seasoned **Project Manager** experienced in providing strategic direction in the design and deployment of technology solutions, I have ...

- Successfully managed customer accounts from defining project requirements through implementation.
- Engineered e-commerce business solutions for myriad organizations from start-up ventures to *Fortune* 500 companies.
- Completed all of the coursework, including specialized electives to obtain the Microsoft Certified Systems Engineer designation.
- Developed comprehensive RFIs and RFPs; selected the most qualified, cost-effective vendor; and directed cross-functional teams to ensure on-time, on-budget implementation.
- Efficiently prioritized projects, developed realistic timelines, and consistently met deadlines.
- Compiled and drove ratification of product requirements.
- Provided technical expertise to sales teams to assist them in closing the sale.

Could your company use a high achiever with a thirst for growth and new challenges? If so, I would like to discuss how my skills and experience could benefit your organization.

I look forward to speaking with you.

Sincerely,

Matthew Sims

Matthew Sims

MS
enclosure

"Cold" Cover Letter to a Potential Employer (Publishing)

An administrative support person who wants to break into the publishing industry—no actual experience, but an avid reader who volunteers time to edit community fundraising publications and newsletters.

Genevieve Stone

245 The Outlook ▪ Glen Cove, New York 11542 ▪ (631) 236-0965 ▪ genstone@aol.com

(Date)

Phillip _____
(Title)
ABC Corporation
1 Industry Plaza
New York, NY 10021

Dear Mr. _____:

In the interest of exploring opportunities in the publishing industry, I have enclosed my resume for your review.

Over the last two years, I have gained valuable knowledge and experience in many aspects of personnel assistance, office procedures, and administrative operations. Recently I volunteered my time to edit a cookbook and have been responsible for editing the newsletter for my sorority. I consider myself a good writer and an avid reader and have always wanted to get into publishing. With my considerable energy, drive, and ability to work long hours, I believe I could make a positive contribution to your organization, and I would appreciate the opportunity to discuss my qualifications at your earliest convenience.

Should any questions arise regarding the information on my resume, or if you need personal references, please do not hesitate to contact me through the address or telephone number listed above.

Thank you for your time and consideration. I look forward to meeting with you.

Respectfully,

Genevieve Stone

Genevieve Stone

GS
enclosure

"Cold" Cover Letter to a Potential Employer
(International Sales)

(Date)

Phillip _____
(Title)
ABC Corporation
1 Industry Plaza
Las Vegas, NV 82341

Dear Mr. _____ :

    I received your name from Mr. _____ last week. I spoke to him regarding career opportunities with _____ and he suggested contacting you. He assured me that he would pass my resume along to you; however, in the event that he did not, I am enclosing another.

    As an avid cosmetics consumer, I understand and appreciate the high standards of quality that your firm honors. As you can see from my enclosed resume, I have had quite a bit of experience in the international arena. My past experience working overseas has brought me a greater understanding of international cultures and traditions, as well as a better understanding and appreciation of our own culture. These insights would certainly benefit a corporation with worldwide locations, such as your own. In addition, I have gained first-hand experience in the consumer marketplace through my various sales positions. I have noticed your recent expansion into the television media and am sure that an energetic individual would surely be an asset to ABC in this, as well as other, projects.

    I would very much like to discuss career opportunities with ABC. I will be calling you within the next few days to set up an interview. In the meantime, if you have any questions I may be reached at the number above. Thank you for your consideration.

Sincerely,

Jennifer Delorean

Jennifer Delorean

JD
enclosure

"Cold" E-Mail to a Potential Employer (Banking)

Having completed a one-year contract, Matthew had been offered a permanent position. However; he was interested in a position in a company that was more financially stable, and one where he could make use of his diverse technology skills.

From: Matthew Lorenzo [bankerpro@hotmail.com]
To: hr@fleetcareers.com
Cc:
Subject: Financial management/Sales orientation

Dear Mr. _____:

Please include my name in your job search database. As requested, I have attached a copy of my current resume.

Banking today is definitely a sales environment. While my marketing skills will always be useful, my interests lead me now to seek a more distinct financial management position such as Controller, Treasurer, or Vice President of Finance.

Since my CPA will be completed in January 20–, my search may be somewhat premature, but my transcript and results, combined with my practical experience, should offset my temporary lack of an accounting designation. I would therefore like you to begin considering me immediately. As an Account Manager, I saw many different industries, and so would not feel constrained to any one sector.

Including a mortgage loan benefit, I am currently earning $4,500 per month plus a car allowance. This should provide you with an indication of my present job level. Your suggestions or comments would be appreciated. I am available for interviews, and can be reached at (516) 555-1212. Thank you.

Yours truly,

Matthew Lorenzo
bankerpro@hotmail.com

"Cold" E-Mail to a Potential Employer (Software Development)

From: Julie Baxter [softwarespecialist@aol.com]
To: hr@developers.net
Cc:
Subject: Developer with quality, productivity, and commitment

Dear Mr. _____:

ABC Corporation caught my attention recently as I began a search for a new employer in the Phoenix area. ABC Corporation is well known in the software industry for quality products and excellent customer service; it also maintains a strong reputation as a great employer. Your organization has created an environment in which people can excel, which is why I write you today.

I am very interested in joining your software development team. I am confident that my background and experience will meet your future needs. My current position is Application Developer for Ascend Corp. I enjoy it very much as it has provided me with extensive hands-on training in Visual Basic and other languages. However, I am ready to get more into the actual software writing, as well as return to the Mesa area. I possess a bachelor's degree in Computer Science as well as training in a variety of programming languages. I am also a fast learner, as demonstrated by my learning Visual Basic quickly after joining Ascend. Additionally, I plan to pursue my master's degree and have begun the application process.

I would appreciate the opportunity to meet with you to discuss your goals and how I can help you meet them. I will call you soon to arrange a meeting at your convenience. In the meantime, please feel free to call for further information on my background and experience.

Thank you for your consideration and reply. I look forward to meeting you in the near future.

Yours truly,

Julie Baxter
(516) 555-1212
softwarespecialist@aol.com

"Cold" E-Mail to a Potential Employer (Internship)

From: David Kent [internationalrelationspro@earthlink.net]
To: hr@internationaljobs.org
Cc:
Subject: Motivated International Relations Intern

Dear Ms. _____:

I am interested in being considered for an internship. I am currently a senior at the University of Denver majoring in International Studies with a concentration in Latin America and a minor in Political Science.

My internships have increased my knowledge of International Relations and have enabled me to make use of my education in a professional environment. I am very serious about my International Relations education and future career and am eager to learn as much as possible throughout my internship. I am interested in working for your organization to gain practical experience and additional knowledge pertaining to my field of study.

My professional and academic background, along with my sincere interest in helping others, has enhanced my sensitivity to a diverse range of cultures. As a highly motivated professional, I enjoy the challenge of complex demanding assignments. My well-developed writing and communication skills are assets to an office environment.

I welcome the opportunity to elaborate on how I could make a substantial contribution to your organization as an intern. I look forward to talking with you soon. Thank you.

Sincerely,

David Kent
(516) 555-1212
internationalrelationspro@earthlink.net

Power Phrases

Consider using adaptations of these key phrases in your "cold" letters to potential employers.

My twenty-two-year operations management career with a multi-billion-dollar _____ company has been at increasing degrees of responsibility. While I have spent the last five years in top management, I am especially proud of my record—I started as a driver many years ago, and like cream, have risen to the top. I have consistently accomplished all goals assigned to me, particularly overall cost reductions, improved productivity, and customer service. Some of my achievements are:

Your recent acquisition of the _____ chain would indicate an intent to pursue southeastern market opportunities more vigorously than you have in the past several years. I believe that my retail management background would complement your long-range strategy for _____ very effectively.

With the scarcity of qualified technical personnel that exists today, it is my thought that you would be interested in my qualifications as set forth in the attached resume.

In approximately three months, I am moving to _____ with my family, and am bringing with me fifteen solid years of banking experience—the last eight in branch operations management. I would like particularly to utilize this experience with your firm.

I have noticed that you conduct laser exposure testing at your facility. If there is a need for laser technicians in this endeavor, I would like to be considered for a position.

As you can see from my resume, I am a psychology major and was president of our debating society in my senior year. I feel both would indicate a talent for sales. I did some selling in my summer job in 20– (ABC Books), and found not only that I was successful, but that I thoroughly enjoyed it.

The position you described sounds challenging and interesting. After receiving your comments about the job requirements, I am convinced that I can make an immediate contribution toward the growth of _____ and would certainly hope that we may explore things further at your convenience.

The opportunity to put to use my medical knowledge as well as my English degree would bring me great pleasure, and it would please me to know that I was bringing quality to your company.

I feel that the combination of _____'s educational environment and my desire to learn as much as possible about the data processing field could only bring about positive results.

If you think after talking to me and reading my resume that there might be an interest with your client company, I would be very interested. I have been put in many situations where I had to learn quickly, and have always enjoyed the challenge.

My accomplishments include:

As my resume indicates, I have demonstrated commitment to clients and to my employer's goals. That track record is consistent in my career endeavors as well as in my life as a whole. I dedicate myself to whatever task is at hand, marshal my resources and stay with the project until it is completed—to my satisfaction. Since my goals and demands are even more stringent than my employers' expectations, I consistently exceed quotas and objectives.

You will notice one common thread throughout my career—I am an administrator and a problem solver.

Currently I am considering opportunities in the $65–$85K range.

My confidential resume is enclosed for your review and consideration.

My current salary requirement would range mid to high $50Ks, with specifics flexible, negotiable, and dependent upon such factors as benefit structure and advancement opportunity.

Having spent several years as a _____, I realize the number of resumes you receive on a daily basis. However, I remember how valuable a few always turned out to be.

I would like the opportunity to discuss with you how we could mutually benefit one another. You may leave a message on my answering machine at my home and I will return the call. I look forward to hearing from you very soon.

I'm a clear communicator equally at ease with senior management, governmental officials and control agencies, vendors and contractors, construction/labor force. I'm a hard-driving manager who is project driven and is accustomed to inspiring the best job performance possible from associates and employees. I'm also creative enough to be in compliance with agency requirements without sacrificing profit or deadlines.

This job does seem to be the right challenge for me; I know that with my strong Java skills and manufacturing background experience I will be an asset to your company.

Hoping to meet you in person, I thank you for your time.

I will be calling you on Friday, August –, 20– to be sure you received my resume and to answer any questions you might have.

I have enclosed a resume which will highlight and support my objectives. I would appreciate the opportunity to meet and exchange ideas. I will call you over the next several days to make an appointment. If you prefer, you may reach me in the evening or leave a message at (516) 555-1212.

"Cold" Cover Letter to Employment Industry Professional (Health Care)

Adam has developed strong relationships with HMOs, hospitals, and physicians throughout his career. He seeks to leverage this experience into a position with an HMO, capitalizing on his expertise in preventative health and chronic illness management programs.

ADAM G. STEVENS

934 Sully's Trail
Pittsford, New York 14534
585-248-0917 / FAX: 585-388-9622
E-mail: adams@cs.com

January 12, 20–

Ms. Greta Pederson, President
Hunter, Gatherer & Recruiter Executive Search, Unlimited
1234 Executive Tower
Rochester, New York 14692

Dear Ms. Pederson:

As an accomplished professional with a 20-plus year track record in the pharmaceutical industry, I believe that I have unique talents that could benefit an HMO or a health care management organization. With this in mind, I have enclosed for your review a résumé that briefly outlines my professional history.

Some of the key capabilities that I can bring to a new opportunity include:

- *Design and implementation of health management programs. I have first-hand experience developing programs for asthma management, and direct the implementation of programs that have delivered substantial savings to client firms.*
- *Managing the development and implementation of web-based services that are new revenue centers for my firm and value-added services to its physician customer base.*
- *Exceptional account relations skills. I currently call on and maintain business relationships with key client contacts at the highest levels.*
- *National certifications from the University of Wisconsin in Quality Management and from the National Heart, Lung & Blood Institute.*

I am confident that my knowledge and expertise would allow me to deliver successful results for one of your clients in the health care industry. I would enjoy speaking with you in person to explore potential opportunities and how I can best serve someone's needs. Please call or e-mail me to arrange a convenient time for us to meet.

Thank you for your time and consideration. I look forward to talking with you soon.

As my employer is unaware of my job search, I trust that you will hold this correspondence in strict confidence and consult with me before releasing my materials to a prospective employer.

Sincerely,

Adam G. Stevens
Enclosure

"Cold" Cover Letter to Employment Industry Professional (Senior Network Control Technician/Administrator)

Peter's goal is to move from a network administrator/tech to a senior position.

PETER M. GUTIERREZ

9999 9th Street, Cactus Center, Texas 79423 • pmgutierrez@sbcglobal.net • 555-555-5555

January 20, 20–

I regard network downtime as unacceptable, yet realize it sometimes happens due to powers beyond my control. I always have contingency plans. —Peter Gutierrez

Placement Services, Inc.
Cactus Center, Texas

RE: SENIOR NETWORK CONTROL TECHNICIAN/ADMINISTRATOR, Cactus Center Area

Dear Personnel Recruiter:

As I consider career options that offer new and challenging opportunities to expand my growth, I am excited by your job posting for Senior Network Control Technician/Administrator. My qualifications and technical background, as well as fieldwork, marketing, and customer service experience, match your requirements for this position. The enclosed résumé reflects the experience and technical training/expertise to provide customized network and hardware/software solutions to meet remote customer needs.

The following *key strengths* also exemplify highly marketable skills and characteristics. I possess:

- *An accommodating attitude and willingness to work hard at any level to accomplish tasks and meet deadlines.*
- *The ability to effectively prioritize tasks and job assignments to balance customer needs with company goals.*
- *Strategic planning to head off downtime and restructure company systems to realize major improvement.*
- *Aptitude for troubleshooting problems, while respecting customers and explaining problems/solutions in simple, illustrative language.*
- *Consultative, straightforward communication techniques that promote development of strong and lasting rapport and trust.*
- *A work ethic that honors integrity and excellence to enhance company distinction.*
- *A persuasive, take-charge style seasoned with a sense of humor for a pleasant work environment.*
- *Psychological insight and a talent for motivating others to work at higher levels to increase productivity.*

An interview to further investigate your needs and my qualifications would be mutually beneficial. I look forward to hearing from you. In the meantime, thank you for your time and consideration.

Sincerely,

Peter M. Gutierrez

Enclosure: Résumé

"Cold" Cover Letter to
Employment Industry Professional (CPA)

THERESE E. MAYSONET

1915 CEDAR COURT • LANSING, MICHIGAN 48910
MAYSONET_ACCOUNTANT@EMAIL.NET

Emily _____   (Date)
(Title)
ABC Corporation
1 Industry Plaza
Detroit, MI 48723

Dear Ms. _____:

As I am just completing the requirements for my MBA in Accounting at City Institute of Technology, I am exploring potential opportunities with a well-established firm that will lead to a career as a CPA. I hope to join an organization where I can learn and grow within the accounting profession and build a long-term relationship. With these goals in mind, I have enclosed for your consideration and review a resume that briefly outlines my credentials.

Some of the key experiences I can bring to an entry-level position with your firm include:

- **Administering Accounts Receivable and Payroll for an engineering firm that was also engaged in construction and some custom manufacturing.**

- **Preparing individual tax returns as part of a volunteer program in conjunction with CIT.**

- **Serving as Treasurer of a campus organization, Delta Beta Gamma, which encompassed maintaining financial records and providing financial reports to the auditing CPA and to the national organization.**

- **Proficiency with basic Windows and Microsoft Office applications, as well as a keen interest in technology and high-tech businesses.**

I am confident that my education and experience to date provide me with skills that would be beneficial to your firm and its clients. I would enjoy speaking with you in person to discuss the possibilities that exist and how I can best serve the needs of your firm and your clients. Please call me at **(516) 555-1212** to arrange a convenient date and time for us to meet. I look forward to opening a dialogue with you soon.

Very truly yours,

Therese Maysonet

Therese Maysonet

TM
enclosure

"Cold" Cover Letter to Employment Industry Professional
(Quality Assurance)

David Jameson
4987 Lubbock Avenue
Centerville, OH 45458
937.555.5264 / cell: 555.555.4652

(Date)

Phillip _____
(Title)
ABC Corporation
1 Industry Plaza
Dayton, OH 45421

Dear Mr. _____:

Reliability. Problem Solving. Attention to Detail. Innovation. These are a few of the many qualities I have developed as a Quality Assurance Technician. If you are looking for a topnotch Quality Assurance Technician, look no further. I have over 15 years experience in quality assurance and quality control and have not only designed better consumer friendly products but have improved sales of existing products.

Because delivering solid productivity increases has been the norm throughout my career in the electronics field, I have achieved superior results at Continuum Biomedical, HMT Technologies, Wheco Electronics, 3M Healthcare, Irwin Magnetic, and Xircom Electronics. As a result, you get a Quality Assurance Technician who is productive from day one. My commitment to you would be the same: simplify processes, improve products, develop workforce competencies, and boost output while completing projects ahead of time and under budget.

Qualifications I can bring to your clients are outlined on the enclosed resume. Given my technical skills, familiarity with the product line, and understanding of your clients' needs, I could step into the position and be of immediate assistance.

Please contact me at my home telephone number to arrange a convenient time to meet. Thank you for your time; I look forward to speaking with you soon.

Yours truly,

David Jameson

David Jameson

DJ
enclosure

"Cold" Cover Letter to Employment Industry Professional
(Executive Computer Specialist)

Kelly L. Hillman

225 Springdale Drive ▪ Pittsboro, NC 27312 ▪ (555) 123-4567

(Date)

Emily _____
(Title)
ABC Corporation
1 Industry Plaza
Greensboro, NC 27345

Dear Ms. _____:

My experience installing and maintaining computer networks, hardware, and software, along with my skills in training users and developing cost-saving applications, are the assets I would bring to the position of Executive Computer Specialist.

I am a Certified Novell Administrator. And my technical skills include expertise in Novell Netware, MS DOS and Windows, as well as experience with hardware including Cabletron, and software including the Microsoft Office Suite.

My computer expertise has saved my employers production time and costs. As a Senior Computer Specialist, I installed a Personal Computer LAN utilizing the Novell Netware Networking System. I saved $35,000 and used the savings to upgrade the equipment installation. Also in that position I designed and implemented a system to cut printing costs. The system is projected to save the government $4 million over four years.

I have also developed software packages, including "point of sale" software and mortgage software, which was for commercial sale.

I believe my skills and experience will make me succeed in the position of Executive Computer Specialist. Kindly review my resume, then contact me at your earliest convenience to schedule a professional interview.

Very truly yours,

Kelly Hillman

Kelly Hillman

KH
enclosure

"Cold" Cover Letter to Employment Industry Professional
(Vice President)

.... **Thomas J. Flokhart**

(Date)

Mr. _____
(Title)
Krieger, Skvetney, Howell
Executive Search Consultants
2426 Foundation Road
Richmond, VA 62362

Dear Mr. _____:

In the course of your search assignments, you may have a requirement for an organized and goal-directed Vice President. My present position provides me with the qualifications and experience necessary to successfully fulfill a Vice President position. Key strengths which I possess for the success of an administrative position include:

- Direct line operations responsibility improving gross margin to 8.0%.
- Planning and developing over $15 million in new construction projects.
- Reduction of departmental operating expenses to 1.1% below budget.
- Negotiating and developing contractual arrangements with vendors.

I have the ability to define problems, assess both large-scale and smaller implications of a project, and implement solutions.

The enclosed resume briefly outlines my administrative and business background. My geographic preferences are the midwest and southeast regions of the country. Relocating to a client's location does not present a problem. Also, I possess an MBA degree from _____ University, and a BS degree in Business Administration from _____University. Depending upon location and other factors, my salary requirements would be between $130,000 and $150,000.

If it appears that my qualifications meet the need of one of your clients, I will be happy to further discuss my background in a meeting with you or in an interview with the client. I will be contacting your office in the near future to determine the status of my application.

Sincerely,

Thomas Flokhart

Thomas Flokhart

TF
enclosure

....
3918 Park Avenue • Roanoke, Virginia 62368 • (703) 926-2457

"Cold" Cover Letter to Employment Industry Professional
(Senior Manager)

Lisa K. Botkin

1003 Farmington Road

Colorado Springs, CO 80031

home: (888) 435-9584

senior manager@yahoo.com

(Date)

Mr. _____

ABC Company

1 Industry Plaza

Los Angeles, CA 90026

Dear Mr. _____:

Mentored by Bob _____, founder of _____, I successfully progressed within his privately held organization for twelve years, serving on the **Board of Directors of 13 separate companies** and holding positions including **Treasurer, Vice President of Finance** and ultimately **President**. During my tenure the company grew from 7 employees to more than 1,000 while **revenues increased from $3 million to $108 million**. My enclosed resume gives further detail.

My reason for contacting you is simple. I am interested in exploring any senior management opportunities which may be available through your organization and would also be interested in interim or consulting roles. Geographically speaking, I have no limitations and am available for relocation throughout the U.S. and abroad. Due to the level and quality of my performance I feel it pertinent to state that I am only willing to consider positions consistent with my current income level. I have the experience, the talent and the energy to turn around, create or grow a dynamic organization.

I have built my career on my commitment and ability to create open lines of communication between the Board of Directors and senior management to **protect the investments of my organization and to assure the attainment of the target return**.

I look forward to hearing from you in the near future to discuss any mutually beneficial opportunities. If you do not at present have a need for a professional with my experience but know of someone who may, please be so kind as to pass my letter and resume on to that individual, or simply call me.

Sincerely,

Lisa Botkin

Lisa Botkin

LB

enclosure

"Cold" Cover Letter to Employment Industry Professional (International Operations)

Franklin Townsend

5555 Andover Avenue • Los Angeles, California 90025
Residence (323) 555-1234 • Mobile (323) 555-5555 • internationaloperations@email.com

(Date)

Ms. _____
(Title)
ABC Corporation
1 Industry Plaza
San Diego, CA 93725

Dear Ms. _____:

Over the years, I have built a successful career in **international operations and project management** on my ability to quickly and accurately assess situations, identify problems and focus on strategies which obtain results. I am currently seeking a challenging opportunity with an internationally focused, growth-oriented organization. I am willing to explore interim assignments and consulting projects as well as senior management opportunities. My enclosed resume details some of my accomplishments and credentials.

I have extensive experience in **diplomacy and international public affairs** dealing with foreign government officials, Heads of State, and Ambassadors as well as Fortune 100 senior executives. Building effective teams and inspiring others to peak performance are among my strengths. I am particularly adept at living and working effectively in foreign countries and with individuals of various cultural backgrounds. As such I am interested in opportunities both in the U.S. and abroad.

Feasibility studies, crisis resolution and international risk assessment are areas where I excel. Unit construction and operations, mining/drilling and industrial equipment procurement, sales and distribution are areas where I may be of particular assistance, but my skills are transferable to virtually any industry.

I look forward to hearing from you to discuss any mutually beneficial opportunities that you may be aware of. Please feel free to send my resume to others who may have a need for a professional of my caliber.

Sincerely,

Franklin Townsend

Franklin Townsend

FT
enclosure

"Cold" E-Mail to Employment Industry Professional
(IT Professional)

From: Jacqueline Smith [smithITpro@mindspring.com]
To: hr@corptech.com
Cc:
Subject: REF: Project management

Dear Mr. _____:

Capitalizing on my success managing IT design and implementation projects for ABC Design Corporation in Anytown, NY, I am seeking a professional opportunity where my project management, customer relations, and organizational skills can benefit your clients. With this goal in mind, I have attached for your consideration a resume outlining my qualifications.

Some of the experiences I would bring to a position with your firm include:

- *Defining project parameters, including interviewing clients to assess goals and objectives, and developing specifications and project deliverables.*
- *Serving on leadership teams that have managed project budgets of up to $10 million to consistently meet customer timeline requirements and budgetary constraints.*
- *Coordinating activities of programmers, Web developers, software engineers, network engineers, graphic artists, and customer representatives to meet project goals.*
- *Testing and validating applications during development stages and upon completion to ensure client objectives are met.*

I am open to relocation anywhere in the United States and would eagerly accept either contract assignments or permanent employment. I believe that my capabilities would allow me to serve your needs and benefit your clients, and would enjoy meeting with you to discuss my qualifications in greater detail. Please contact me via phone or e-mail to arrange an initial interview at your convenience.

Thank you for your time and consideration. I look forward to speaking to you soon.

Sincerely,

Jacqueline Smith
(516) 555-1212
smithITpro@mindspring.com

"Cold" E-Mail to Employment Industry Professional (Computer Professional)

From: Sally Winston [computerpro@earthlink.net]
To: mcooper@isculptors.com
Cc:
Subject: Technology guru, plus global experience

Dear Ms. _____:

My broad background in all aspects of computers, from design and installation through user training and maintenance, coupled with my business operations expertise, are the assets I would bring to a position with one of your clients.

Currently I hold a management level position with MainLine Graphics, a firm that designs and builds flight simulators for U.S. and foreign governments. I provide the electronics expertise in completing approximately 12 major projects annually, which means I conceptualize the simulators' computerized mechanisms, direct the design and manufacturing processes, then install and test the systems at clients' sites around the globe.

In addition to providing technical expertise, the other major aspect of my job involves aggressively targeting new business. At a point when MainLine was facing an essentially saturated U.S. market, I designed and implemented an Internet Web site, then had it translated into several languages to target international clientele. The site generated 80% of our new business within one year.

Other assets I would bring to this position include skill in relocating entire company computer systems from existing facilities to new or expanded sites, as well as experience servicing all major brands of PCs. I am extremely familiar with nearly every computer-associated component, program, or operating system on today's market.

Thank you in advance for taking a few moments to review my resume. I am confident that the experience you'll find outlined therein will be valuable to your firm. Kindly contact me at your earliest convenience to schedule a professional interview.

Best regards,

Sally Winston
(516) 555-1212
computerpro@earthlink.net

"Cold" E-Mail to Employment Industry Professional
(Programmer/Analyst)

From: Suresh Gupta [certifiedprogrammer@yahoo.com]
To: hr@techvibes.com
Cc:
Subject: REF: Programming assignments

Dear Ms. _____:

My certification in computer programming, along with my professional background in electro-mechanical engineering, are among the primary assets I would bring to a programmer/analyst position with one of your clients.

As part of my training at Computer Institute in South Fork, NJ, I was required to design, write, code, edit, and modify an e-commerce Web site. The project succeeded not only because of my skill in applying my technical knowledge, but also because of my strict attention to detail.

Currently I'm employed at Dynamic Pharmaceuticals in Price Point, NJ, executing experiments on electrical/mechanical equipment I was involved in manufacturing to ensure conformance to customers' specifications.

I am also committed to furthering my professional education, which is key for success in this field. I plan to augment my knowledge by attending and completing relevant courses.

I am confident this background well equips me for success with one of your clients. Kindly review my resume, then please contact me at your earliest convenience to schedule an interview.

Very truly yours,

Suresh Gupta
(516) 555-1212
certifiedprogrammer@yahoo.com

"Cold" E-Mail to Employment Industry Professional
(IT Management)

From: Maria Costas [ITexpert@aol.com]
To: cfloyd@mtechit.com
Cc:
Subject: Top productivity enhancement professional

Dear Mr./Ms. _____:

Leading information technology projects for high-growth companies is my area of expertise. Throughout my career I have been successful in identifying organizational needs and leading the development and implementation of industry-specific technologies to improve productivity, quality, operating performance, and profitability.

In my current position at XYZ company, I have initiated and managed the technological advances, administrative infrastructures, training programs, and customization initiatives that have enabled the company to generate over $3 million in additional profits in the past year. The scope of my responsibilities have included the entire project management cycle, from initial needs assessment and technology evaluations through vendor selection, internal systems development, beta testing, quality review, technical and user documentation, and full-scale, multi-site implementation.

My technological and management talents are complemented by my strong training, leadership, and customer service skills. I am accustomed to providing ongoing support and relate well with employers at all levels of an organization, including senior executives. Most notable are my strengths in facilitating cooperation among cross-functional project teams to ensure that all projects are delivered on time, within budget, and as per specifications.

Originally hired for a one-year contract at XYZ company, I have been offered a permanent position within the company. However, I am interested in greater challenges and would welcome the opportunity to meet with you to determine the contributions I can make to your client. I will call you next week to set up an appointment.

Sincerely,

Maria Costas
(516) 555-1212
ITexpert@aol.com

"Cold" E-Mail to Employment Industry Professional
(Systems Integration)

From: Michael Wilson [systemsintegrationpro@hotmail.com]
To: hr@sap-si.com
Cc:
Subject: Onstar engineer plus more

Dear Company Representative:

My solid background in electrical engineering supported by extensive management and product development experience are key assets that I can contribute to your client's future success.

Throughout my career I have worked with cutting-edge technologies, including **embedded microprocessors, RF, telecommunications,** and **wireless,** in the development and manufacture of products for varied industries. In all of my positions, integrating software, firmware, and hardware to create unique applications has been a key strength. Some of these applications that proved quite marketable include development of custom instrumentation and a PC-based network for tracking vehicles in transit. In addition, I have also played an important role in both the sales and customer support process, helping A+ Corp. win its largest municipal contract with the city of New Orleans.

Currently, I am exploring opportunities in the telecommunications industry where I can contribute significant expertise in systems integration. I welcome the opportunity to meet with you to explore areas of mutual benefit. Attached is my resume for your review.

In order to present my credentials more fully, I will follow up with you to answer any questions you may have. Thank you for your consideration.

Sincerely,

Michael Wilson
(516) 555-1212
systemsintegrationpro@hotmail.com

"Cold" E-Mail to Employment Industry Professional (Systems Administrator)

From: Dae Sung Kwan [systemsspecialist@mindspring.com]
To: gdawson@stokely.com
Cc:
Subject: Sys admin/people skills/military background

Dear Ms. _____:

If you seek a new Systems Administrator who is more than just technically oriented, but also people oriented, then we have good reason to meet. As you'll find on my attached resume, I possess extensive technical skills and experience. What is more difficult to portray on a brief resume is my people skills.

Several colleagues, supervisors, subordinates, and end-users have commended me for my interpersonal skills. I am dedicated to helping others with their technical issues and sharing my knowledge to help them complete their work more efficiently. My job is to serve as a support person, there to keep the system operating smoothly for end-users, as well as to provide them training. I also understand that most technical projects are a team effort. Again, I have been recognized for my abilities as a team player as well as a team leader. I have a proven track record in taking projects and running with them, but the successes are a result of the combined efforts of the whole team. Whether it's a matter of motivating others, coordinating tasks, or just doing my part, I can do it.

My technical skills speak for themselves. My primary focus has been on Windows NT. In fact, I am currently pursuing my Microsoft Certified Systems Engineer designation. My plans are to attain this at about the time I leave the military. I will be able to bring this added expertise to an employer.

A meeting at your convenience would be greatly appreciated. Please feel free to contact me to schedule a time or to gain further information on my background. I am sure you will agree that I am right for the job after reviewing my resume and meeting with me in person.

Thank you for your time and prompt reply. I look forward to meeting you in the near future.

Best regards,

Dae Sung Kwan
(516) 555-1212
systemsspecialist@mindspring.com

POWER PHRASES

Consider using adaptations of these key phrases in your "cold" letters to employment service professionals.

I am an optimist, thrive on challenges, lead by example, and readily adapt to situations. If your client—international or domestic—would benefit from these kinds of qualities we should get to know each other. If you will call or write at your convenience, I look forward to telling you more about my background.

As a dedicated listener, I am usually designated for client/customer relations and produce notable results in client/customer retention—even under the least favorable conditions.

An industry association referred to _____ as an active and selective executive search firm, and mentioned your name because of your work in logistics. I liked that referral and think our meeting would be mutually beneficial.

I would like to talk with you personally to further discuss our meeting. I suggest next week, the week of October –, when you have a free minute. I have asked my staff to forward your message immediately in case I am unavailable when you call. I look forward to hearing from you.

Please include my name in your job search database.

Including a mortgage loan benefit, I am currently earning $4,500 per month plus a car allowance. This should provide you with an indication of my present job level. Your suggestions or comments would be appreciated.

For 25 years, my family operated one of the most prestigious landmark inn/restaurants on Long Island. From the age of 6, I was a part of the family workforce—I couldn't wait to "help." That attitude pervades my work ethic and I'm grateful for the training that helped me to develop an attitude of service, teamwork and pride in performance and product.

One of your clients is looking for me, if not today then sometime in the near future. I know good people are hard to find because I've had to find them myself.

I have the depth of experience it takes to make a positive contribution.

Income is in the mid-five figures, but the right opportunity is the motivating factor. References and resume are available. With my well-rounded professional background I look forward to a new and interesting career opportunity through your firm.

I'm a natural "enroller" because my enthusiasm is contagious and I personally project credibility—people are inclined to (1) cooperate and participate wholeheartedly on projects with which I'm involved, (2) favorably consider products I recommend, and (3) be open to my efforts on their behalf when they experience problems or dissatisfaction.

The following are some highlights of my track record for your consideration:

I understand your clients frequently ask you to locate senior operating executives with much higher than average ability to accomplish difficult jobs quickly and profitably.

It is my goal to play an integral part in the development, operation and success of a small to mid-sized company where the diversity of my experience and the level of my commitment can be used to their fullest advantage and I can have the satisfaction of seeing the results of my efforts . . . really impacting profitability!

Please call at your convenience this week so we can explore potential opportunities more fully. Use the home number, please; our company's uncertain financial status is stirring up the office rumor mill. Thank you for your time and attention.

I am a motivated and dedicated leader. Many of my staff have worked for me from 10 to 30 years. My enthusiasm for meeting goals and accomplishing objectives has been contagious, and I know how to reward outstanding performance without disturbing a profit and loss balance. My employees and I thrive on a "family" environment with no loss of respect or production.

As a former business owner, I am well aware of the needs, concerns and challenges facing management. By the same token, I am accustomed to operating with the best interests of the total business in mind and at heart, as well. I operate expeditiously, constantly seeking the best use of time, effort, resources and money . . . for my staff and myself.

My experience as an entrepreneur as well as an employee of a powerful, demanding employer gives me the unique ability to empathize the needs of management as well as the aggressiveness necessary to represent management effectively.

I'm seeking an opportunity to join an employer that can benefit from my expertise and experience while offering me the opportunity for challenge, continued professional growth, as well as commensurate compensation.

I'm a dedicated listener and an accomplished problem solver, always seeking to assist clients in accomplishing their mission. My clients experience and express a sense of trust and confidence in me and my recommendations because my sincerity and my efforts invested on their behalf are evident and consistent. They never have a doubt that I really care and will operate in their best interests.

Broadcast Letter (Faculty Position)

This instructor was awarded the faculty position she aspired to,
and she also was asked to chair the Humanities Department.

SARA ANNE STEEL

9999 Old Mill Road • Paintbrush, NM 77777
(999) 999.9999 • sasteel55@mindspring.com

May 3, 20–

Human Resources Office
RIO GRANDE UNIVERSITY
900 W. Casa Ave.
Yellow Creek, New Mexico 99999

I am interested in ideas,
not merely visual products.

—Marcel Duchamp

Dear Human Resources Coordinator:

An instructor in good standing at Rio Grande University, I am very interested in transitioning from painting, design, and art appreciation instructor to your recently posted **Jewelry Repair and Design Faculty position**. I was thrilled to discover an **exceptional match between your requirements for this opening and my skills and qualifications**. The enclosed curriculum vitae reflects a progressive career path and a credible candidate for this position. Qualifications follow:

Your Requirements:	**My Qualifications:**
MFA in Metal	MFA in Jewelry/Metalsmithing from Freemont Art University of New York, 1997.
Bench work/experience with jewelry repair practices	Jewelry repair and bench work for local retail jeweler. Experience includes stone setting, soldering, pearl bead stringing, ring sizing, jewelry designing, and riveting. Consider value and safekeeping.
Teaching, jewelry design education, and curriculum development	Two years' teaching experience. Comprehensive knowledge of casting gained through education, freelance, and contract work includes wax carving, wax chasing, and mold making.
Excellent communication skills	Comprehend the English language. Excellent oral and written self-expression. Give clear instructions and relate well to students. Relaxed communication style fosters encouragement and support. Subscribe to open-door policy.
Commitment to working with a diverse population	Successfully teach and interact with physically and mentally challenged individuals, as well as people of all ages from varied backgrounds and cultures.
Ability to manage projects and set specific objectives.	Extremely goal-oriented, giving particular attention to planning and follow up for positive results. Day planner and "to-do" lists spark productivity. Experience coordinating special events such as art shows, parties, and dinners.

Page 1 of 2

Besides these qualifications, I am an avid photographer, have an interest in gemology, and produce an average of one large art object a month. Personal qualities include a cheerful, energetic demeanor, positive attitude, dedication, self-sufficiency, and creative/innovative idea generation. I am passionate about art, teaching, and mentoring, and enjoy the two-fold return of the enthusiasm I bring to class.

Additionally, positive feedback from both peers and students precedes me:

- "I have never seen painting so strong from the art department," and "you are raising the bar."
- "I got more from this class (Painting I) than most others I've had."
- "This was the most exciting/stimulating class I've taken in 1½ years."
- "It was nice to see your work and know that it came from someone as normal as the rest of the world."
- "Your help contributed most to my learning. You were not afraid to help in any way you could."

Comments like these are especially fulfilling. Other job satisfaction comes from observing facial expressions when students finally comprehend a theory or concept and helping students discover and expand their creativity.

I am willing to handle the responsibility and safety issues involved in running a jewelry/metals lab and believe properly taught techniques and procedures are of vital importance. The prospect of teaching in my field and being on the ground floor of future jewelry department development energizes me. I am confident I will continue to offer a fresh perspective to course and curriculum development at Rio Grande University and look forward to a personal interview to further discuss your needs. Thank you for your time and consideration.

Sincerely,

Sara Anne Steel

Sara Anne Steel

Enclosure: Résumé

Broadcast Letter (Assistant Director of College Housing)

Used a side-by-side comparison to effectively illustrate her qualifications for the position.

BRENDA YOUNG

254 Dunhill Lane • Brentwood, NY 11717 • (631) 999-8866 • studentlife@college.edu

Miss Christine Timmons
Assistant Director for College Housing
State University of New York at Long Island
777 North College Road
Brookhaven, NY 11724

January 12, 20–

Re: Reference Code: TC-E-5556E2

Dear Miss Timmons:

In response to your ad for an Assistant Director of College Housing advertised in Sunday's *Newsday*, I have enclosed my resume for your review. To further illustrate my qualifications, the following outlines the scope of my experience as it pertains to the position's requirements.

Your requirements	My qualifications
• Bachelor's degree or four years of experience in lieu of degree.	• Master's degree in Clinical Counseling; • Eight years of combined experience in resident hall administration and counseling capacities.
• Promote and develop educational programming and maintain extensive budget.	• Plan, develop, and implement educational programs, and manage an operational budget.
• Administration of three to five residence halls housing approximately 1,000 students.	• Administration of residence halls housing up to 500 college students.
• Supervise, develop, and evaluate three to five full-time resident hall directors.	• Supervise, develop, and evaluate 26 Resident Advisors with direct responsibility for four RAs and a Head Resident Advisor (HRA).
• Develop departmental policies and procedures, manage area office including billing, occupancy, and facilities records.	• Direct all aspects of front desk management and facilities maintenance operations.
• Assist in the development and leadership of departmental committees, and serve as manager for student conduct cases	• One year as VP of Committees and Organizations for the Student Government with the State University of New York at Suffolk.

Thank you for your review and consideration. I look forward to hearing from you soon.

Sincerely,

Brenda Young

Brenda Young

Broadcast Letter (Financial Planning Professional)

The employer was so impressed with the detail of the cover letter that he offered a position to this applicant at the initial interview.

David Meyers

310 E. 127th Terrace ▪ Kansas City, MO 64141

Phone: 816-555-6226 ▪ Cell Phone: 913-555-3588 ▪ E-mail: meyerstown@juno.com

September 19, 20–

Prudential Financial
David Borgrum, Manager
347 W. 47th Street
Kansas City, Missouri 64164

Dear Mr. Borgrum,

The Rock. Prudential is known internationally by this symbol of security and permanence, the assurance to their clients the company will always be there. The corporate slogan "Growing and Protecting Your Wealth" can only be accomplished through principled management, effective investment strategies, and ethical financial planners.

The relationship. With corporate scandal and financial malfeasance perceived to be the norm, now, more than ever, a relationship built on integrity and mutual respect is paramount to success in the financial services industry. As a goal-oriented financial planning professional who possesses strong marketing and communication skills, I am confident upon review of my qualifications you will find I have the solid combination of experience and achievement that Prudential looks for in its representatives.

My qualifications include:

- ✓ Series 7 and 66 Licensing.
- ✓ Registered Investment Advisor.
- ✓ B.A. in Economics.
- ✓ Commitment to client satisfaction and quality service through needs assessments.
- ✓ Demonstrated results in business development and execution of marketing strategies.
- ✓ Effective communication and presentation skills necessary to articulate product benefits clearly and accurately to clients.
- ✓ Outstanding time management and organizational ability.
- ✓ A willingness to "go the extra mile" for client and corporation.

The consultation. Inherent to every successful consultation, is my obligation to obtain a comprehensive financial background in order to meet the clients' future needs and objectives. Performing an effective client needs assessment, gives me the decisive edge when the client makes their financial planning decisions. Furthermore, I am skilled at new business development, cold calling and seminar presentations. Employers and colleagues have consistently praised my attention to detail, hard work ethic and ability to deal with the most complex client engagements.

Please contact me at your earliest convenience to set up an interview concerning employment opportunities within your company. I look forward to hearing from you.

Sincerely,

David Meyers

David Meyers

Broadcast Letter (Heavy Equipment Operator)

Relocating to Northern Florida and wants to secure a position that
could capitalize on his diverse range of skills.

.... **JACK L. CROUTHER**

Dear Sir or Madam:

Please accept the enclosed resume in application of your Heavy Equipment
Operator position advertised in The Times Journal.

My diverse range of experience includes over ten years of experience operating and maintaining heavy equipment. In my current position, I operate backhoes,
loaders, lulls, Gallion cranes, Ditch Witch trenchers (large and walk-behind), fork
lifts, street sweepers, and bucket trucks. In addition, I supervise the troubleshooting, maintenance and repair of all of the department's equipment.

Of equal importance are my supervisory and leadership skills where I have
managed multiple crews of up to 40 employees. Being extremely diligent, I have
assumed responsibility for overseeing and monitoring various projects and issues
which affect the daily operations, efficiency, and profitability of the company. I
am recognized by senior management for consistently completing projects on time
and within budget.

My transition through several trades during my career has developed my
strong multi-tasking abilities which have proven to be an asset in my current
position. Additional areas of experience include plumbing, irrigation, landscap-
ing, electrical work, fiber optics, and carpentry. In each of these areas, I have
received training and have worked independently.

If you are in need of a person with my skills, I would welcome the opportunity
to meet with you to determine the contributions I can make to your company.

Thank you for your consideration.

Sincerely,

Jack L. Crouther

Jack L. Crouther

....
11 Oaklawn Boulevard • Orlando, Florida 33082
Phone: (386) 749-2430 • Cell: (386) 147-5874 • jlcrouther@yahoo.com

Broadcast Letter (Executive Chef/Hotel/Restaurant Manager)

Michael started as a chef and went into the management side of the restaurant.
He is now looking to work for a multirestaurant chain, in a management capacity.

Michael J. Fisher C.M.C.

56 Madison Avenue
Summit, New Jersey 07901
(908) 277-8796

Dear Sir/Madam:

I am confident that my extensive experience as an executive chef and hotel/restaurant manager would serve as an asset to a position in your organization. My career began 23 years ago as an apprentice training under several notable internationally known chefs. Since that time I have been involved extensively in the area of food services management and marketing.

I am currently General Manager and Corporate Executive Chef of Hague Nieuw-York. In 1999, I was hired to start up this 225-seat restaurant. The casual dining establishment is part of Avanti Brands, Inc., USA. I am responsible for all financial reporting and instituted key control systems to meet the standards of the parent company. Additional achievements include gaining excellent media publicity, creative menu development, and directing on- and off-site catering for many New York City premieres. I was asked to coordinate all aspects of our new construction and assist in the design aspects of the kitchen.

As Director of Operations for Town Square Katering and Times Square Restaurant in Hoboken, New Jersey, my staff and I expanded the business to accommodate parties ranging from 10 to 4,000 people and grossed over $1.5 million in sales.

Working as Vice President of Operations and Executive Chef for Pine Ridge Country Club, I oversaw all profit and loss functions for a 165-seat à la carte restaurant and a 1,000-seat banquet facility. The club had an 18 hole Championship Golf Course that I managed, with an active membership of 1,000 members.

I gained extensive international experience working as Executive Chef for Ordini's, a five-star-rated restaurant in New Zealand, I prepared food for the Prime Minister, various heads of state, and visiting dignitaries. I obtained my New Zealand Master Chef's Certification. In addition, I served as an Executive Pastry Chef and Chef for a Hawaiian hotel owned and operated by the Sheraton Corporation.

Thank you for your consideration. I look forward to speaking with you personally regarding my qualifications and how I can contribute positively as a member of your management staff.

Sincerely yours,

Michael J. Fisher

Michael J. Fisher C.M.C.

Broadcast Letter (Maintenance Mechanic)

Elizabeth was a school bus driver who transitioned into a warehouse position, and eventually into a higher-paying maintenance mechanic position. After a downsizing, she wishes to continue her mechanical career.

ELIZABETH DENTON

1814 TAYLOR DRIVE ~ NORTH BRUNSWICK, NJ 08902
(732) 821-7227 (H) ~ (732) 406-1927 (C) ~ E-MAIL: LIZDENT3@MSN.COM

RE: Maintenance Mechanic

Dear Sir/Madam:

As a professional **Facilities** and **Maintenance Mechanic**, I understand that success depends on several factors. These include timely upkeep of machinery maintenance and repair, supervision of maintenance programs, and monitoring outside contractors. My extensive hands-on experience as a mechanic has allowed me to ensure timely completion of projects and adherence to corporate safety requirements.

Throughout my career I have been promoted and have acquired increasing responsibilities within every position. In my latest position as a Mechanic for Heinz Foods, I had the reputation for excellent machinery knowledge and a keen attention to detail.

Heinz Foods is downsizing the plant in Edison, NJ, and I have accepted a voluntary separation package from the company. I would like to continue my career with a new company offering me new challenges.

Thank you for your consideration. I possess excellent hands-on knowledge as well as supervisory expertise, and I look forward to meeting with you personally so that we may discuss how I may make a positive contribution to your team.

Very truly yours,

Elizabeth Denton

Elizabeth Denton

Enclosure

Broadcast Letter (Database Engineer)

Edward Kumamoto
kumamotoed@islandnet.com

P.O. Box 775
Mililani, Hawaii 96789

Home: 808-555-4563
Cellular: 808-555-5457

(Date)
Phillip _____
(Title)
ABC Corporation
1 Industry Plaza
Honolulu, HI 96772

Dear Mr. _____:

Empowering your employees with the information and tools necessary to make better strategic business decisions is very likely to improve your company's competitive advantage and profitability. I can do this through insightful strategic planning and the delivery of superior data warehouse and decision support systems.

My extensive career experience in data warehousing, database administration, and business systems development, coupled with my commitment to exceed customer expectations and my focus on achieving sustainable strategic competitive advantage, are the primary assets I would bring to your Director of Database Engineering position. I have successfully delivered numerous data warehouse projects that were effectively aligned with company strategic objectives. I am also highly skilled at directing teams on complex initiatives and improving processes, communication, teamwork, and quality.

As a senior-level employee of R & M Information Technology, Inc., I have established an excellent track record for successfully managing large complex projects. Notably, I managed a $10 million development project for Management Source One, building and implementing their first enterprise data warehouse and certain downstream divisional data marts. So successful was this project that within three months after implementation it established itself as the recognized supreme source of accurate company data for all of Management's North American business units. Additionally, it met tight service level commitments over 97% of the time and experienced no downtime due to programming error.

As a Project Leader/Manager for Churchman's Business Systems, Inc., I also managed the development of a large data warehouse. I led the design and development efforts for this data warehouse of sales information for their Specialty Products division. This was the first data warehouse developed at Churchman's that successfully met user expectations.

An additional asset I would bring to your organization is competency in correlating data warehousing functions with overall company goals. I am skilled in providing counsel to senior managers and executives and adept at monitoring data warehouse systems to continually ensure their value and usefulness to an organization as a whole.

I am confident that this experience well equips me for success as your Director of Database Engineering. Kindly review my resume, then please contact me at your earliest convenience to schedule a professional interview.

Sincerely,

Edward Kumamoto

Broadcast Letter (Senior Technical Sales)

STEPHANIE PAIGE NEWMAN

15 Jasper Loop ▪ Ft. Thomas, Kentucky 91075 ▪ (859) 386-2276
techsales@aol.com

Emily _____   (Date)
(Title)
ABC Corporation
1 Industry Plaza
Louisville KY 91057

Dear Ms. _____:

As a seasoned Technical Sales and Marketing Consultant, I've generated considerable new business for my previous employers, and now I'd like to do the same for you. For the past 15 years I have pursued an increasingly successful career in telecommunications sales and marketing. Among my accomplishments are:

SALES
Qualified to spearhead the entire sales cycle management process, from initial client consultation and needs assessment through product demonstration, price and service negotiations, and final sales closings.

MARKETING
Success in orchestrating all aspects of developing a gainful marketing strategy, from competitive market intelligence and trend analysis, product development, launch, and positioning to distribution management and customer care.

TELECOMMUNICATIONS & NETWORK SOLUTIONS
Recognized for pioneering technology solutions that meet the needs of complex customer service, logistics, and distribution operations. Able to test operations to ensure optimum systems functionality and availability, guide systems implementation across multiple platforms, and deliver user training and support programs that outpace the competition.

I hope you will contact me in the very near future. You'll find my address and telephone number listed above. I would welcome the opportunity to contribute my skills to the success of your marketing team and look forward to learning about any available opportunities in your corporation.

Very truly yours,

Stephanie Newman

Stephanie Newman

SN
enclosure

Broadcast Letter (Telecommunications)

Tom Clancy

444 55th Street • Springtown, TX 77333 • telecompro@aol.com
Home: (281) 000-0000 • Work: (281) 000-0000 • Cell: (713) 000-0000

(Date)

Emily _____
(Title)
ABC Corporation
1 Industry Plaza
Houston, TX 77521

Dear Ms. _____:

If you need someone with proven international success who will really listen to your clients' needs and has leaped over cultural barriers to forge some of the most profitable technical opportunities in the telecommunications field, I am your #1 choice for any opportunity in international or domestic sales or marketing.

Since 1994, my work in strategic partnering, developing alliances, creating new opportunities, and exceeding multinational clients' expectations has helped my employers more than double their sales. However, follow-up, tenacious attention to detail, and my ability to listen have critically solidified long-standing relationships with major players worldwide.

With a global leader in telecommunications, I received 3 promotions in 4 years due to my success in managing contacts, motivating staffs, and implementing marketing campaigns that delivered ROI threefold.

Since 1998 I have ...

- Marketed a full range of data and voice communication services to multinational corporations and Internet service providers in Japan, Southeast Asia, Canada, and Western Europe.
- Brought in 28 new global accounts representing up to a 250 percent increase in business—currently handle brand management efforts for DWDM on pace to exceed annual goal; managed 20 accounts requiring broadband connectivity to international locations.
- Created the first transcontinental ATM circuit and earned one of the most prestigious awards in the company.
- Trained technical associates in ATM and employed knowledge of DWDM, SONET, SDMS, and TCP/IP technology to create some of the most cost-effective networks on the planet.

If these proven successes sound like a go-getter you need on staff ...

- Consider that, in just 2 years with a system software developer, I added $1.5M in new business, trained an all-Japanese staff in direct marketing principles, and launched direct sales campaigns that increased client awareness of our services.

Page 1 of 2

Additionally, my efforts with an international contractor ...

- Partnered the parent company with Japan-based joint venture interests that enabled the first US-built airport in Japan.
- Kept Japanese executives and high-ranking government officials apprised of progress—and landed 2 additional opportunities for a total of $10M in business in just a year.

Technically speaking ...

- I have worked with ATM, Frame Relay, Private Line, SONET, DWDM, SNA/SDLE, SDMS and IP, and managed networks and a diverse array of hardware and software packages—in addition to holding numerous Novell and Windows specialized certifications.

I love calling on clients who have been abused by other reps, because I know my negotiating skills, ability to cross cultural barriers and generate win-win opportunities will get the decision-maker to sign every time.

Reviewing my attached resume, you will note doctoral, master's, and bachelor's degrees—and a host of quantifiable results and technical training that serve only to enhance my drive and enthusiasm. I will gladly set aside time to meet with you and discuss how my knowledge of technology, client relations, and strategic partnering can become your biggest asset.

I will take the liberty of contacting you on Monday at 10 a.m. If you need to reach me, please feel free to contact me at 281-000-0000. Thanking you in advance for the opportunity to meet with you, I am,

Sincerely yours,

Tom Clancy

Tom Clancy

TC
enclosure

Broadcast Letter (Senior R&D Engineer)

Samantha Robinson

11825 Rambling Rose Lane • Valley Glen, California 91405
(818) 555-5555 • R&Dpro@email.com

**SENIOR R&D ENGINEER ... patent holder ... launched x# new products...
recognized worldwide ... created win-win alliances ... cornered global markets...**

(Date)

Phillip _____
(Title)
ABC Corporation
1 Industry Plaza
Sacramento, CA 91401

Dear Mr. _____:

If your R&D-to-market time needs a sense of urgency, creativity, and a seasoned coordinator of people and priorities, I am one individual you need to discuss the ABD POSITION with. Here's why:

- STRATEGIC PLANNING: Etched long- and short-term technological plans that kept a $2B manufacturer ahead of its competition since 1999

- COORDINATED RESOURCES: 20+ years in planning, reviewing, and benchmarking technical performance, meeting budgetary goals, and coordinating interlaboratory and interdepartmental efforts

- IGNITED STAFFS' CREATIVITY: Led efforts and piqued an in-house multidisciplinary R&D staff's synergy; got x# new products to market

- ENRICHED KNOWLEDGE: Trained sales, marketing, and technical staffs since 1995; well-known for abilities to communicate new ideas, selected for numerous assignments in product training worldwide

- MOVED THE MARKET TO OUR PRODUCT: Recognized expert—created the need for cutting-edge technology in the cutting tool market by featuring results in technical articles for leading publications

- INTEGRATED OPERATIONS: 1 of 2 individuals to integrate a newly acquired company's R&D with parent company's

- IGNORED STIGMAS: First person to involve marketing with R&D-created pathway between R&D and marketing, bringing projects to market in record time; landed $10 million+ in new accounts—only non-salesperson to get a one-of-a-kind annual sales award

- IMPECCABLE RECORD: Achieved 70 to 80 percent first-time success rate in field testing for all products developed; hold x# US patents; consulted worldwide by engineers and scientists; published; presenter at technical conferences since post-doctoral fellowship

Samantha Robinson
2 of 2

Reviewing my credentials and past results, you will note they occurred in the XYZ field. However, I am confident the core *technical, interpersonal, and organizational expertise I bring to your staff and customers would easily retrofit* at ABC CORPORATION.

If you need *a driven problem solver who can get your people moving to the work*, I am readily available to discuss how I can channel my more than two decades of success as your ABD POSITION at ABC CORPORATION. I will be in the area next month, and would prefer to meet with you then.

I am in a position to move to the Bay area, and *am ready to demonstrate how I can reignite your R&D efforts and create a flurry of opportunity*. Should you need added information, please do not hesitate to contact me at 818-555-5555 or R&Dpro@email.com.

Sincerely,

Samantha Robinson

Samantha Robinson

SR
enclosure

Broadcast Letter (Multilingual Sales Manager)

Robert Rodriguez

555 15th Street Apartment, 5A ~ Hoboken, New Jersey 07030
Cell: 201-555-5555 ~ Pager 201-555-4444 ~ E-mail: robrodriguez@hotmail.com

**Fluent in Spanish . . . time management skills . . . 8 years front line experience . . .
service-oriented positions . . . trainer . . . presentation expertise . . .**

(Date)

Emily _____
(Title)
ABC Corporation
1 Industry Plaza
Trenton, NJ 07028

Dear Ms. _____:

If you know your *customers and operations deserve attention to detail*, as well as a high-energy individual who is *fluent in Spanish and makes people a #1 priority*, I am one individual you need to interview for an ZYX position at ABC Corporation.

Reviewing my credentials, you will note I have taught high school since 1996. This exposure to *daily planning, keeping people motivated and moving to the work* can be an immediate asset at ABC, and here are some areas up-front that align with your needs . . .

—SUCCESS IN DIRECT COMMUNICATION: Whether with students, decision-makers or the general public, my presentation skills kept people interested, involved and properly served . . .

—MULTILINGUAL ABILITIES: Fluent in Spanish, Japanese and Russian—despite having a Spanish-only background, mastered the dialects of Russian and Japanese and was teaching classes upon hire at a school district . . .

—ALWAYS LOOKING FOR IMPROVEMENTS: Successfully integrated technology with additional conversational strategies . . . working for a distributor as an undergraduate, took initiative to revamp routing—increased productivity and service . . . increased a student's competency from 31 percent to 100 percent while an undergrad . . .

—FOCUS ON SERVICE: Made individual needs a priority since 1996 as a teacher—adept in varying approach per individual personalities and priorities . . .

—MOTIVATED: Worked up to 30 hours weekly while pursuing degree . . . proven abilities to juggle diverse assignments opened door for additional assignments and leadership roles . . .

I seek to channel my communication, presentation, customer service, training and organizational skills, and the ZYX opportunity at ABC Corporation matches my goal for a transferable opportunity. *You would benefit from someone with a proven track record in front line positions, and your customers and operations will have a team player who knows how to set goals, meet goals, and keep customers' needs at the forefront.*

Page 1 of 2

I will take the liberty of contacting you on _____ at _____ to confirm your receipt of my information and briefly discuss how my energy and talents could be your asset. I would also like to arrange our meeting at that time. Should you need to reach me sooner, I can be contacted at 201-555-5555 or robrodriguez@hotmail.com.

Best regards,

Robert Rodriguez

Robert Rodriguez

RR
enclosure

Broadcast Letter (Management)

LORI PAULEY
....
6777 ELGIN STREET • MIAMI, FL 99844 • (555) 555-5555

(Date)

Phillip _____
(Title)
ABC Corporation
1 Industry Plaza
West Palm Beach, FL 99831

Dear Mr. _____:

People will only give you what you're willing to accept. That's why my staffs employed "The Golden Rule" every day, treating customers the way they themselves would like to be treated.

If you need someone with a technical background who has hired and kept top talent challenged and on their toes to deliver exemplary service, then consider that in 20+ years...

—I translated my knowledge of physics and business into profits and operational success— for my staffs, my employers, and myself.

—I took on the lead engineering position in my second year with an industry giant, skipping over the traditional 12-year career path—I simply outworked everyone and never said I couldn't do something or get it done on time or within budget.

—I earned full latitude in decision making after proving my team's understanding of a new target market's needs—I introduced more products than my successors, improved processes, and cut manufacturing and warranty costs by roughly $1M the first year.

—Operations I had an impact on experienced extremely low employee turnover—and employees met or exceeded customer expectations 100 percent of the time.

I've made sure my staffs are so service-oriented that the customer doesn't have to ask for warranty repairs or "the next step"—they have the answers or already have performed the warranty work.

And when my name is on a project, it always is on schedule within budget—and is a winner...

—When a relationship with a specialty manufacturer ended, I spearheaded development of an intake manifold line, analyzed and negotiated manufacturing costs, and selected vendors—and launched an 18-unit product line in 18 months that led the industry.

—The first race manifold we developed took the first 5 Chevrolet finishes in the 1985 Daytona 500 without prior testing by participating teams.

Page 1 of 2

If you seek someone with the work ethic of a business partner, then I am your top choice for the _____ opportunity with the ABC Corporation. I fully understand the nuts-and-bolts of customer service, and certainly can combine my financial know-how with proven success in the field at ABC.

Right now I'm ready to step down from entrepreneurial management, simplify my role, and do "one or three things" well for an organization that values integrity, hard work, and creativity.

If I sound like the person you need at ABC, then contact me right away to discuss the _____ opportunity. I can be reached at 555.555.5555 after 6 p.m. Monday through Friday, or at my place of business at 555.555.1212 during regular business hours. I will take the liberty of contacting you on Monday at 10 a.m. to briefly screen my qualifications and arrange our interview.

Yours truly,

Lori Pauley

Lori Pauley

LP
enclosure

Broadcast Letter (HR Generalist)

Elliott Davidson
744 Haven Road
Millertown, NH 55599
(555) 555-5555 • davidsonhrpro@msn.com

HR GENERALIST
9 years advising senior decision-makers on employee matters...
5 years in benefits administration for $1B company and 5 affiliates...
15 years delivering HR presentations...
Open enrollment/benefits processing for professional employees...
13 years grievance/disciplinary meeting involvement...
10+ years training/development, entry through professional levels...
Worked through mergers and reorganizations...
Created award-winning concept for enrollment booklet...
Earned highest ratings throughout career...

(Date)

Phillip _____
(Title)
ABC Corporation
1 Industry Plaza
Concord, NH 55587

Dear Mr. _____:

    If your organization seeks someone to advance your human resource programs, consider my proven track record. I am ready for a challenge with ABC Corporation, as your recent growth needs someone acclimated to working with new subsidiaries and maintaining the bottom line. I absolutely am ready to step in as your Human Resource Director at ABC Corporation, as my commitment extends to all areas you seek to address.

    I bring you and your employees objectivity, knowledge of policy/procedure implementation and interpretation, and hands-on work in an ever-emerging climate. Here are some highlighted abilities that can be put to work immediately at ABC Corporation...

    MET THE CHALLENGE: With little notification, stepped in and was an asset in a HR Directorship capacity; administered $20M in health and welfare benefits; initiated multi-tier health care plan to better suit regional product needs

    BENEFITS: 5 years working with open enrollment for all levels of employees—restructured benefits during 3 internal reorganizations

Page 1 of 2

REMAINED FLEXIBLE: Adapted to the needs of entrepreneurial organizations while continuing a career with conservative major utility company

LEADERSHIP: Entrusted to step in for superiors due to track record in HR; #1 person consulted by senior managers of a $1B parent company and its 5 affiliates regarding HR or benefits; met with bargaining unit leadership, discussed and resolved grievances and complaints

COMMUNITY INVOLVEMENT: Accepted leadership role in United Way Campaign, keynote speaker for regional fundraising appearances

TRAINING/DEVELOPMENT: Delivered HR and benefits presentations since 1995, safety training, 2 years

OVER/ABOVE: Traveled over 3-year period to help a newly formed company whose explosive growth took them to 2,000 employees in 3 years (coordinated staffing and benefit enrollment while maintaining existing workload); singled out for HR support for special finance division structure, took on policy making/interpretation and HR

If you need someone seasoned in policy making who can interface with decision-makers and keep you 100 percent compliant with federal regulations, I am one individual awaiting your call for an interview.

I prefer to take the lead in contacting you, so I will call on Monday at 10 a.m. to brief you on how my background can be an immediate asset and arrange our meeting. I can forward a resume for your review immediately. Should you need to reach me sooner, I am at 555-555-5555.

Sincerely,

Elliott Davidson

Elliott Davidson
ED

~ **Benefits Enrollment** ~ **Multi-Tier Coverage** ~ **Labor Relations** ~ **Grievances** ~ **Arbitration** ~ **Job Bidding** ~ **HCFA, HIPAA, COBRA Regulations** ~ **EEOC/PHR Compliance** ~ **Unemployment Compensation** ~ **Sexual Harassment** ~ **Safety Training** ~ **Background Investigations** ~

Broadcast Letter (Operations Manager)

A downsized environmental operations manager trying to get back into a tight job market after 9/11.

Diane Baldwin
897 Station Street ▪ Brookfield, OH
330.555.4888 ▪ operationsmanager@alphone.net

(Date)

ABD Corporation
1 Industry Plaza
Cleveland, OH 44429
Attention Ms. Emily_____

Dear Ms._____:

Do you need an experienced, versatile individual who can improve bottom-line profits? I can offer innovative ideas to the position of Operations Manager—ideas that can benefit a service-driven, quality-oriented company like yours. No one has money to burn in a tough economy, which is why adding an already-skilled manager to your staff can reduce time and money.

The match between your needs and my talents is ideal. Why? Because my strengths lie in understanding the labor and manufacturing operations that design, build, install and manage equipment for environmental and production improvements. I am a leader both by example and through effective management of individuals and teams. In short, I have the drive and vision to make a positive difference in any organization.

Dozens of proposed projects have been successfully implemented due to my established reputation for the quality of work completed. The work performed under my direction has come in at, or below, budget and we meet project deadlines.

The enclosed resume summarizes my qualifications and achievements. I would be glad to discuss any of this information with you as an opportunity of employment. Because "proven skills" are best explained in person, I look forward to our conversation and will call early next week to schedule our meeting. Thank you for taking the time to review my resume and for your consideration.

Sincerely,

Diane Baldwin

Diane Baldwin

DB
enclosure

Broadcast Letter (Pharmaceutical Sales)

·· **Rebecca Marks**

(Date)

ABC Laboratories
1 Industry Plaza
Philadelphia, PA 16175

Ladies and Gentlemen:

ABC Laboratories is one of the fastest-growing companies in the United States.
Your achievements are impressive, and I am eager to make a contribution to your
professional team as a Pharmaceutical Sales Representative. Given a chance,
based on my enthusiasm and desire to excel, **I can make a positive difference in
your company!**

As a recent graduate, my professional job experience is limited. However, I believe
that you will find that I exhibit intelligence, common sense, initiative, maturity,
and stability. Various jobs over the last ten years have required a good attitude
and keen interpersonal skills. These jobs, along with my education, life's experiences and extensive travels, have not only enlightened me intellectually, but have
also given me a totally different paradigm compared with other candidates.

Analyzing an audience is of utmost importance as a sales representative. As
the daughter of a physician, I had great exposure to the medical environment.
I strongly believe this gives me insight into the way physicians think—that
patients' needs come first. Therefore, effective presentations of products must be
made in a timely, succinct, and caring manner for successful sales in this industry. My desire is to stay close to the medical field, and working in a pharmaceutical company is exactly where I aspire to be!

After reviewing the enclosed resume, please contact me at (724) 555-9821 to
arrange an interview. Because "proven skills" are best explained in person, I
look forward to discussing how my qualifications can meet your personnel needs
and contribute to your company's important mission.

Sincerely,

Rebecca Marks

Rebecca Marks

RM
enclosure

···
298 Jefferson Street • Wheatland, Pennsylvania 16161 • 724-555-9821

Broadcast Letter (Information Technology Program Manager)

DARRYL C. WARREN

51 Plantation Road, Apt. 7-C
Durham, NC 27706

(444) 555-4444
ITpro@yahoo.com

(Date)

Mr. Philip _____
CIO
ABC
1 Industry Plaza
Winston-Salem, NC 27561

Dear Mr. _____:

May I ask your advice and assistance?

As a result of J.P. Morgan's merger with Chase Manhattan Bank, I am confidentially exploring my opportunities. Although I am confident that I will be offered a role in the new organization, I am currently assessing where I can make the optimal contribution.

I am an Information Technology Program Manager. In this role, I have led the development of key financial systems and strategic business plans, co-managed the seamless migration of two divisions to another state and founded the PeopleSoft Wall Street Networking Group—delivering noteworthy cost savings and productivity gains. For the past 11 years, I've had dream jobs with leading firms like J.P. Morgan and Andersen Consulting. I have been entrusted with the direction of large scale, global projects. Many times, I learned "on my feet"—to implement new systems, design testing methods, manage resources, repair damaged vendor relations for mutual gain and to meet a wide array of challenges. My career has accelerated based on the results, as you'll note from the accomplishments in my enclosed resume.

I'm considering transferring my skills and experience to an organization where I can continue to be a team player and visionary leader for state-of-the-art technology programs, and where I'll also continue to learn new functional and technical areas. My expertise and interests are in the financial service industry.

I would greatly appreciate a few minutes of your time to discuss my options and glean any suggestions you can offer. I'll phone you in a few days to see if we can schedule a brief meeting.

Thanks very much.

Regards,

Darryl Warren

Darryl Warren

DW
enclosure

Broadcast Letter (Vice President of Operations)

A retiree in his late fifties, Barry is still interested in full-time employment and wants to communicate this to his contacts without giving the impression that he is "old" and "set in his ways." The tone of the letter is intended to be energetic and full of youthful enthusiasm.

Barry D. Hargrove

781 Forest Lane • Palmdale, CA 93591 • (447) 447-4477 • operationsvp@yahoo.com

(Date)

Philip _____, (Title)
Artesia Drilling Equipment
1 Industry Plaza
Modesto, CA 95354

Dear Mr. _____:

Problem - Action - Results. It is a simple formula, and one that I have implemented successfully throughout my long career in manufacturing. A former business associate passed your name on to me after commenting that my business philosophy and style reminded him of a CEO he had heard speak at a conference in Houston. That CEO was you.

It has been several years since I took my first job as a machinist back in Watertown, New York, but I have never lost my enthusiasm for finding faster and better ways to accomplish goals while cutting costs. I have worked my way up through the ranks from Foreman, to Plant Supervisor, to Manufacturing Engineer, to Director of Operations, and finally Vice President of Operations. Taking a swing at every new idea that came my way, I may have missed a few, but overall my batting average has been good:

- led a $340M manufacturing firm to earning ISO9002 certification on first attempt;
- revitalized operations at a plant site in Mexico by implementing a comprehensive employee training program;
- increased profits by 200% by identifying and rectifying problems with production and delivery at a Seattle manufacturing facility.

I believe strongly in teams and am comfortable working with R&D, engineering and marketing professionals. My colleagues have expressed appreciation for my direct and honest approach to people and problems.

Between jobs now, I am planning a fishing excursion on the Gulf. I will be arriving in Galveston on March 20th and would like to get together with you to explore potential opportunities with Artesia Drilling Equipment. It would be great to meet over lunch. I will give you a call the morning of the 22nd to see if that can be arranged.

I'm sending along my resume to lay a foundation for our meeting. I look forward to meeting you and exchanging ideas.

Sincerely,

Barry Hargrove

BH
enclosure

Broadcast Letter (Consultant)

A retired executive who wants to approach companies directly
and offer her unique expertise on a contract or consulting basis.

Elizabeth H. Jameson

49 IVANHOE COURT ◆ MONROE, NJ 08831 ◆ HOME: 732.658.6762

(Date)

Philip _____, (Title)
ABC Company
1 Industry Plaza
Ewing, NJ 08812

Dear Mr. _____:

- **Is your organization fully prepared to safeguard its technology services, information, and facilities in the event of a disaster?**
- **Are you taking full advantage of high-value and cost-effective vendor agreements?**
- **Do you benefit from high team performance and low turnover?**

If you have answered "No" to any of the above questions, then allow me to introduce myself and the expertise I can offer your organization. With a proven and award-winning track record of achievement, I offer a unique combination of expertise in disaster recovery/business continuity planning, vendor management/negotiations, and team leadership. I am currently offering my services to organizations within the Durham region, and would like to draw your attention to the value I offer.

Put simply, my expertise is delivering results. In previous positions, I have designed, implemented, and optimized comprehensive enterprise-class disaster recovery and information security procedures, saved millions in vendor negotiations and third-party service agreements, and led a variety of cross-functional teams to consistently achieve and exceed organizational mandates.

If the following interests you, I invite you to review the attached resume which further illustrates my experience, achievements, and expertise:

- **Expert in Disaster Recovery, Information Security, and Business Continuity**—expertise includes planning, protection, and off-site recovery of technology services, databases, and facilities

- **Superior contract procurement, negotiation, and vendor management capabilities**—proven record for negotiating agreements that improve service quality and save millions in vendor costs

- **Strong, decisive, and motivating leader**—reputation for building and leading high-performance teams to breakthrough achievement

- Available for **full-time, part-time, contract, and consulting opportunities**

Page 1 of 2

If you believe that you could benefit from a highly motivated and talented professional with a reputation for generating results, then I would welcome the opportunity to meet and discuss the specific value I can offer your organization.

I thank you for your consideration and I look forward to speaking with you soon.

Sincerely,

Elizabeth Jameson

Elizabeth Jameson

EJ
enclosure: Resume

Broadcast Letter (Project Manager)

MICHAEL J. SALINGER

1 Colonial Drive • Metropolis, LA 70114 • (504) 123-4567

(Date)

Dear Employer:

Because of current market conditions and high unemployment, I am sure you have many candidates and few **Project or Training Manager** positions to fill. With this letter and resume, please allow me to add to your cadre; but, may I also give a few reasons why you might want to call me ahead of other qualified candidates should an appropriate position become available?

You will note that my educational and professional **background is broad** and includes experience in post-secondary organizations, community colleges, business, and the military. Because of this range of experience, I am able to bring **insight and the ability to relate well to individuals at all levels and from diverse backgrounds**.

Working within for-profit organizations has enabled me to develop an **eye for the bottom line**. Whether it be budgetary or profit-enhancing, I am continually evaluating systems and methods to make them more efficient and productive.

Incredulous as it may sound, I appreciate and welcome change. I am **known for my abilities as a change agent**. However, while I may embrace change—technologically or otherwise—I recognize that many do not. Therefore, from a management standpoint, I look for ways to make transitions more tolerable for the people in my charge.

While my resume is comprehensive, it does not fully demonstrate the manner in which I have achieved success. My character, personality, and the ability to effectively lead a project or team could be evidenced in a personal meeting. Therefore, I would welcome an interview to further discuss your needs and my qualifications. Thank you for your time and consideration.

Respectfully,

Michael Salinger

Michael Salinger

MS
enclosure

185

Broadcast E-Mail
(Senior Buyer/Purchasing Agent/Purchasing Manager)

From: Kalista Jabert [purchasingpro@earthlink.net]
To: humanres@aeiusa.com
Cc:
Subject: Smart Purchasing Choice

Mr./Ms. _____:

SENIOR BUYER * PURCHASING AGENT * PURCHASING MANAGER

Do you cringe at the high costs your company incurs for goods and services?

Do you need someone who will maximize vendor resources, working hard to secure lower-cost, longer-term contracts?

Do you need someone on board who will immediately slash supply costs and streamline purchasing operations?

With more than 20 years in purchasing, retail sales management, store expansions, and new product research and market launch, I believe I may offer just what you're missing.

In my esteemed career with Major Company, a premier auto parts and accessories distributor, I have:

- Directed procurement of over $200M of goods and services, accounting for 60% of MC's total purchasing budget.
- Launched 3 private label programs, garnering $500K in additional profits during the first year of distribution.
- Recouped $300K in stolen merchandise and prosecuted the employees responsible.
- Generated $3M in savings by cultivating partnerships and negotiating long-term contracts with key suppliers.

With the right opportunity, I'd be perfectly willing to relocate. With regard to salary, I understand that flexibility is essential and would consider a compensation package appropriate for a person with my outstanding qualifications and dynamic track record of accomplishments.
If you're tired of seeing your company's profits slip through your fingers, call me today to schedule a business meeting. I can't wait to discuss how I can benefit your purchasing operation right away. I can be reached at (516) 555-1212 to arrange our interview.

Very truly yours,

Kalista Jabert
(516) 555-1212
purchasingpro@earthlink.net

Broadcast E-Mail (New Product Marketing)

From: Elizabeth Stettin [marketingexpert@aol.com]
To: bmathis@planetrecruit.com
Cc:
Subject: Real Marketing Savvy

Dear Mr. _____:

If you are looking for a successful executive to take charge of new product marketing, you will be interested in talking to me.

Ten years of experience in every aspect of marketing and sales in different industries gives me the confidence to be open to opportunities in almost any field. My search is focused on companies that innovate, because I am particularly effective at new product marketing. I have successfully managed new product-marketing research, launch planning, advertising, product training, and sales support, as well as direct sales. In my current position with XYZ Company, I created several products and marketing approaches on which other operating divisions in the company based their programs.

My business education includes a Marketing MBA from _____ University's School of Management, and provides me with a variety of useful analytical tools in managing problems and maximizing opportunities. My superior sales track record guarantees that I bring the reality of the marketplace to each business situation; I know what sells and why.

Currently, my total compensation package is in the low seventies; I am looking for a company that rewards performance consistently.

Since I am currently weighing several interesting opportunities, please contact me immediately if you are conducting any searches that might be a good fit. Relocation is no problem.

Thank you in advance for your consideration.

Sincerely,

Elizabeth Stettin
(516) 555-1212
marketingexpert@aol.com

Broadcast E-Mail (Senior Marketing Executive)

From: Joshua Michaels [marketingexec@yahoo.com]
To: hr@quantumcorp.com
Cc:
Subject: Ref: Your Marketing Executive Search

Dear Mr. _____:

I recently learned of your firm's excellent record of matching senior marketing executives with top corporations. I also have learned that you have an officer-level marketing assignment in process now—I am a serious candidate for your client's vacancy. Please consider some successes:

- After joining _____ as Marketing Director, I revitalized a declining processed-meats product category in less than a year, introducing better-tasting formulas and actually reducing product costs by over $100,000. Dramatic new packaging enhanced appetite appeal, and fresh promotion strategies doubled previous sales records.

- I have carefully crafted and fine-tuned many new product introductions and line extensions, such as _____ turkey, _____ processed meats, and _____'s deodorant maxi-pads.

- My sales/marketing experience dates from 1990, when I formed a direct sales company to pay for my _____ MBA (now the top-rated program in the U.S.A., I'm proud to say). Much of my subsequent success springs from strong working relationships with sales management and joint sales calls with field reps and marketing brokers. I have designed events like the _____ program, and _____'s sponsorship of the Indy 500 Williams racing team.

- I have a strong personal and professional interest in consumer electronics. I consult professionally and have successfully adapted marketing techniques for home and commercial satellite systems, "high-tech" audio/video, and radio communications equipment.

Please inform your client that I am fluent in French and I quickly absorb other languages. If your client challenges executives with the greatest of responsibilities and rewards them for remarkable performance, please contact me as soon as possible. I'll quickly repeat my past successes.

Sincerely,

Joshua Michaels
(516) 555-1212
marketingexec@yahoo.com

Broadcast E-Mail (Logistics)

From: Leonard Curtis [logisticspro@earthlink.net]
To: careers@ryder.com
Cc:
Subject: A logical choice for your client

Dear Mr. _____:

An industry association referred to your organization as an active and selective executive search firm, and mentioned your name because of your work in logistics. I liked that referral and think our meeting would be mutually beneficial.

I have a successful career of using logistics to cut costs and improve profits, usually in concert with other parts of the business. For example:

- I supervised the start-up of several remote offices to assist our plants in improving their distribution operations. By offering customized service, and through sharp negotiations, we saved over $500 million in various operations and warehouse costs.

- I directed the efforts of sizeable computer resources in the design and installation of a major application that saved $2.5 million in carrier costs. The application became the standard throughout the company's forty-six locations.

- Working with International Sales, I have established various Quality Control programs that have improved the timeliness and accuracy of product and paperwork delivery. Customer complaints plummeted to virtually zero, and remain there today.

A recent reorganization has reduced the number of senior management positions available within my company. I have concluded that another firm may offer a position and career advancement more in line with my personal expectations.

I would like to talk with you further. I suggest next week, the week of October 29, when you have a free minute. I have asked my staff to forward your message immediately in case I am unavailable when you call. I look forward to hearing from you.

Sincerely,

Leonard Curtis
(516) 555-1212
logisticspro@earthlink.net

Broadcast E-Mail (Vice President Asset Liquidation)

From: Gene Harrison [assetliquidationpro@mindspring.com]
To: cklause@cmaauctions.com
Cc:
Subject: Asset liquidation challenge? Get this guy!

Dear Mr. _____:

In recent years, as the Vice President of Lease Asset Liquidation with XYZ U.S.A., I successfully engineered the recovery of $23 million in assets, almost three times the original buyout offer of $8 million. Throughout my career I have been instrumental in developing and implementing workout and liquidation strategies and as such I have earned a strong reputation as a professional who gets the job done.

My reason for contacting you is simple. I am interested in project opportunities that will serve both to challenge and to utilize my abilities in asset liquidation management. My current project will be completed within the next four to six weeks. I am currently considering offers and intend to make a decision by February 1st.

The attached summary details some of my accomplishments. I look forward to hearing from you to discuss any mutually beneficial opportunities. Please feel free to pass along my resume to others who may have a need for my professional assistance.

Sincerely,

Gene Harrison
(516) 555-1212
assetliquidationpro@mindspring.com

POWER PHRASES

Consider using adaptations of these key phrases in your broadcast letters.

I hope this summary describes my experience and provides you with a better understanding of my capabilities. Thank you for your help.

If you feel that any of the strengths outlined in my resume could make a valuable contribution to your organization, please contact me to let me know of your interest.

Recently I read about the expansion of your company in the _____ Sun. As the _____ industry is of great interest to me, I was excited to learn of the new developments within ABC Corporation.

I feel confident that a short conversation about my experience and your growth plans would be mutually beneficial. I will be calling you early next week to follow up on this letter.

Currently, my total compensation package is in the low $70s; and I am looking for a company that rewards performance consistently.

I'm a responsive and responsible listener, maintaining a gracious and empathetic attitude, creatively troubleshooting, thoroughly researching options and making well thought-out recommendations designed to establish and enhance customer/client relationships.

I am available for relocation and travel and am targeting compensation in the $50K range.

I fervently request more than your cursory consideration; I request your time to verify my claims. YOUR TIME WILL NOT BE WASTED.

Superior recommendations from industry leaders as well as verifiable salary history is available.

I hope you will not think me presumptuous in writing directly to you; however, in view of your position, I am led to believe that you are more aware of your organization's telecommunications personnel requirements than anyone else.

I am confident that with my experience I can make a significant contribution to your organization.

Throughout my career, I've been fortunate to represent quality merchandise and services and have learned just how to present them in their most favorable aspects. I know how to evaluate competition, to assess consumer/market needs, exploit a market niche, maximize profit margins, create and maintain a reputation for dependability and excellent service.

I am a self-starter looking to join a reputable firm, one that could benefit from an individual who is ready to give 110 percent. With over three years of sales experience, I have developed excellent interpersonal, organizational, and communication skills. I am a hard-working individual who is motivated by the knowledge that my earnings are directly related to the time, energy, and effort that I commit to my position.

I am personable, present a highly professional image, and deal effectively with both peers and clientele. I am confident you will agree that I should be representing your firm and not your competition. My salary requirements are negotiable. I will call you this week to set up a mutually convenient time for an interview.

Since beginning with ABC Company, my average commission has progressed from $400 to $650 weekly. My current salary or commission requirement would range upward of the mid-$20Ks, with specifics flexible and negotiable.

I look forward to hearing from you in the near future to schedule an interview at your convenience, during which I hope to learn more about the position, your company's plans and goals, and how I can contribute to the success of your team.

I am grateful for that environment and the faith that was demonstrated in my capabilities. I automatically moved into the role of Executive Assistant, constantly seeking ways to limit expenses, cut costs and generate additional profit for the company. I was exceptionally successful in that endeavor—while managing 5 operations, 3 warehouses, 6 Warehouse Managers and a staff of 60.

I am appreciative of the time you've spent reviewing this letter (and the accompanying material). I hope to hear from you in the very near future to arrange to meet in person and discuss just how my qualifications may be of value to your organization.

Networking Letter (Managerial/Administrative Position)

A colleague that Maurice hasn't spoken to in several months has been nominated for a prestigious award. He decides to capitalize on an opportunity to renew the acquaintance and enlist her help in his job search.

Maurice DuMaurier
1360 French Court
Rochester, New York 14692
585-258-1693

January 12, 20–

Ms. Philippa Consodine, President
Rochester Regional Industrial Management Council
1000 Main Street
Rochester, New York 14600

Dear Philippa,

Congratulations on your nomination for the Athena Award. Even though you were not the ultimate winner, the nomination itself demonstrates the high degree of professional excellence you have achieved.

It's been a while since we've chatted, and I wanted to bring you up to date on what I've been doing. After leaving The Highlands, I explored several options before accepting a position as Director of Human Resources for Jefferson County. Unfortunately, the daily drive to Port Charles, among other factors, proved to be untenable—particularly during the winter months—and I have left that position.

This puts me back in the job market, and I am writing to inquire if you are aware of any managerial/administrative positions that would capitalize on my skills. I have enclosed for your reference an updated résumé that includes my recent experience.

Reiterating some of the key capabilities that I can bring to a position, consider the following:

- **Excellent team building and leadership skills**
- **Superb interpersonal skills and supervisory experience**
- **Developing and implementing human resource policies**
- **Extensive knowledge and experience in the healthcare arena**

I am convinced that my experience and professional diligence could be an asset to one of the IMC's member firms, and would appreciate any referrals you may be able to give me for potential employment opportunities. I will contact you to arrange a convenient date and time when we might renew acquaintances. In the meantime, feel free to pass my résumé on to anyone who may have an appropriate opportunity, or give me a call at 585-258-1693.

Thank you in advance for your assistance. I look forward to talking with you soon.

Sincerely,

Maurice DuMaurier

Enclosure

Networking Letter (Administrative Assistant)

This "insider" networking letter positions well for an administrative assistant, especially since this firm values foreign language proficiency in German and French.

Susan Jacobsen

43 Beacon Court, Robbinsville, NJ 08691 ▪ (609) 371-2324

April 26, 20–

Mr. Tom O'Kane
Head of Human Resources
Firmenich Incorporated
P.O. Box 5880
Princeton, NJ 08543

Dear Mr. O'Kane,

Kirsten Alexander of Human Resources suggested that I contact you in regard to applying for a position as an **Administrative Assistant**. If you have need of a well-qualified professional with German and French language skills and experience in office administration, customer service, sales, training, and marketing, then we have good reason to meet.

My resume is enclosed for your review. Highlights include:

✓ Over eight years' experience in organization, coordination, communication, and customer service. Consistently focus on creating and maintaining excellent client relationships, and training others in successful techniques to do the same.

✓ A resourceful problem-solver with a track record of getting positive results, such as a 75% collection rate on accounts 90 days past due.

✓ Ability to build confidence and trust at all levels, and demonstrated experience in supporting cooperative, results-oriented environments.

✓ Proven communication skills, including fluency in French and German.

My career success has been due in large part to supporting teams, as well as internal and external customer relationships, and tackling persistent problem areas with creative approaches. I am seeking the opportunity to transition my experience, skills and enthusiasm into a new organization where I can continue to contribute to bottom-line results while growing professionally.

Should my qualifications meet with your needs, I would be available to schedule a meeting immediately. I will call your office next week to answer any questions you may have and to set up a mutually convenient appointment. Thank you for your consideration.

Sincerely,

Susan Jacobsen

Susan Jacobsen

Enc. RESUME

Networking Letter (Internship/Employment)

A letter from a Japanese exchange student pursuing either an internship
or employment in a new program on campus.

November 14, 20–

Ms. Deborah Marks
Chairman, Creative Media Academy
University of the Northwest
6543 Campus Road, Jones Hall 322
Seattle, Washington 98155

Dear Ms. Marks:

Since meeting you earlier this year at the Korean Film Festival we have
exchanged e-mails and met several times. We have discussed our mutual interest
in the Japanese movie industry and its future in the global entertainment business. You know well my vision of integrating Japanese gaming and animation
technologies into filmmaking.

Over the course of our conversations, you have mentioned that there might be
an opportunity for an internship or, possibly, employment in the Creative Media
Academy. I am very interested.

I offer negotiation, persuasion, and liaison abilities; and management, leadership,
and communication skills. I have also proven that I can use my bilingual proficiency to enhance international relations. Please see my résumé for examples of
how I have used these abilities in the past.

I believe that my unique strengths can contribute to the growth of the Creative
Media program, particularly if you are able to secure departmental status. I welcome the opportunity to discuss my continued involvement in your program.

Sincerely,

Motoshi Mori

Motoshi Mori

Enclosures: 2-page Résumé
             Addendum of Completed Coursework

Networking Letter (Computer and Information Systems Manager)

A letter sent to follow up a meeting with a medical school dean.

DAVID KENT

1623 St. Louis Way • Honolulu, Hawaii 96813
808-555-6256 • dkent@alohanet.com

January 14, 20–

John Jones, M.D.
Dean, School of Medicine
University of Hawaii
1234 East-West Circle
Honolulu, Hawaii 96822

Dear Dr. Jones:

Perhaps you remember our chance meeting at the Bio Asia-Pacific Conference at the Sheraton Waikiki on August 18 and 19, 20–. In our brief conversation, I shared with you the idea of utilizing Web Development as an administrative tool. You expressed interest in the possibility of implementing such a system within the School of Medicine.

May I suggest a formal meeting to explore the idea?

I have some exciting and creative ideas, which may encourage you to take the next step towards realizing the positive impact a content management system would have in the School of Medicine. This would also be a great opportunity for us to discuss your goals and how an administrative intranet would help you reach them in a more timely and cost-effective manner.

In addition, there has recently been spirited discussion within the IT community on the topic of organizational continuity and its potential vulnerability due to advances in technology. I think you'll find the specific strategies I have to share with you worthy of consideration.

If you recall, my background is in Web Planning and Development, with specific skills in developing administrative intranets and public web sites, and designing web-based software to address the internal and external reporting needs of organizations.

Enclosed is my résumé attesting to my experience and specialties. I will contact you within the next few days to discuss the possibility of meeting with you.

Respectfully,

David Kent

David Kent
Computer and Information Systems Manager

Enclosure: Résumé

Networking Letter (Management)

SHARI T. MALSCH

717-755-1369 (Cell) • 717-845-5856 (Home) • managementpro@email.com
202 Mason Street • Atlanta • GA • 30605

(Date)

Philip _____, (Title)
ABC Company
1 Industry Plaza
Atlanta, GA 30601

Dear Mr. Harmond:

It has been said, *"in today's world there are two kinds of companies—the quick and the dead."* I propose the same is true of managers. I am a dynamic management professional with extraordinary team building and interpersonal skills, and thrive in a fast-paced environment that is constantly moving and producing solid bottom line results. I relish a challenge and will never run from a difficult situation. In fact, if you want a successful completion, you can count on it, accurately, timely, and right the first time.

In addition to solid people skills, I posses an extensive management background in International Affairs. While living in Germany for five years, I had the opportunity to study the language and culture. Bilingual with excellent comprehension of both German and English, my translation skills are strong in both languages. I also have conversational knowledge of French. Having held direct responsibility for commercial dealings with the UK, Ireland, and Germany, my knack for capturing key client relations with diverse cultures and people is intense. I would like to bring my business savvy and management/marketing skills to your firm.

My experience spans industries such as Real Estate Development, International Affairs and Procurement; however I am an ideal candidate for a company that values a well-rounded staff who can step in wherever needed and isn't afraid to learn. Dedicated to doing whatever it takes to achieve outstanding results, I will lead your team to meet tight deadlines. In short, I will not let you down.

My resume is enclosed for your consideration. I look forward to meeting with you to discuss your needs and the immediate impact I will make to your organization.

Best regards,

Shari Malsch

Shari Malsch

SM
Enclosure

Networking Letter (Chief Financial Officer)

Primarily a treasury executive, Paul was seeking a broad-based
senior finance assignment and was offered a CFO position.

PAUL A. GERARDI

16 MAIN STREET • ST. PAUL, MN 55401 • 612-624-2817

Dear _____:

Perhaps your company could benefit from a strong chief financial officer with a record of major contributions to business and profit growth.

The scope of my expertise is extensive and includes the full complement of corporate finance, accounting, budgeting, banking, tax, treasury, internal controls, and reporting functions. Equally important are my qualifications in business planning, operations, MIS technology, administration, and general management.

A business partner to management, I have been effective in working with all departments, linking finance with operations to improve productivity, efficiency and bottom-line results. Recruited at The Southington Company to provide finance and systems technology expertise, I created a solid infrastructure to support corporate growth as the company transitioned from a wholesale-retail distributor to a retail operator. Recent accomplishments include:

- **Significant contributor to the increase in operating profits from under $400K to more than $4M.**
- **Key member of due diligence team in the acquisition of 25 operating units that increased market penetration 27% and gross sales 32%.**
- **Spearheaded leading-edge MIS design and implementation, streamlining systems and procedures that dramatically enhanced productivity while cutting costs.**

A "hands-on" manager effective in building teamwork and cultivating strong internal/external relationships, I am flexible and responsive to the quickly changing demands of the business, industry and marketplace. If you are seeking a talented and proactive finance executive to complement your management team, I would welcome a personal interview. Thank you for your consideration.

Very truly yours,

Paul Gerardi

Paul Gerardi

Enclosure

Networking Letter (General)

Linda Brown
310 Hickory Valley Avenue
Nashville, Tennessee 37201
(615) 555.3471

(date)

Mr. Philip _____
1 Industry Plaza
Memphis, TN 37259

Dear Philip,

Congratulations on your re-election. I hope this letter finds you and your family well and that you have an enjoyable holiday season.

I am writing to update you on my job search. You may recall from our last discussion that I am now focusing on obtaining an hourly position with basic benefits that will sustain me until such time as I am ready for retirement (in three to five years).

As you recommended, I have applications on file with the Town of Anytown for various hourly positions and have corresponded with various department heads, in each case indicating my flexibility and strong interest in making a meaningful contribution to smooth operations within one of their departments.

Philip, I genuinely appreciate the advice and assistance you have offered to date. Once again, I am requesting that if you are aware of any other avenues I should be pursuing, please let me know. I believe I have skills and experience to offer and can be an asset to someone in just about any position requiring maturity, reliability, and dedication.

Thank you, again, for all your help, and "Merry Christmas."

Sincerely,

Linda Brown

Linda Brown

Networking Letter (Accounting)

ROBERT A. DOWNEY

24 Autumn Drive ▪ Seattle, Washington 98101 ▪ (206) 730-2187
accountingpro@aol.com

(date)

Mr. Philip _____
ABC Manufacturing
1 Industry Plaza
Olympia, WA 98501

Dear Mr. _____:

As a motivated accounting professional with proven capabilities in financial analysis and accounting management, I believe that my education and experience could benefit your company. For this reason, I have enclosed a resume for your review, which outlines my relevant experiences.
Some key qualifications that may be of interest to your firm include:

- **Extensive experience in providing timely and accurate financial reports utilizing a variety of applications and procedures. I have managed accounting functions for a manufacturing firm with over $100 million sales. I advanced quickly in the finance department and have gained a wide range of experiences, primarily focusing my efforts on analyzing, reporting, and planning.**

- **Absolute reliability and dedication to efficiency. As key financial analyst, I have worked closely with controllers and managers in monitoring financial input/output, streamlining financial reporting processes, and meeting aggressive deadlines for delivering information and analyses. I am also knowledgeable and current on legislative and regulatory requirements.**

- **Long-term vision. I have participated in both strategic planning for long-term marketing, and in annual budget preparation. My analyses and input have contributed to the successful outcomes of external audits, annual reviews, and budgeting processes in domestic operations.**

- **Proficiency in current business applications, including CODA, DCS, 4TH Shift, FAS1000, MP 2, FOCUS, and Microsoft Office.**

I have a strong desire to move into a business environment where my skills can be fully utilized in effectively furthering a leading firm's business objectives. I am confident that my knowledge and expertise, along with my dedicated professionalism, would allow me to make a significant contribution to your company's ongoing success. I would enjoy meeting with you to further discuss the possibilities. Please contact me to arrange a convenient date and time for an interview.
Thank you for your time and consideration. I look forward to speaking with you soon.

Sincerely,

Robert Downey

Enclosure

Networking E-Mail (Employee Benefits Administration)

From: Angela Sullivan [benefitsspecialist@hotmail.com]
To: awilliams@tcm.com/hr-careers/
Cc:
Subject: Great to talk to you again!

Dear _____:

It was a pleasure to speak with you on the telephone recently and, even more so, to be remembered after all these years.

As mentioned during our conversation, I have just recently reentered the job market and have ten years of experience with a 3,000-employee retail organization in the area of employee benefit administration. My experience includes pension plans, and dental, life, and disability insurance. I have been responsible for all facets of management of the company plan, including accounting, maintenance, and liaison with both staff and coverage providers.

My goal is to become a Benefits Manager in a larger organization with the possibility of advancement in other Human Resources areas. My preference is to remain in the Metropolitan _____ area.

For your information, attached is my resume. If any situations come to mind where you think my skills and background would fit or if you have any suggestions as to others with whom it might be beneficial for me to speak, I would appreciate hearing from you. I can be reached at the telephone number listed below.

Again, I very much enjoyed our conversation.

Yours truly,

Angela Sullivan
(516) 555-1212
benefitsspecialist@hotmail.com

Networking E-Mail (Publishing)

From: Robert Render [publishingpro@aol.com]
To: hr@pennwell.com
Cc:
Subject: Thanks for all the help ;-)

Dear _____:

It was a pleasure to meet with you for lunch today. I am grateful for the time you took out of your busy schedule to assist me in my job search.

It was fascinating to learn about the new technology which is beginning to play a major role in the publishing field today. I have already been to the bookstore to purchase the book by _____ which you highly recommended. I look forward to reading about his "space age" ideas.

I will be contacting _____ within the next few days to set up an appointment. I will let you know how things are progressing once I have met her.

Thanks again for your help. You will be hearing from me soon.

Yours sincerely,

Robert Render
(516) 555-1212
publishingpro@aol.com

POWER PHRASES

Consider using adaptations of these key phrases in your networking letters.

It was good talking with you again. As promised, I am enclosing a copy of my resume for your information. If any appropriate opportunities come to your attention, I would appreciate it if you would keep me in mind.

After you have had a chance to look over the resume, please give me a call.

I am beginning to put some "feelers" out in advance of the completion of my degree in December.

I do not intend to target any specific type of job. I am open to most anything that my qualifications will fit. My only criteria are the following:

I would appreciate any advice and/or referrals you might be able to give me.

I am looking for a position in management and would appreciate any assistance you could provide.

As always, it was good to talk with you. Your positive outlook is catching. I've been called the eternal optimist, but I always feel more upbeat after a conversation with you.

Many thanks for the words of encouragement and taking the time from your busy schedule to help me. It truly is appreciated. I have never faced an unemployment situation like this before.

It was a pleasure to speak with you on the telephone recently and, even more so, to be remembered after all these years.

For your information, enclosed is my resume. If any situations come to mind where you think my skills and background would fit, or if you have any suggestions as to others with whom it might be beneficial for me to speak, I would appreciate hearing from you. I can be reached at the telephone numbers listed above.

He assured me that he would pass my resume along to you; however, in the event that it has not reached you yet, I am enclosing another.

Perhaps you know of a company that could use this scope of experience. In this regard, I enclose a copy of my resume outlining a few of my more significant accomplishments.

My objective is to find a _____ level position at a marketing driven company where my skills can contribute to the firm's growth and profitability.

I am not limited by location and would consider the opportunity wherever it presents itself.

First of all, let me sincerely thank you for taking the time and trouble to return my call last Monday. I found our conversation informative, entertaining, and (alas) a little scary. Needless to say, I genuinely appreciate your prompt response and generous, helpful advice.

Again, a thousand thanks for your time and consideration. If I might ask you one last favor, could you please give me your opinion of the revision? A copy is, as usual, enclosed.

I am writing to you in response to our recent conversation over the telephone. I thank you for your time and your advice. It was most generous of you and sincerely appreciated. Please accept my apologies for invading your privacy. I anticipated an address for written correspondence from an answering service.

I look forward to hearing from you on your next visit to _____.

I hope you'll keep me in mind if you hear of anything that's up my alley!

I recently learned that your firm is well connected with manufacturers in the _____ area and does quality work. We should talk soon, since it's very likely we can help each other. I'll be in the office all next week and look forward to hearing from you. I have alerted my secretary; she'll put your call right through.

_____ suggested that I contact you regarding employment opportunities.

After many years in the _____ community, I have decided that a career change is due in order to use my interpersonal skills to their fullest.

Follow-Up Letter (after telephone contact) (Fundraising Consultant)

From an applicant who has had too many jobs in too few years, this letter
was designed to get two competing "partners" to bring her on board.

.... **Lanina Crowne**

Wednesday, 02 May 20–

Ms. Patty Martineau
Vice President
O'Neill & Associates
Three Peachtree Avenue, NE
Atlanta, Georgia 30305-3001

Dear Ms. Martineau:

Thank you for making time to explore how I could help O'Neill & Associates as
your newest Fundraising Consultant.

I've already starting thinking about how I might be most productive—right from
the start. Of course, my ideas must be preliminary; I don't know exactly how
your organization works. Nevertheless, I would value your reactions to the preliminary thoughts you'll find in the next paragraphs.

I want each of your clients to see the tailored solutions we provide as a rapid,
seamless, continuing operation that guides them through the complex world of
modern fundraising. In fact, I want them to think of us as their "sole source"
for the resources they must have to grow financially and operationally. If we are
to speak with the one voice the clients should demand, then our business model
requires close teamwork between Ms. O'Neill, you, and me.

In the meantime, I am modifying my own continuing professional development
program to concentrate on fundraising from a consultant's perspective. I've begun
to look through the literature and contact professional organizations to hear about
the latest trends directly from industry leaders. Later, I'll use what I learn to
reevaluate my own successes in campaigns done with and without consultants.

I appreciate your vote of confidence in recommending that I meet with Ms.
O'Neill. And I want to make that interview just as useful for her as possible.
Toward that end, may I call in a few days to get your reactions to the prelimi-
nary thoughts I've outlined above?

With many thanks for all your help...

Sincerely,

Lanina Crowne

Lanina Crowne

....
1000 New College Way • Cumming, Georgia 30041
[678] 555-5555 (Home) • lcc@randomc.com

Follow-Up Letter (after telephone contact) (Adjunct Faculty)

STEPHANIE A. MONACO

862 Lafayette Parkway
Rochester, New York 14625
(585) 586-2389

EDUCATOR/ADVOCATE/MENTOR
"Every leader a teacher, every teacher a leader, every student a success."

Emily _____   (Date)
(Title)
ABC Community College
1 Industry Plaza
Princeton, NJ 08540

Dear Ms. _____:

I enclose my resume in follow-up to our conversation last week regarding the adjunct adult education position currently available at Anytown Community College. I appreciate very much your offer to forward my credentials to the appropriate individual.

With a master's degree in Education Administration, Principal of Administration and Supervision certification through the state of New York, plus four years of cumulative experience in the classroom, I believe I possess the expertise and qualifications that are critical to leading your organization's adult students to successfully achieve their educational goals.

What do I offer your students?

- Effective listening and communication skills—a demonstrated ability to provide individualized instruction based on students' interests and needs.
- Encouragement and motivation—a creative, inviting atmosphere of interaction and participation.
- Sincere desire to reach them on a level they can understand, no matter what age, skill level, or cultural background.

I am excited at the opportunity to work with adult students, because I recognize that they are in that classroom because they want to be there. The adult population brings a unique flavor of enthusiasm and motivation that energizes and inspires me as an instructor and makes me eager to go above and beyond expectations to help them reach their goals.

In terms of salary, I realize that flexibility is essential and am therefore open to discussing your organization's compensation package for an individual with my distinctive talents. If you believe that I could play an important role on your educational team, please call me at (585) 586-2389 to arrange for an interview.

Sincere regards,

Stephanie Monaco

Stephanie Monaco

SM
enclosure

Follow-Up Letter (after telephone contact) (Legal Assistant)

JAMES PENSON
2279 Reynolds Road, Ocala, Florida 33739
(352) 796-4476 legalpro@aol.com

(Date)

Phillip _____
(Title)
ABC Corporation
1 Industry Plaza
Orlando, FL 33576

Dear Mr. _____:

Thank you for returning my telephone call yesterday. It was a pleasure speaking with you, and as promised, a copy of my resume is enclosed. As I mentioned, I have been working in law firms since the end of February, as well as working on weekends and in the evenings for over one year. At present, I am looking for a second or third shift to continue developing my word-processing and legal skills.

Although the majority of my positions have been more managerial and less secretarial, I have developed strong office skills over the years. While I was attending both undergraduate and graduate school, I worked as Administrative Assistants to Deans and Department Heads, in addition to working in other professional capacities.

_____ speaks very highly of me, and if you need to confirm a reference with him, please feel free to contact him at _____. In addition, I would be happy to furnish you with names of people I have worked for within law firms over the past year.

Within the next day, I will be contacting you to arrange a convenient meeting time to discuss the position you now have available. However, if you would like to speak with me, feel free to contact me at 352-796-4476.

Thank you again for calling yesterday. I look forward to speaking with you on the telephone, and meeting you in person.

Sincerely,

James Penson

James Penson

JP
enclosure

Follow-Up Letter (after telephone contact) (Purchasing)

CHERYL BLOOM
··
89 PINE ROAD • OMAHA, NE 68117 • (555) 555-5555

(Date)

Bob _____ - (Title)
Krieger, Skvetney, Howell
Executive Search Consultants
2426 Foundation Road
Lincoln, NE 68154

Dear Mr. _____:

In reference to our telephone conversation, enclosed is my _____ resume. I believe the one you have is written toward a sales and marketing position.

Since we last spoke I have been working as a business consultant for the _____ group of companies on projects in a number of different areas outlined below.

- Elected to serve as the Vice Chairman of the _____ Chapter 11 bankruptcy creditors committee including the two primary subcommittees reviewing offers to purchase the _____ operations.

- Spearheaded and supervised upgrading of the _____ companies' communications systems, including printing and copy machines, telecommunications systems, computer hardware and software systems, computer scanning system, computer filing system, and fax and modem transmission systems.

- Set up and implemented an auto and entry floor mat marketing program for _____ including pricing and product displays for retail sales outlets.

- Researched, purchased and installed a bar code labeling program for the companies' products, including label set up and printing systems to allow them to sell their products to _____.

- Participated in the design and layout of a new logo for _____ division including specifications for all letterheads, forms, and printed communications materials.

- Provided major input for a factory-paid _____ point-of-sale system to display custom automotive floor mats.

Most of my projects should be wrapped up by the end of November, and so I will be looking for another company who could utilize my broad range of experience. Please let me know if you think you might have something for me.

Sincerely,

Cheryl Bloom

CB
enclosure

Follow-Up Letter (after telephone contact) (Manager)

Andrew T. Bestwick
653 Lassiter Drive
Lake Wylie, SC 29710
(803) 458-8004
managerpro@aol.com

(Date)

Bob _____
(Title)
Krieger, Skvetney, Howell
Executive Search Consultants
2426 Foundation Road
Columbia, SC 29753

Dear Mr. _____:

THANK YOU for allowing me to tell you a little about myself. I have just completed my MBA (December, 20–) and would appreciate the opportunity to talk with your client companies who are in need of an experienced and seasoned manager. Whether the need is for general (operational) management, products, marketing, or sales, my substantial background in management, marketing, and technical products should be very valuable to your clients.

I have enclosed two resumes (marketing-oriented and operational-oriented) with some other information which you may find useful. With eyes firmly welded to the bottom line, I offer: the ABILITY to manage, build, and quickly understand their business; EXPERIENCE in domestic and international corporate cultures; INTELLIGENCE and the capacity to grasp essential elements; and the WILLINGNESS to work hard, travel, and relocate.

Realizing that most of your clients aren't looking for VPs, I'm not necessarily looking for fancy titles (but I am promotable). What I am looking for is that special position which will offer not only a challenge but a career opportunity with long-range potential. I know my successes will bring them (and me) rewards.

Resumes and letters are brief by their very nature and cannot tell the whole story. I will be happy to discuss with your client and you how my commitment to them will help solve their needs or problems and will definitely make good things happen! After all, isn't that the bottom line?

May we work together?

Very truly yours,

Andrew Bestwick

Andrew Bestwick

AB
enclosures

Follow-Up E-Mail (after telephone contact) (General)

From: James Young [jyoung@earthlink.net]
To: hr@agcocorp.com
Cc:
Subject: Glad we finally caught up

Dear Ms. _____:

I appreciate the time you took yesterday to discuss the position at _____. I recognize that timing and awareness of interest are very important in searches of this type. Your comment regarding an attempt to contact me earlier this summer is a case in point.

Attached, as you requested, you will find an outline resume. I also believe that my experiences as a director of physical plant services are readily transferable to a new environment. I believe that I can contribute a great deal to the satisfaction of your client's needs.

Realizing that letters and resumes are not an entirely satisfactory means of judging a person's ability or personality, I suggest a personal interview to discuss further your client's needs and my qualifications. I can be reached directly or via message at (516) 555-1212, so that we may arrange a mutually convenient time to meet. I look forward to hearing from you. Thank you for your time and consideration.

Sincerely,

James Young
(516) 555-1212
jyoung@earthlink.net

Follow-Up E-Mail (after telephone contact) (Arts Management)

From: Jasmine Morgan [promotionspro@yahoo.com]
To: ewoods@maoriartspromos.com
Cc:
Subject: Thanks from a motivated flack!

Dear Ms. _____:

Per yesterday's conversation, I am forwarding a copy of my resume and am looking forward to our meeting in the very near future.

As we discussed, the positions that interest me are as follows:

Event/Arts Management
Promotions/Advertising/Public Relations
Corporate Training

I am a fanatic about image, excellence, and attention to quality and detail. As my academic and career background reveal, I have the tenacity of a rat terrier when it comes to task accomplishment.

I have never held an "eight-to-five" job and would most likely be bored to death if I had one. Therefore, I am looking for something fast-paced and challenging to my gray matter that will allow growth and advancement and an opportunity to learn. I am in my element when I am in a position to organize . . . the more details the better!

I'll give you a buzz on Tuesday, March –th to try to set an appointment for further discussion.

Sincerely,

Jasmine Morgan
(516) 555-1212
promotionspro@yahoo.com

POWER PHRASES

Consider using adaptations of these key phrases in your follow-up letters after phone calls.

As you requested in our telephone conversation this morning, I am enclosing a copy of my resume for your review.

As you can see from my resume, I have some excellent secretarial experience.

I'll give you a buzz on Tuesday, March —th, to set an appointment for further discussion.

In reference to our telephone conversation, enclosed is my sales and marketing resume; I believe the one you have is written toward a purchasing position.

I am a bright, articulate, and well-groomed professional with excellent telemarketing skills, sales instincts, and closing abilities. I am seeking a dynamic position with a reputable firm. I would like to meet with you in person to discuss how I could contribute to the effectiveness of your clients' operations.

Please remember me if something arises that would tie in with my background.

My many long-term professional relationships would benefit any employer in this area.

I'd like to meet with you to tell you more about my background and to show you some of the training and marketing materials I've developed. This would give you a better picture of my capabilities.

As you suggested when we spoke last week, I have enclosed my resume for your review and consideration. I contacted you on the recommendation of _____ of _____, who thought that you may have an interest in my qualifications for a position in the near future.

I have long admired _____ for its innovations in the industry, and I would consider it a tremendous career opportunity to be associated with your organization.

Follow-Up Letter (after face-to-face meeting) (Library System Director)

Victoria was genuinely impressed with the facility she visited, but also recognized she could help them improve by applying her management experience.

Victoria Leung
64 West Blossom Circle ▪ Brighton, New York 14618 ▪ (585) 586-5803

January 12, 20–

Ms. Louisa May Prescott, President
Orchard County Library Board
West View Library
One Orchard Parkway
MacIntosh, New York 14782

Dear Ms. Prescott:

Thank you for the opportunity to visit your facilities and discuss the Director's position with you. I enjoyed meeting you and the other trustees, as well as Sylvia Morrison and members of the library staff. I was impressed with your outline of the position and believe that I possess the capabilities to successfully lead the Orchard County Library system well into the 21st century.

My tour of three of your branches and my conversations with several staff members made it easy for me to understand how you have achieved your national ranking. As someone with over 20 years in the library field, and experience visiting literally hundreds of library branches in the course of a year, I was favorably impressed with the design and space utilization of your branches. The cordiality of your staff members and the fine way in which the facilities are maintained are also quite impressive. Your "Friends" organization and Foundation also appear to be real assets to the library.

Some key talents that I can bring to this leadership position include:

- *Establishing a strategic vision and motivating staff to pursue that vision.*
- *Maintaining productive rapport with advisory boards, and successfully interacting with governmental entities and the community at-large to achieve library goals.*
- *Developing information technology plans that have prepared libraries for the 21st century and that anticipate the changing technological landscape.*

I remain most interested in this position and am confident that my knowledge and expertise would allow me to exceed your expectations in this leadership role. I look forward to further discussing my candidacy with you soon.

Sincerely,

Victoria Leung

Victoria Leung

Follow-Up Letter (after face-to-face meeting) (Sales)

A two-point letter: (1) reinforces the point that he was successful in sales, even though he hadn't ever worked in pharmaceutical sales, and (2) moves the hiring official to make a decision.

··· **NORMAN CORNFELD**
75 Willow Street • Crenshaw, Alabama 36078 • 334.555.5555 • ncorn72@aol.com

Friday, July 20, 20–

Mark Pugh
Area Manager
Aventis Pharmaceuticals
609 Greenwich Circle
Birmingham, Alabama 35243

Dear Mr. Pugh:

Thank you for making time to meet with me this morning. Even during our interview, it struck me how good a match I think I am for Aventis. And on the way home, I began to formulate a plan to be productive for you from the first day, based on how I might meet your special needs. Here's what I've come up with so far:

Your needs	My capabilities
• Good track record	• Bringing in twice my sales quotas for four consecutive years. • Being my organization's top producer in those same four years.
• Communication skills that build sales	• Capturing sales with presentations before busy decision makers.
• Good work ethic	• Turning around a market that had been stagnant for 15 years. • Regularly overcoming strong sales resistance.

I can offer everything you see above because I show the benefit of what I sell—not just to the end user, but to the people who deliver those benefits. That's a direct parallel with an Aventis strength.

I've already spoken with your Dothan representative. And I'm looking forward to my "ride along."

At this point, most applicants would ask you to contact them if you have questions. I want to do something different. Please consider this question: What additional information do you need from me to choose me as the best candidate for the position?

Sincerely,

Norman Cornfeld

Follow-Up Letter (after face-to-face meeting) (Loan Processor)

Richard had to overcome the effects of a prolonged slowdown in his industry—portfolio management—and convince the decision maker that his skills were transferable and he could master the intricacies of new product lines he had never worked with before.

RICHARD WEIGMAN

1100 Apartment A
Patton Street
Montgomery, Alabama 36100

[334] 555-5555 (Home)
[334] 555-8888 (Office)
rweigman@hotmail.com

Wednesday, 13 June, 20–

Malcolm S. McLeod
Vice President
Alabama Home Mortgage Lending
1200 17th Street, South
Birmingham, Alabama 35205

Dear Mr. McLeod:

Thank you for meeting with me this afternoon. I think Alabama Home Mortgage Lending and I are a good match if I can be your newest loan processor.

In fact, as I was driving back to Montgomery, I began to plan how I might be productive for you right from the start. My ideas are, of course, preliminary. But I would value your reactions to this tentative plan:

- I would start by introducing myself to every "player." I want them to think of me as Alabama Home Mortgage Lending. And I want to find out what their special needs are before any rush requirements come up. When they need answers, I want them to remember two things: my name and my phone number.

- I have already started my plan to master FHA requirements. As first step, I'm jotting down the kinds of questions I must have the answers to so I can process FHA loans fast and right the first time. I want Alabama Home Mortgage to be the "provider of choice" in the eyes of buyers, agents, closing attorneys—in short, anyone who wants quality loan processing services. If I am successful, I hope our percentage of revenue for FHA loan processing grows steadily.

As you asked me to, I plan to call on Friday. And I've already thought of the question I would most like to ask. Here it is: Will the plan I've outlined above work for Alabama Home Mortgage faster and better than any plan suggested by the other candidates you've interviewed?

Sincerely,

Richard Weigman

Follow-Up Letter (after face-to-face meeting) (Concierge Associate)

Lacking professional experience as a concierge, Olivia was sure to remind her interviewers of her related volunteer work, enthusiasm, education, international travel experience, and multilingual communication skills. Notice how she copied ("cc") her interviewers.

Olivia Beth Copperfield

2 Jenkins Place
Brentwood, NY 11717
(631) 455-2344
worldtraveler@sky.net

February 19, 20–

Ms. Janet Berlinger
Human Resources Specialist
The Marriott Wind Watch Hotel
1717 Motor Parkway
Hauppauge, NY 11788

Dear Ms. Berlinger:

Thank you for the opportunity to participate in a follow-up interview with you and your supervising managers, Mr. Sean Johnson and Mrs. Rita Bronson to further discuss the possibility of my joining your hospitality team as Concierge Associate.

As discussed during our meeting, The Marriott Wind Watch Hotel is the ideal work environment for me to express my enthusiasm for working with people as well as put to use my education in psychology and business administration. I feel strongly that my volunteer work experience at The New York Hilton and my personal experiences acquired over the years while traveling worldwide will prove especially valuable in this highly visible position. Combined with an ability to communicate effectively in Spanish, French, and Italian, I feel I would make a significant contribution to The Marriott Wind Watch Hotel.

Please note that my availability is immediate. If you need to contact me, I can be reached at the above telephone number. Thank you again for your time and consideration. I hope to speak with you soon.

Sincerely,

Olivia Beth Copperfield

Olivia Beth Copperfield

cc: Mr. Sean Johnson
     Mrs. Rita Bronson

Follow-Up Letter (after face-to-face meeting) (Merchandise Manager)

This thank-you letter capitalizes on reinforcing the "fit" between the potential job and her qualifications, as well as introducing some areas overlooked in the interview.

DEBORAH DEVEREAUX

555 MAIN STREET, LAWRENCEVILLE, NJ 08648
(609) 771-5555 HOME • EMAIL: DDEVE@BOL.COM

November 9, 20–

Ms. Melinda Newby, Director
Human Resources
Universal Stores
1700 Primary Place
Princeton, NJ 08540

Dear Ms. Newby,

Thank you for the opportunity to interview for the **Merchandise Manager** position. You were extremely generous with your time and I was impressed with the warmth and efficiency of your office, and your genuine interest in acquainting me with the company's concepts and goals.

My background is unique – it does not fit into a traditional career mold – yet it encompasses a very diverse exposure in Home Furnishings and Ready-to-Wear. As we discussed, my extensive experience with the type of clientele your company targets has prepared me to quickly "come on board" your team. My sales record of $279,000 (2003) demonstrates that I can produce immediate value, as well as train new sales reps in highly effective merchandising and closing techniques.

What I did not stress is that I also have built an arsenal of skills around quantitative, technical processes involved in merchandising dollar planning. For example, I have developed six-month dollar merchandising plans for the RTW division of Chic Apparel, and classification planning which established the focus on merchandise categories, prices, styles, sizes and colors.

I have always strived to achieve high quality results by knowing the customer well, anticipating profitable market trends and never forgetting the store image. Offering wide, but well-edited, assortments of multiple classifications so that one-stop shopping can easily occur has been my hallmark. Such high standards have been central in all of my work, whether with a major retail department store, New York City wholesale showroom, or upscale home furnishings boutique. Your corporate environment and company goals appear to reflect those same high standards and I am eager to join your team.

I am very interested in this position and would like to touch base with you next week to check on the progress of your search. Thanks again for the opportunity to interview.

Sincerely,

Deborah Devereaux

217

Follow-Up Letter (after face-to-face meeting)
(Manufacturer Representative)

Anthony Ruggerio

4 Edgewood Court

Dover, NJ 00000

Home Phone: (555) 555-5555 • Cell Phone: (555) 555-5555

February 28, 20–

Ms. Kathleen McMann
General Manager
Panoramic Imaging
975 17th Street
Morris, NJ 00000

Dear Ms. McMann:

Thank you for allowing me to interview with you on Friday, February 23rd, for the Manufacturer's Representative position. Everything I learned from you about Panoramic Imaging leads me to believe that this is a progressive company where I could fully utilize my skills and make a valuable contribution. In fact, I have not been this determined or excited about a job since I started my business 25 years ago.

As I mentioned to you, I am sales oriented and have a solid technical background in printing. I relate well to printers at any level, from pressmen to owners. In my sales activities with John Watkins when he was a printing buyer at Dart Industries, I found him to be very demanding and hard to please. One of the reasons why I was successful in acquiring and retaining his business was my constant commitment to customer service. Whenever there were any questions, I never failed to answer them promptly.

During our discussion, you seemed to express a concern about my lack of experience with dealers. Although I had not mentioned it at the time we spoke, I have had long-term relationships with dealers like Arvine, and have bought approximately $1 million worth of equipment from them, starting with my first press and expanding to 20 over the years. I am certain that with my persistency and follow-through, I know I can handle dealers at the sales and service end. Rest assured that I would keep you informed of my progress on a daily basis. Nothing would be done without you knowing about it. My first priority will be to make you look good.

Among my major strengths, I am goal-driven, self-motivated, have a strong work ethic, and an ability to learn quickly. My training period would be brief, and I would use my own time to familiarize myself with your equipment and product line. In addition, I am accustomed to long hours and have no objection to the travel requirements throughout the Middle Atlantic states or being away from home four days a week.

Coming from a medium-sized company, it would be an honor to work at Panoramic Imaging, and I am hopeful that I would have the chance to be a member of your team. Please do not hesitate to call me if you have any further questions or need additional information from me.

I look forward to your positive decision about my candidacy.

Sincerely,
Anthony Ruggerio

Follow-Up Letter (after face-to-face meeting) (General)

MARCY SMITH
222 East Ninth Street – Maryland Heights, MO 63146
999-555-4444 – marcysmith@msn.com

(Date)

Phillip _____
(Title)
ABC Corporation
1 Industry Plaza
St. Louis, MO 63141

Dear Mr. _____:

Thank you very much for taking the time to meet with me today. I enjoyed our discussion, and I'm now even more excited about the possibility of working for ABC and with your team.

It was great to learn that you are embracing technology as it relates to your business—both in terms of day-to-day operations and the future delivery of ABC's programs (e.g., on-the-spot training). I am very interested in, and have an affinity for, computer technology and would love to be a part of your efforts in this area.

I am confident that I could make a strong contribution to the continued growth of ABC. As we discussed, I have related experience in all of the required areas for the position. In addition, I look forward to taking a project management approach to establishing the new system for the delivery of the assessment workshops to your key client. This process would allow me to ensure that I am meeting your objectives and getting a system "up and running" within an established time frame. Having done this, I would continually review for improvement and focus on managing the enhancement of customer service.

I remain very interested in the position, and I look forward to hearing from you soon. If you require additional information in the meantime, I may be reached at (999) 555-4444.

Sincerely,

Marcy Smith
Marcy Smith

MS

Follow-Up Letter (after face-to-face meeting) (Librarian)

The interview in this case was by a committee and very structured, leaving the candidate with the feeling that there was more she would have liked to have said. This thank-you letter conveys some of these ideas. The result: the candidate was hired for this high-level position.

... Mary Kelner

(date)
Mr. Philip _____
(Title)
ABC State Librarian
State Library of ABC
Wichita, KS 66627

Dear Philip:

Thank you for the opportunity to meet with you and the selection committee on Monday. I enjoyed our discussion of the Associate State Librarian for Library Development opening. I was impressed with your vision for this individual's role.

Based on our conversation, I believe that I possess the capabilities to successfully meet your expectations for this key position with the State Library.

To reiterate the experiences I bring to this opportunity, please note the following:

- Promoting programs and fostering working relationships with over 1,000 member libraries in all major segments of the field. These activities also encompass extensive community outreach.

- Providing strategic vision and mission, and motivating staff to pursue visionary goals. In two leadership assignments, I have recognized staff for their efforts and given them the guidance and direction that has delivered exceptional program results.

- Managing capital projects and spearheading information technology initiatives. These encompassed upgrades to comply with ADA access requirements, renovations that improved space utilization, and leading efforts to incorporate technology into library settings.

- Supervising departments in urban and suburban settings to address a broad range of competing priorities. Among these experiences was the supervision of an Interlibrary Loan department serving 100 individual branches in a five-county area.

I am most interested in this position and am confident that my track record at Ledgerock demonstrates my capacity to "hit the ground running," and apply my leadership, enthusiasm, and expertise to furthering the mission of state libraries in this development role. I look forward to continuing our discussions in the near future.

Sincerely,

Mary Kelner

Mary Kelner

...
113 Normal Avenue, Topeka, Kansas 66612
(785) 757-5555 Home • librarianspecialist@optonline.com

Follow-Up Letter (after face-to-face meeting)
(Construction Manager)

Leonard Curtis

123 Circle River Drive • Littleton, CO 81579
555.555.5555 • constructionmanager@msn.com

(Date)

Emily _____
(Title)
ABC Corporation
1 Industry Plaza
Craig, CO 81625

Dear Ms. _____:

We had the opportunity to speak briefly at last week's Chamber of Commerce meeting concerning the Construction Management position you are seeking to fill in Vancouver. I appreciate you filling me in on the details of the project and have enclosed my resume as you suggested.

As we discussed, I am well acquainted with ABC Corporation's brand and store concept, and I am excited to learn of the company's expansion plans over the coming decade. With my background in construction, maintenance, and project management as well as operations and strategic leadership, I believe I am primed to play a key role in this growth.

As Chief Executive Officer of Superior Landscape Design, I have been instrumental in leading the company to phenomenal success within a very short time, building the organization from start-up into a solid revenue generator reputed throughout the Pacific Northwest as an aggressive competitor in markets crowded by multimillion-dollar, nationally recognized companies.

I am currently in the process of selling the company and have been exploring opportunities with dynamic, growth-oriented organizations like yours that could benefit from my broad-based expertise in operations, organizational management, finance, and business development. Complementing my diverse leadership background is expertise in all the fundamentals of construction management, including the ability to see projects through to completion while exceeding quality standards.

Perhaps one of my strongest assets is my ability to cultivate long-lasting relationships with clients through attentive, direct communication. I have been highly successful at defining complex project plans, establishing budgets, outlining scope of work, and directly soliciting qualified contractors utilizing the bid process. I also offer extensive experience navigating through the paperwork and bureaucracy, forging productive alliances with key regulatory agencies to streamline permitting and licensing and to facilitate expedited project starts.

I would enjoy the opportunity to speak with you again in greater detail. Could we meet for lunch on Friday? I'll call your assistant in a few days to confirm the appointment.

Best regards,

Leonard Curtis

Leonard Curtis

Follow-Up Letter (after face-to-face meeting)
(Executive Assistant)

Janice Moss
55 Cherrytree Circle
Ashland, KY 41101
(606) 555-5555

(Date)

Phillip _____
(Title)
ABC Corporation
1 Industry Plaza
Lexington, KY 41235

Dear Phillip _____:

The time I spent interviewing with you and Sandra gave me a clear picture of your company's operation as well as your corporate environment. I want to thank you, in particular, Phillip, for the thorough picture you painted of your CEO's needs and work style.

I left our meeting feeling very enthusiastic about the scope of the position as well as its close match to my abilities and work style. After reviewing your comments, Phillip, I think the key strengths that I can offer your CEO in achieving his agenda are:

- Experience in effectively dealing with senior level staff in a manner that facilitates decision-making.
- Proven ability to anticipate an executive's needs and present viable options to consider.
- Excellent communication skills—particularly, the ability to gain feedback from staff and summarize succinctly.

Whether the needs at hand involve meeting planning, office administration, scheduling or just serving as a sounding board, I bring a combination of highly effective "people skills" and diversified business experience to deal with changing situations.

With my energetic work style, I believe that I am an excellent match for this unique position. I welcome an additional meeting to elaborate on my background and how I can assist your CEO.

Sincerely,

Janice Moss

Janice Moss

Follow-Up Letter (after face-to-face meeting)
(Management Information Systems)

CHRISTOPHER FALK

5555 VALLEY VIEW AVENUE • RESEDA, CALIFORNIA 91335 • (818) 555-5555

(Date)

Bob _____
(Title)
Krieger, Skvetney, Howell
Executive Search Consultants
2426 Foundation Road
San Jose, CA 95113

Dear Mr. _____:

Thank you for meeting with me this morning. Our associate, _____, assured me that a meeting with you would be productive, and it was. I sincerely appreciate your counsel, insight, and advice.

I have attached my resume for your review. I would appreciate any feedback you may have regarding effectiveness and strength. I understand you may not have any searches under way that would be suitable for me at this time, but I would appreciate any future considerations.

As we reviewed this morning, I seek and am qualified for senior MIS positions in a medium to large high-tech manufacturing or services business. I seek compensation in the $150,000-and-above range and look to report directly to the business CEO. These requirements are somewhat flexible depending on a number of factors, especially potential, of a new position. My family and I are willing to relocate to any area except New York City.

Please consider any associates, customers, or friends who may have contacts that would be useful for me to meet with. I have learned how important networking is, and will really appreciate some assistance from a professional like you.

Thanks again, Mr. _____, and please let me know if I can be of service to you. I wish you and your colleagues continued success and look forward to a business relationship in the future.

Best regards,

Christopher Falk

Christopher Falk

CF
enclosure

Follow-Up Letter (after face-to-face meeting) (Assistant)

MELANIE SHREVE
34 Oakwood Road
Provo, Utah 84062
(801) 555-3443

(Date)

Emily _____
(Title)
ABC Corporation
1 Industry Plaza
Salt Lake City, UT 84037

Dear Ms. _____:

Thank you for the opportunity to discuss the position of Assistant.

ABC Corporation is involved in one of the most pressing concerns of today: environmentally safe methods of disposing of solid waste materials. The challenge of creating proper disposal systems is paramount. I look forward to being a part of an organization that is focusing on furthering the technology needed to enhance our environment.

At ABC Corporation I would be able to:

- Be a productive assistant to management
- Be a part of a technologically developing industry
- Be in a position to learn and grow with the opportunities presented by your company
- Be involved in the excitement of a new expanding company

The skills that I have to offer ABC Corporation are:

- Professionalism, organization, and maturity
- Excellent office skills
- Ability to work independently
- A creative work attitude
- Research and writing skills
- Varied business background
- Willingness to learn

Again, thank you for considering my qualifications to become a part of your organization.

Sincerely,

Melanie Shreve

Melanie Shreve

Follow-Up Letter (after face-to-face meeting) (Sales)

A follow-up on a meeting Carol arranged with a targeted employer. While there was
no position currently available, she nevertheless wants to "sell" her suitability.

CAROL ANN CONASTA

43 Meadow Lane ~ Ludlow, MA 01056

(413) 589-2222 ~ salespro@comcast.net

(Date)

Philip _____
(title)
ABC Company
1 Industry Plaza
Boston, MA 01059

Philip,

First of all, thank you. I thoroughly enjoyed our meeting last Wednesday, and greatly
appreciate your insight and the time taken to discuss where I might best fit in to the ABC
team. Your professionalism and willingness to share what you know put me instantly at ease,
and I am now even more motivated to be part of ABC's success.

Let me begin by restating how flattered I am that you saw such potential in me. I likewise
feel confident that I have the management and leadership expertise, marketing skills, and
business development experience to be successful, and I see tremendous opportunities for
ABC in the future.

However, as we discussed, I understand that my first step is to make my mark as a member
of the Road Crew and am equally excited at the opportunity to make an impact on the front
line. I realize that you are not currently in the position to make such an offer, but I want to re-
emphasize my enthusiasm to join the ABC team wherever you feel I could add value.

If you will, I'd like to take a moment of your time to re-state a few key points:

- I possess the drive, commitment, and strong people skills required to make an impact
  in this industry.

- I offer proven business development, sales, and revenue building experience.

- I know what it takes to get results, both out of myself and from others, and have
  proven again and again to be the "go to" person when results are expected.

I hope that you and I have the opportunity to continue our discussions and, once again, I
appreciate the time you spent to meet with me. I wish you continued success in all your efforts
and look forward to seeing you at the Sales Excellence seminar at the end of July.

Sincerely,

Carol Ann Conasta

Carol Ann Conasta

CC

Follow-Up E-Mail (after face-to-face meeting) (General)

From: William Long [w_long@hotmail.com]
To: jones@alphavax.com
Cc:
Subject: Great meeting! Can we talk again Tuesday?

Dear Mr. _____:

I appreciate the time you took today interviewing me for the position. I hope our 2-hour meeting did not throw off the rest of the day's calendar. I trust you will agree that it was time well spent, as I sensed we connected on every major point discussed.

Your insight on e-commerce was intriguing. My history in hi-tech, manufacturing, and bio-medical industries and background in technology solutions seems to be a good match with the opportunities available in your company. As I mentioned, at Continuum Biomedical I initiated the marketing stratagems that opened our markets to Latin America. What I failed to mention is that I also have contacts with some e-commerce investors developing online portals targeted to Latin Americans.

I am very interested in the position and would like to touch base with you on Tuesday to see where we stand.

Sincerely,

William Long
(516) 555-1212
w_long@hotmail.com

Follow-Up E-Mail (after face-to-face meeting) (Sales Manager)

From: Damien Chavez [salespro@aol.com]
To: mgabor@lds.com
Cc:
Subject: Thanks for an exciting meeting. Next steps?

(date)

Mr. Philip _____
(title)
ABC Corporation
1 Industry Plaza
Anytown, NY 12096

Dear Mr. _____:

I thoroughly enjoyed our meeting on Wednesday. After learning more about the ABC Corporation and its goals, the prospect of joining the organization as the Western Region Sales Manager is even more exciting.

One of the most important things I have learned in my 20+ years in sales is to listen to what the customer needs. I have always taken pride in designing customized solutions that not only meet the clients' objectives, but also are competitive in price. This philosophy has enabled me to exceed corporate expectations for 17 consecutive years. In addition, I have managed to convert about 65% of my clients to "repeat order" accounts, an objective you indicated was a high priority for your sales team in ensuring the company's continued growth.

ABC Corporation's Western Region Sales Manager position is an important cornerstone in the company's overall growth plans for the new fiscal year. The company is poised to make significant strides to gain ground on the competition and the West Coast territory will be instrumental in making the corporate goals a reality. I am excited about contributing my expertise, meeting ABC's customers, and building long-term client relationships.

Thanks again for your time. I am certain that I can be a valuable asset to your sales team, and I look forward to having the opportunity to contribute to ABC's growth.

Sincerely,

Damien Chavez
(516) 555-1212
salespro@aol.com

Follow-Up E-Mail (after face-to-face meeting) (Senior Counselor)

This e-mail shows how her skills and experience in counseling matched this particular job opening and would be an asset to the agency and its clients.

From: Susan Goodman [skilledcounselor@earthlink.net]
To: cpatterson@couns.edu.msu
Cc:
Subject: Looking forward to next week

Dear Ms. _____:

I would like to thank you for affording me the opportunity to meet with you to discuss the Senior Counselor position with your organization. I have long been an admirer of your services and commitment to the community. I am very confident that my education, experience and counseling skills will enable me to make an immediate and long-term contribution to your mental health program.

The position we discussed seems well suited to my strengths and skills. My counseling and teaching background includes an emphasis on the family unit and its influence and relationship to each client's needs and therapy.

I am looking forward to seeing you, again, next week. If you require any additional information before then, please feel free to call. Thank you for your time and consideration.

Sincerely,

Susan Goodman
(516) 555-1212
skilledcounselor@earthlink.net

Follow-Up E-Mail (after face-to-face meeting)
(Management)

From: Henry Jacobs [hjacobs@yahoo.com]
To: jjordan@forman.com
Cc:
Subject: The right choice for program development

Dear Mr. _____:

The position we discussed Friday is a tremendously challenging one. After reviewing your comments about the job requirements, I am convinced that I can make an immediate contribution toward the growth and profitability of ABC Corporation.

Since you are going to reach a decision quickly, I would like to mention the following points, which I feel qualify me for the job we discussed:

1. Proven ability to generate fresh ideas and creative solutions to difficult problems
2. Experience in the area of program planning and development
3. Ability to successfully manage many projects at the same time
4. A facility for working effectively with people at all levels of management
5. Experience in administration, general management, and presentations
6. An intense desire to do an outstanding job in anything which I undertake

Thank you for the time and courtesy extended me. I will look forward to hearing from you.

Sincerely,

Henry Jacobs
(516) 555-1212
hjacobs@yahoo.com

Follow-Up E-Mail (after face-to-face meeting)
(Corporate Graphic Design)

From: Melissa Harris [graphicdesignpro@earthlink.net]
To: rmatthews@redgraphic.com
Cc:
Subject: Let's keep in touch

Dear Mr. _____:

It was a pleasure speaking with you regarding my search for a position in Corporate Graphic Design. Thank you for your initial interest.

The position I am looking for is usually found in a corporate marketing or public relations department. The titles vary: Graphic Design Manager, Advertising Manager, and Publications Director are a few. In almost every case the job description includes management and coordination of the corporation's printed marketing materials, whether they are produced by in-house designers or by an outside advertising agency or design firm.

I would like to stay in the _____ area; at least, I would like to search this area first. My salary requirement currently is in the $_____ range.

My professional experience, education, activities, and skills uniquely qualify me for a position in Corporate Graphic Design. My portfolio documents over eight years of experience in the business, and includes design, project consultation, and supervision of quality printed material for a wide range of clients.

I hope you will keep me in your files for future reference. I will telephone your office next week to discuss my situation further.

Sincerely,

Melissa Harris
(516) 555-1212
graphicdesignpro@earthlink.net

Follow-Up E-Mail (after face-to-face meeting)
(General)

From: Joseph Winger [jwinger@hotmail.com]
To: hr@banacorp.com
Cc:
Subject: I listened . . . here's the result!

Dear Ms. _____:

It was a pleasure meeting with you last week in your office. I appreciate the time you spent with me, as well as the valuable information you offered. As we discussed, I have adjusted my resume in regard to my position with _____. I have attached the new resume with this e-mail so that your files can be updated.

_____, please allow me to thank you again for the compliment on my ability to present a strong interview. Please keep this in mind when considering me for placement with one of your clients.

Sincerely,

Joseph Winger
(516) 555-1212
jwinger@hotmail.com

Follow-Up E-Mail (after face-to-face meeting)
(Entry-Level)

From: Dana Sorrensen [dsorrensen@mindspring.com]
To: djackson@allianz.com
Cc:
Subject: Thanks from a quick study

Dear Mr. _____:

I would like to take this opportunity to thank you for the interview Wednesday morning at _____, and to confirm my strong interest in an entry-level position with your company.

As we discussed, I feel that my education and background have provided me with an understanding of business operations which will prove to be an asset to your company. Additionally, I have always been considered a hard worker and a dependable, loyal employee. I am confident that I can make a valuable contribution to your Group Pension Fund area.

I look forward to meeting with you again in the near future to further discuss your needs.

Sincere regards,

Dana Sorrensen
(516) 555-1212
dsorrensen@mindspring.com

Follow-Up E-Mail (after face-to-face meeting)
(Auditing)

From: Alex Davis [auditpro@earthlink.net]
To: hr@sunstar.com
Cc:
Subject: Very motivated by meeting you

Mr. _____ :

Thank you for allowing me the opportunity to meet with you to discuss the IT Audit position currently available at Wilde Manye. The position sounds very challenging and rewarding, with ample room for growth. I feel my background and qualifications prepare me well for the IT Audit position we discussed.

I am committed to the ongoing development of my audit skills and feel I could work well with your focused audit staff at Wilde Manye. I look forward to hearing from you.

Sincerely,

Alex Davis
(516) 555-1212
auditpro@earthlink.net

POWER PHRASES

Consider using adaptations of these key phrases in your follow-up letters after face-to-face meetings.

Thank you for meeting with me this morning. Our associate, _____, assured me that a meeting with you would be productive, and it was. I sincerely appreciate your counsel, insight, and advice.

I have attached my resume for your review. I would appreciate any feedback you may have regarding effectiveness and strength. I understand you may not have any searches under way that would be suitable for me at this time, but I would appreciate any future considerations.

Please consider any associates, customers, or friends who may have contacts who would be useful for me to meet with. I have learned how important "networking" is and will really appreciate some assistance from a professional like you.

Thanks again, _____, and please let me know if I can be of service to you. I wish you and your colleagues continued success and look forward to a business relationship in the future.

In addition to experiencing a very enjoyable and informative interview, I came away very enthusiastic about the position you are seeking to fill.

I hope _____'s consideration of candidates will result in our being together again soon.

During my drive home I savored the possibility of working for _____ in the _____ area, and I must say it was an extremely pleasing thought.

I look forward to meeting with you again and hope our discussion will precede a long-term working relationship.

I am looking forward to meeting _____ on August – at 10:00 A.M., at which time I will convince her of my abilities and prove I am the most qualified person for the position.

It was a pleasure meeting with you last week in your office. I appreciate the time you spent with me, as well as the valuable information you offered.

I hope you will take a few moments to review my resume and place it in your files for future reference. I will telephone your office next week to discuss my situation further.

Gone but not forgotten ...

Thank you for our time together this afternoon. What I lack in specific experience in your business I more than make up for with my people power and my proven record of achievement, energy, and just pure tenacity.

Given the opportunity, I can succeed in your office. That makes you and me both successes. Is that worth the investment in training me?

I would like to take this opportunity to thank you for the interview this morning, and to express my strong interest in the position with _____.

I would welcome the opportunity to apply and to further develop my talents within your company.

Through my conversations with you and Mr. _____, I felt that the company provides exactly the type of career opportunity that I am seeking, and I am confident that I will prove to be an asset to your organization.

I trust our meeting this morning helped you further define the position. First and foremost, however, I hope that you came away from our meeting with a vision that includes my filling one of the many offices in _____. I certainly did.

I would like to take this opportunity to thank you for the interview on Thursday morning. I was very impressed with the operation, and I am enthusiastic about the prospects of joining your team.

Since we spent so much time discussing the subject, I have enclosed ...

I look forward to hearing from you again to further discuss the position. Through my conversations with you and _____, I felt ...

After reviewing your comments about the job requirements, I am convinced that I can make an immediate contribution toward the growth and profitability of _____.

Since you are going to reach a decision quickly, I would like to mention the following points, which I feel qualify me for the job we discussed:

The position in the _____ area is very attractive to me.

The interview confirmed that I want this career opportunity. Specifically, I want to work in the _____ department for you and _____. That is the simplest way to say it. I will call you this week to see what the next step is in the process.

Again, thank you for your time and interest.

It was indeed a pleasure to meet with you after working with you by telephone several years ago.

Thank you for taking time out of your busy schedule to meet with me on Tuesday, December –, 20–. I left the interview with an extremely favorable impression of your company.

I would like to take this opportunity to thank you for the interview on Friday morning, and to confirm my strong interest in the _____ position.

A career opportunity with _____ Corporation is particularly appealing because of its solid reputation and track record in research and development. I am confident that the training program and continued sales support will provide me with the background that I need to succeed in a _____ career.

I look forward to discussing my background and the position with you in greater detail.

I want to take this opportunity to thank you for the interview on Tuesday afternoon, and to confirm my strong interest in the position of _____ with XYZ Health Care Agency.

From our conversation, I feel confident in my ability to reach and exceed your expectations.

I am looking forward to spending a day in the field with a _____ representative. I will telephone you later this week to set up an appointment for my second interview.

Thank you for the time during my visit to _____ yesterday. I enjoyed our conversation at lunch and learned more about personal trust and investment services.

Thank you for your time and interest today. As I indicated, I am very new to this game of searching for employment and it is nice to start this effort on a positive note.

I am eager to hear from you concerning your decision; I know that you have several other candidates to meet with, so I will wait patiently. Good luck to you in your interview process; I know it must be difficult. Again, thank you so much for your time and consideration. I would welcome the opportunity to work for your company.

_____, the visit with you left me feeling positive about the possibility of working for _____. I would appreciate an opportunity to join your staff, and look forward to hearing from you.

"Resurrection" Letter (HR Position)

Kenyon knows this decision maker personally. Although he didn't get the job, he wants to keep the lines of communication open and hopes to be considered for other positions in the town government.

··· **KENYON P. STEWART**

January 13, 20–

Mr. Eric Pedersen, Supervisor
Town of Winterland
One Municipal Parkway
Winterland, New York 14528

Dear Eric:

Congratulations on the selection of your new Director of Human Resources! I hope this new person meets your expectations and I wish you every success.

I appreciate the chance to apply for the position and am grateful for the consideration you have given me throughout this process. Although I am obviously disappointed at not being the successful candidate, I remain interested in potential opportunities with the Town of Winterland. If for any reason you decide it is necessary to reopen the search at any time, please be aware that I am still interested in the position on either an interim or permanent basis.

In the meantime, should there be openings for support positions within the HR Department, or positions in other departments of the Town government, I would like to be considered for such opportunities.

Eric, as we have discussed in the past, I am a team player and believe that I have a contribution to make. At this stage of my career, I would be happy to accept something other than a managerial position and am convinced that my organizational skills, communication skills, and flexibility would make me an asset to any organization. If you know of other openings, either within governmental agencies or the private sector, I would be most appreciative if you could pass that information on to me.

Thank you for all your time and consideration. I look forward to speaking with you again soon.

Sincerely,

Kenyon

··
98 Meadowlark Lane • Penfield, New York 14526 • 585-388-5712

"Resurrection" Letter (Lift Line Driver Position)

After interviewing with the hiring authority and complying with their requests, this candidate is having trouble getting them on the phone. This letter is meant to get their attention.

Percival T. Morgan

3918 Calkins Road
Pittsford, New York 14534
585-248-5439
PercyMorgan@rochester.rr.com

January 2, 20–

Mr. Jefferson A. Bertram
Bureau of Human Resources
Genesee Regional Transit Authority
One Main Place
Rochester, New York 14692

Dear Mr. Bertram:

You may recall that we met on December 23rd regarding opportunities for Lift Line Operators. Following our meeting, I obtained a **CDL-B Learner's Permit with Passenger and Air-Brake endorsements.**

I am writing to reiterate my sincere interest in a **Lift Line Driver** position and hope to speak with you soon to learn what my next steps would be in order to further my candidacy.

Please contact me at **585-248-5439**. I look forward to talking with you soon.

Sincerely,

Percival T. Morgan

Percival T. Morgan

"Resurrection" Letter (Community Empowerment Team Director Position)

Another candidate was selected for the position that Madison interviewed for. Because he remains a city employee and hopes for other opportunities, he wants to both thank the mayor for the interview and keep his name (and qualifications) at the top of the mayor's mind for future consideration.

Madison P. Aldridge
45 Northern Crescent
Syracuse, New York 13081
315-286-4952

January 12, 20–

Hon. Michael Anderson, Jr., Mayor
City of Syracuse
City Hall
Syracuse, New York 13288

Dear Mayor Anderson:

Thank you for the opportunity to interview for the Community Empowerment Team Director position. I genuinely appreciated the chance to discuss your vision for the CET program.

Although another candidate was ultimately selected for this important position, I was pleased to be among the short list of applicants under consideration.

As we have discussed, I believe that my nine years' experience with the City of Syracuse provide me with a wealth of knowledge and expertise that can be beneficial to the City. I continue to be committed to the mission of the CET program, but also wish to offer myself as a candidate for other roles where my capabilities can further the objectives of the City.

To briefly reiterate, some of the qualities that I can bring to a new position include:

- **Strategic vision, creative energy, and strong leadership skills.**
- **Capacity to build collaborative teams across public, private, and government sectors.**
- **Excellent project management capabilities.**
- **Ability to build employee morale and inspire team members to strive for excellence.**
- **Innovative problem-solving skills.**

Please keep me in mind if other opportunities should arise where my talents would be an asset, particularly as you move ahead with implementation of The Syracuse Renaissance Vision. I would enjoy speaking with you further to discuss how I can best serve the City of Syracuse's needs.

Thank you, again, for your consideration.

Sincerely,

Madison P. Aldridge

Madison P. Aldridge

"Resurrection" Letter (Stevedore)

This is a follow-up letter to several telephone conversations with the best contact within the target company, the company president.

CASEY SMITH

· ·

1234 MAIN STREET, #4 • HONOLULU, HAWAII 96813
HOME: (808) 555-5555 • CELLULAR: (808) 555-5551

November 14, 20–

Mr. Gregory Roberts
President, Roberts Line Shipping, Ltd.
P.O. Box 5555
Honolulu, Hawaii 96855

Dear Mr. Roberts:

Firstly, I want to thank you for the time you spent with me in recent telephone conversations. I know you are a very busy person.

On August 4 I attended the stevedore recruiting event at the Oahu Convention Center. I submitted my résumé and spoke very briefly with a representative. In the short time I chatted with her I did my best to communicate my interest in, and qualifications for, the job. However, due to the overwhelming number of applicants there just wasn't sufficient time to convey how qualified I really am.

With that in mind, I have enclosed my brief résumé for your review. To summarize:

- I have an extensive history of working safely around heavy equipment.
- I am in outstanding physical condition.
- I am a very reliable and dedicated employee.
- I have received first aid, CPR, and terrorism awareness training.

This résumé is only a hint of who I am—words on paper cannot replace a personal conversation. Therefore, would you please consider my request for a face-to-face interview so that you may evaluate my qualifications, abilities, drive, and enthusiasm for yourself?

I will make myself available for any time that you can take out of your schedule. Thank you for your consideration, and I look forward to possibly meeting with you in the near future.

Respectfully,

Casey Smith

Casey Smith

Enclosure: résumé

"Resurrection" Letter (Social Worker)

Having already interviewed with Mr. Thornson, Beth started the letter in an upbeat, informal manner to re-establish a rapport. The indication that he thought she was well suited at the time of their initial interview was an effective way to sell herself.

BETH ANDERSEN
77-42 Gateway Circle
Bay Shore, NY 11706
(631) 665-9992
BAndersen@4kidsake.net

February 16, 20–

Mr. William Thornson
Foster Care and Adoption Coordinator
Little Lamb Foster Care & Adoptive Services
290 Brentwood Road
Brentwood, NY 11717

Dear Mr. Thornson:

Talk about small coincidences. I bumped into Father O'Brien at church this past Sunday and learned that St. Mary's is opening a new foster care division this coming March. One word led to another, and he informed me that Little Lamb Foster Care & Adoptive Services is in desperate need of social workers and foster/adoptive care counselors to fill several positions.

You might not recall my name, but hopefully I can help you to remember our meeting. I participated in an interview with you in early May of 20– for the position of Foster Care Counselor with Little Lamb's Brentwood facility. We discussed my involvement with St. John's Youth & Family Counseling Program at great length, and agreed I would be well suited for a similar position with Little Lamb as an Adoptive Care Counselor. Unfortunately, the lack of state and federal funding was reduced that month leaving Little Lamb with no other choice but to put a freeze on hiring.

As you can imagine, I am thrilled to learn of Little Lamb's new foster care program, and would welcome the opportunity to meet again to pick up where we left off. For your convenience, I am enclosing my updated resume for your review.

Thank you for your reconsideration. I look forward to speaking with soon.

Sincerely,

Beth Andersen

Beth Andersen

"Resurrection" Letter
(Wholesale Market Manager)

Leanne K. Boardman

617 Van Winkle Drive ▪ Keller, IN 46185 ▪ (888) 449-2200 ▪ marketmanager@email.com

(Date)

Phillip _____
(Title)
ABC Corporation
1 Industry Plaza
Indianapolis, IN 46222

Dear Mr. _____:

I understand from _____ of _____ that the search is continuing for the Wholesale Market Manager position at _____ Bank & Trust. As you continue your search, I would like to ask that you keep in mind the following accomplishments and experiences that I would bring to the job:

1. Maximized relationships and increased balances through the sale of trust and cash management products.

2. Captured largest share of public funds market in _____ within three years and captured a disproportionate market share of insurance companies in _____.

3. Developed cash management and trust products tailored to the needs of my target market.

4. Marketed services through mass mailings and brochures, through planning and conducting industry-specific seminars, and through active participation in target market's industry professional organization.

5. Direct experience in all phases of wholesale commercial banking, including: market segmentation, prospecting, building and maintaining customer relationships, lending, and the sale of non-credit products and services.

Sincerely,

Leanne Boardman

Leanne Boardman

LB

P.S. I will call you next week, after you have seen the other candidates, to continue our discussion. In the meantime, please be assured of both my competency and commitment.

"Resurrection" Letter (Construction Manager)

(Date)

Alice _____
(Title)
Krieger, Skvetney, Howell
Executive Search Consultants
2426 Foundation Road
Atlanta, GA 30605

Dear Ms. _____:

    I am writing to you to follow up on the initial inquiry I wrote to you on July –th, 20–. At that time I forwarded you a cover letter and resume. I am in the construction management and business management fields. Since I have not had a response I can only assume that you do not have any currently active searches that meet my qualifications in process or that my file has been deactivated.

    I am still in the market for an executive position that matches my qualifications and abilities. I am open to relocating throughout the United States and overseas. If any positions become available, I would be interested in hearing from you. If you need an updated resume, please write or call me and I would be most happy to forward you any information required.

Sincerely,

Eric L. Ross

Eric L. Ross

ER

P.S. I'll call in a couple of days to follow up on this letter.

"Resurrection" Letter (Entry-Level)

Elizabeth A. Andrews

307 West Ivy Lane • Meridian, Idaho 83642

(Date)

Bob _____
(Title)
Krieger, Skvetney, Howell
Executive Search Consultants
2426 Foundation Road
Boise, ID 83712

Dear Mr. _____:

I feel I should more thoroughly explain why I am willing to take even an entry-level position considering all my past experience. And that's just it—past experience.

For the past three years I ran my own small business, which, of course, kept me out of the job market. Meanwhile, computers took over the world! Fortunately, since moving here and doing temp jobs, I have gotten hands-on experience in data entry. I have also taken and finished a private course in Microsoft Word. So I guess that makes me computer literate, if not entirely experienced.

Nevertheless, I'm in no position to be proud or disdainful of clerical jobs, as I realize I must start somewhere. Fortunately, I enjoy all facets of office work (even filing), so that would not be a problem. I have enough faith in myself and my ability to learn quickly to know that some form of upper movement would be possible for me ... eventually.

Incidentally, even though I am on a temp job this week and possibly next, I do have an answering machine I check every couple of hours during the day. So please leave a message and I'll return your call soon after.

Thank you, and I look forward to hearing from you. I have enclosed another copy of my resume for you.

Sincerely,

Elizabeth Andrews

Elizabeth Andrews

EA
enclosure

"Resurrection" E-Mail (Account Executive)

From: Katherine Knockwood [accountexecutive@aol.com]
To: hr@incentivedepot.com
Cc:
Subject: Thanks from Katherine, I'll be the next one

Mr. _____ :

I wanted to thank you for the interview we had on March –th, 20–. The position that was being offered sounds like something I would be interested in. However, I do understand your reasons for not choosing me for the position, and I thank you very much for your honesty.

Perhaps when you are looking for an account executive with five years of experience instead of ten, you will bear me in mind. I am determined to be your choice. I hope the fact that I came in a close second to someone with twice my chronological experience will help you keep me in mind.

I look forward to hearing from you, and thank you again for your time. With your permission I will stay in touch.

Sincerely,

Katherine Knockwood
(516) 555-1212
accountexecutive@aol.com

"Resurrection" E-Mail (Programmer)

From: Robert Zelinski [programmerpro@yahoo.com]
To: hr@jitmfg.com
Cc:
Subject: Oh the software we could create!

Dear Ms. _____:

I must have been one of the first people you spoke with about the job posting, because at the time you seemed very interested in me. However, when I called you back, you had received so many calls for the position, you didn't know one from the other. That's understandable, so I hope I can stir your memory and, more importantly, your interest.

When I spoke with you I got the feeling we could both benefit from working together. I am a computer enthusiast, always looking for new applications and ideas to implement on the computer. I have a solid programming and project development background in both the Windows and Macintosh worlds. What's even better is my hobby: my work. I spend countless hours in one way or another doing things which concern computing.

You had asked if I had children and I do: a four-and-a-half-year-old daughter and a four-and-a-half-month-old daughter. You had some ideas for children's software and thought having kids would help when working on such software. My oldest uses _____ on my Macintosh at home and double-clicks away without any assistance from my wife or myself. She has learned a great deal from "playing" with it and is already more computer literate than I ever expected. We need more software like _____ to help stir the minds of our kids.

I have attached a resume for your perusal. But in case you don't want to read all the details, here it is in short:

- I have 6 years programming and development experience in Windows.
- I have 3 years programming and development experience on the Macintosh.
- I am currently the Senior Developer for Macintosh programming here at _____ Corp.

I look forward to speaking with you again, so please don't hesitate to call me, either at home (516-555-1212) or at work (516-555-1213) anytime.

Regards,

Robert Zelinski
(516) 555-1212
programmerpro@yahoo.com

"Resurrection" E-Mail (Product Manager)

From: Amanda Jones [ajones@hotmail.com]
To: jkline@activeproducts.com
Cc:
Subject: We will work together!

Dear Ms. _____:

Four months ago you and I discussed an opportunity at Active Products, and you were kind enough to set up meetings with _____ and _____. Shortly thereafter, as you know, I accepted a position with _____, where I am now.

For reasons I will go into when we meet, I would like to reopen our discussions. If you think such a conversation would be mutually beneficial, I hope we can get together. I'll call next week to see when you have a half hour or so of free time.

Sincerely,

Amanda Jones
(516) 555-1212
ajones@hotmail.com

POWER PHRASES

Consider using adaptations of these key phrases in your resurrection letters.

I turned down your job, but for reasons I will go into when we meet, I would like to reopen our discussions. If you think such a conversation would be mutually beneficial, I hope we can get together. I'll call next week to see when you have a half hour or so of free time.

As you continue your search, I would like to ask that you keep in mind the following accomplishments and experiences that I would bring to the job.

I am still in the market for an executive position that matches my qualifications and abilities. I am open to relocating throughout the United States and overseas. If any positions become available, I would be interested in hearing from you.

I look forward to hearing from you, and thank you again for your time. With your permission I will stay in touch.

I hope I can stir your memory and, more importantly, your interest.

I look forward to speaking with you again, so please don't hesitate to call me either at home or at work anytime.

Rejection of Offer Letter (Public Library Director)

Tamara has decided to take another position. As a courtesy, she wants to tell Blossom City that she's no longer interested in the position, while keeping her name alive for any future opportunities.

Tamara L. Salinger

622 Cromwell Drive • Pittsford, New York 14534 • (585) 248-7042

January 12, 20–

Mr. Henry O. Felix, President
Blossom City Public Library Board of Trustees
447 South Avenue
Blossom City, New York 13901

Dear Mr. Hastings:

Thank you for taking the time to meet with me recently to discuss the position of BCPL Director. I genuinely appreciated the opportunity to meet with the Board and the Search Committee to learn about the position. I was very favorably impressed with the Blossom City Library System and believe that if selected, my contributions would have significantly enhanced your organization's success.

However, I am writing to ask that my name be withdrawn from further consideration for the Director's position at this time. I have recently been offered another challenging and rewarding opportunity. The relative time frames involved have made it necessary for me to render a decision without further delay, and I have chosen to accept the offer.

Had circumstances permitted, I believe that it would have been productive to continue our discussions and am confident that we could have arrived at a mutually beneficial arrangement. I would be most interested in applying and interviewing for the position should there ever be another search for a Director at some future date.

I wish you the best of luck in your current search, and much success in the future. Thank you, again, for your time and consideration.

Sincerely yours,

Tamara L. Salinger

Tamara L. Salinger

Rejection of Offer Letter (Team Supervisor)

This candidate interviewed for a position that turned out to be below his level of experience and at a salary well below his expectations. He didn't want to slam the door shut on other opportunities, but couldn't accept the position offered.

Ms. Lucretia A. Selander
Program Director
Salinas Group, Ltd.
443 Electronics Parkway
Liverpool, New York 13088

Dear Ms. Selander:

Thank you for your e-mail message updating me on the status of the telecommunications project we discussed in our recent telephone conversation.

Although I genuinely appreciate your consideration for the Team Supervisor position, at this time, I feel it is in my best interest to seek a position more closely aligned with my level of experience and demonstrated managerial skills.

I remain most interested in opportunities with Salinas Group, and would ask that you keep my name in consideration for other positions that would more fully capitalize on my knowledge and expertise.

Thank you for your time and interest.

Sincerely,

Christopher J. Franz

Christopher J. Franz

Rejection of Offer Letter (General)

AUDREY M. LAURENCE

968 Pleasant Avenue • Rochester, New York 14622
(585) 248-9917 • alaurence@rochester.rr.com

(Date)

Phillip _____
(Title)
ABC Corporation
1 Industry Plaza
Buffalo, NY 14657

Dear Mr. _____:

It was indeed a pleasure meeting with you and your staff to discuss your needs for a _____. Our time together was most enjoyable and informative.

As we have discussed during our meetings, I believe a purpose of preliminary interviews is to explore areas of mutual interest and to assess the fit between the individual and the position. After careful thought, I have decided to withdraw from consideration for the position.

My decision is based upon the fact that I have accepted a position elsewhere that is very suited to my qualifications and experiences.

I want to thank you for interviewing me and giving me the opportunity to learn more about your facility. You have a fine team, and I would have enjoyed working with you.

Best wishes to you and your staff.

Sincerely,

Audrey Laurence

Audrey Laurence

AL

Rejection of Offer E-Mail (Department Manager)

From: Allen Meriden [managementpro@earthlink.net]
To: hr@seatoncorp.com
Cc:
Subject: With regret for the present and sincere hope for the future

Dear Ms. _____:

I would like to take this opportunity to thank you for the interview on Thursday morning, and to express my strong interest in future employment with your organization.

While I appreciate very much your offer for the position of Department Manager, I feel that at this stage of my career I am seeking greater challenges and advancement than the Department level is able to provide. Having worked in _____ management for over four years, I am confident that my skills will be best applied in a position with more responsibility and accountability.

As we discussed, I look forward to talking with you again in January about how I might contribute to ABC Corporation in the capacity of Unit Manager.

Sincere regards,

Allen Meriden
(516) 555-1212
managementpro@earthlink.net

POWER PHRASES

Consider using adaptations of these key phrases in your rejection of offer letters.

It was indeed a pleasure meeting with you and your staff to discuss your needs for a _____.

Our time together was most enjoyable and informative.

After careful thought, I have decided to withdraw from consideration for the position.

As we discussed, I look forward to talking with you again in _____ about how I might contribute to _____ in the capacity of _____.

Acceptance Letter (Marketing Research Manager)

JULIE GREGORIO
3339 Elldin Street
Portland, ME 04412
(207) 555-5555

(Date)

Ms. Emily _____
ABC Financial Services Group
1 Industry Plaza
Bangor, ME 04401

Dear Ms. _____:

Thank you for your positive response to the Marketing Research Manager position. I am delighted to accept your offer of employment and look forward to "jumping in head first" into the various projects we discussed during our meetings, especially sales forecasting and strategic market planning for ABC's core product line.

I am honored that your organization feels that I am the right person to lead your marketing research efforts, and am confident that I can deliver the results Radiant wants. As I mentioned in our telephone conversation yesterday, I am constantly in touch with what the competition is doing with the goal of placing my team's effort higher in the market place to yield maximum results.

Per your instructions, I will contact Mary Smith, Human Resources Manager, on Monday morning to arrange an orientation appointment. I look forward to meeting with you after that to discuss in detail my ideas for meeting the objectives we explored in our interviews.

Sincerely,

Julie Gregorio

Julie Gregorio

JG

Acceptance Letter (Managing Consultant)

Jacqueline Mains

788 Port Republic Road ▪ Port Republic, NJ 08241

(609) 652-5555 Residence ▪ managingconsultant@comcast.com

(Date)

Dear Philip,

I want to thank you for the privilege of joining your staff as Managing Consultant. Your flexibility and cooperation in the counter negotiations was encouraging. Thank you for making every effort to make the pending transition a smooth one.

Per your requests, I am providing this letter, for my official file.

"In that your organization is a competitor of my previous employer, and in that this organization seeks to maintain goodwill and high levels of integrity within the industry, it should be duly noted, that neither you nor any representative of your organization, sought me as a prospective employee. It was my identification of a possible position, and solely my pursuits toward your company, that resulted in my resignation as Senior Director, to join your firm as Managing Consultant."

If I can provide additional clarification on this matter, or assist in protecting the ethics of your company, notify me at your convenience. I look forward to starting with your team on the 15th of July. Until then . . .

Respectfully yours,

Jacqueline Mains

Jacqueline Mains

JM

Acceptance Letter (Vice President)

.... **Victor L. Williams**
555 Hillcrest Circle
Dearborn, Michigan 48121

(Date)

Emily _____
(Title)
ABC Corporation
1 Industry Plaza
Detroit, MI 48227

Dear Ms. _____:

This letter will serve as my formal acceptance of your offer to join your firm
as Vice President of _____. I understand and accept the conditions of
employment which you explained in your recent letter.

I will contact your personnel department this week to request any paperwork
I might complete for their records prior to my starting date. Also, I will schedule a physical examination for insurance purposes. I would appreciate your
forwarding any reading material you feel might hasten my initiation into the
affairs of _____.

Yesterday I tendered my resignation at _____ and worked out a mutually acceptable notice time of four weeks, which should allow me ample time
to finalize my business and personal affairs here and be ready for work at
_____ on schedule.

You, your board, and your staff have been most professional and helpful
throughout this hiring process. I anxiously anticipate joining the ABC team
and look forward to many new challenges. Thank you for your confidence
and support.

Yours truly,

Victor L. Williams

Victor L. Williams

JS

Acceptance E-Mail (General)

From: George Keller [gkeller@mindspring.com]
To: pwalters@raytheonco.com
Cc:
Subject: Yes! Absolutely! I accept!

Dear Mr. _____:

I would like to express my appreciation for your letter offering me the position of _____ in your _____ Department at a starting salary of $53,000 per year.

I was very impressed with the personnel and facilities at your company in Dallas and am writing to confirm my acceptance of your offer. If it is acceptable to you I will report to work on November 20, 20–.

Let me once again express my appreciation for your offer and my excitement about joining your engineering staff. I look forward to my association with ABC Corporation and feel my contributions will be in line with your goals of growth and continued success for the company.

Sincerely,

George Keller
(516) 555-1212
gkeller@mindspring.com

POWER PHRASES

Consider using adaptations of these key phrases in your acceptance letters.

I am delighted to accept _____'s generous offer to become their _____. All of the terms in your letter of October 13th are amenable to me.

My resignation was submitted to the appropriate managers at _____ this morning, but we are still working out the terms of my departure.

I am eagerly anticipating starting my new position, particularly at a firm with _____'s reputation. During the interim, I will stay in direct contact with _____ to assure a smooth initiation at _____. Thank you again for this opportunity.

We are still working out the terms of my departure from _____, but it is safe to say that I will report to _____ no later than November –th. It should be possible to confirm a starting date early tomorrow morning. I will telephone you directly when my erstwhile managers and I have a departure schedule completed.

_____ has scheduled my pre-employment physical for _____, and I do not expect any problems to arise. I have found several possible housing alternatives that I will be investigating and I do not expect any problems here, either.

I appreciate the confidence you demonstrated by selecting me to be _____.

I am confident that you made an excellent choice.

I feel that I can achieve excellent results for your firm, and I am looking forward to working with you. I am also anxious to get to know you and your corporation better.

This letter will serve as my formal acceptance of your offer to join _____. I understand and accept the conditions of employment that you explained in your recent letter.

I will contact your personnel department this week to request any paperwork I might complete for their records prior to my starting date. Also, I will schedule a physical examination for insurance purposes. I would appreciate your forwarding any reading material you feel might hasten my initiation into the affairs of _____.

Yesterday I tendered my resignation at _____ and worked out a mutually acceptable notice time of four weeks, which should allow me ample time to finalize my business and personal affairs here, relocate my family, and be ready for work at _____ on schedule.

You, your board, and your staff have been most professional and helpful throughout this hiring process. I anxiously anticipate joining the _____ team and look forward to many new challenges. Thank you for your confidence and support.

I look forward to making a contribution as part of your team.

I look forward to the challenges and responsibility of working in this position.

Negotiation Letter (General)

Betsy Kimble
121 Eight Mile Drive   555-555-4567
Haddenville, VT 05600   bkimble@aox.com

(date)

Mr. Philip _____
(Title)
ABC Corporation
1 Industry Place
Montpelier, VT 05602

Dear Philip,

I want to thank you for your invitation to join the ABC family. I have reviewed the offer of position and compensation, as presented in your letter dated _____. I would like to ask for clarification on a few items prior to providing you with a "formal acceptance." While none of these items are necessarily "deal breakers," I believe they will enable both parties to begin the partnership more informed of mutual goals and expectations.

Per the breakdown provided:

- I accept the 401(K) plan as proposed
- I accept the paid holiday and personal days plan as proposed
- I accept the educational reimbursement plan as proposed
- I accept the Direct Payroll Deposit plan as proposed (if elected)
- I accept the Medical, Dental, Vision, Pharmacy, and Life Insurance benefits as proposed, contingent on factors clarified below.

Points of Clarification:

- What is available in regards to "Stock Options"?
- What are the "standard hours of operation" for ABC employees?
- Would it be possible to have a "Performance Evaluation" at the end of 6 months?
- I would like to structure the vacation days as follows: 3 days in remainder of year 20–, One week during calendar year 20–, Two weeks during calendar years 20– to 20–, Three weeks beginning January of 20–.
- In light of the "out of pocket expenses" anticipated correspondent to the medical benefits, how might we agree to get the annual base salary to $35,000? I am open to a number of different options to achieve this goal, including profit sharing, commission, or 5% annual bonus arrangement.

Page 1 of 2

261

I am excited about the long-term possibilities that exist at ABC. As you can see by my level of interest, I intend to partner with you for a long tenure of success. I believe my skills will be an enhancement to the existing leadership. My presence will enable you and others to focus on new aspects of business development and achieve corporate goals and objectives that will be beneficial to us all. Again, I want to thank you for the gracious offer. I look forward to finalizing these minor details very soon.

Sincerely yours,

Betsy Kimble

Betsy Kimble
BK

Negotiation Letter (Sales)

Eden Miller

67 Walden Road • Somers, TX 89776 • (555) 555-5555 • e-mail: salespro@aol.com

(Date)

Dear Mr. _____,

I have reviewed your letter and the specific breakdown regarding compensation. I believe there to be a few items to clarify, prior to providing you with a formal acceptance. I do not consider any of the items to be "deal breakers" in any way. I also do not perceive them to be issues that cannot be discussed, as we are in fact, moving ahead.

The primary concern has to do with the commission structure, as opposed to salary plus commission, to which I have grown accustomed. I am therefore asking for a one-time initial payment to me in the amount of $5,000. I am trying to diminish some of the "exposure" that I may experience in the transition from one office to another. I also believe exposure will be felt as a shift occurs from receipt of compensation on a monthly basis, when I am currently accustomed to a biweekly format. Lastly, I am hoping to afford your company the opportunity to share some of the "risk" in this process and show some "short-term good faith" toward what I hope will be a long-term relationship of success, productivity, and increased profitability.

The second clarification revolves around the 401K program; the percentages, time frames, and terms. This is something we can discuss over the course of the next two weeks. You may even be able to pass something specific on to me in writing.

With these two concerns articulated, I want you to know that I will be meeting with the owner of our company tomorrow morning, to discuss my plans for departure. In fairness to him and to my current client load, I could not start full-time with you for 21 days.

I would like to set a time for us to have dinner one evening next week, so you can meet my wife and we can talk a bit less formally.

Looking forward to what lies ahead,

Eden Miller

Eden Miller

EM

263

Negotiation Letter (Senior Lab Specialist)

MITCHELL T. NORDSTROM

621 SAWMILL ROAD • HAMLIN, NEW YORK 14464
(585) 964-1298 (DAYS) / (585) 964-45201 (EVENINGS) • LABSPECIALIST@CS.COM

(date)

Philip _____
ABC
1 Industry Plaza
Jamaica, NY 11434

Dear Philip:

I want to thank you for the time that we were able to spend together last week. I was encouraged by the invitation to join the ABC family as Senior Lab Specialist. The position, responsibility, and geography are consistent with my career goals and objectives. Based on the information that you gave to me, there are a number of items for clarification, prior to providing you with a formal acceptance. None of the items listed are necessarily "deal breakers," but they are essential to us beginning this tenure with full disclosure of mutual expectations and responsibilities. Items for clarification are as follows:

- Detailed description of insurance benefits

- Realistic analysis of the corporate stock and 401(K) plans

- Written explanation of educational reimbursement allowance

- The mobility plan seems very reasonable, but would like specifics on the Permanent Work Relocation (Is it an allowance or reimbursement of actual expenses incurred in the move?)

- Detailed explanation of the Variable Pay Plan

This final item is significant, as it will impact the "full compensation potential" and modify the suggested salary. In our conversations, I communicated to you that I was making $32K while working part-time and going to school. The salary offer is substantially lower and represents a pay cut. My goal is to discern how feasible it will be for me to meet my financial obligations.

I am interested in your company and this position, but am finding it difficult to give serious consideration to anything less than $40K salary plus benefits. I am hoping to discover a variety of vehicles that will enable you to help me achieve that goal, so that I can help you accomplish your growth and profit targets.

I look forward to discussing these issues with you in the very near future and trust that we will soon be working together in the best interest of Philip _____, Mitchell Nordstrom, and ABC Incorporated.

Respectfully Yours,

Mitchell Nordstrom

Mitchell Nordstrom

MN

Negotiation Letter (Product Specialist)

MARY A. MARTIN

717-755-1369 (Cell) • 717-845-5856 (Home)
productspecialist@email.com
202 Springhill Street • Greenville , SC 29681

(Date)

Philip _____
(Title)
ABC Corporation
1 Industry Plaza
Columbia, SC 29170

RE: Product Specialist/ABC Team

Dear Philip:

Thank you for your offer of employment with ABC Corporation. Your state-of-the-art company would afford me the opportunity to make a contribution while continuing to grow professionally in an ever-evolving industry. I am confident that my strong work ethic would enhance the ABC Team.

As you know from our previous conversations, I have outstanding skills and abilities that I can bring to ABC. First and foremost is my hands-on experience in the medical field. I have a proven track record of relating well to other medical professionals and accommodating their needs. It is my understanding that as Product Specialist, my expert communication skills will be tantamount to performance success. With my experience in troubleshooting technical problems, I know that technology can be learned but becomes utilitarian only when it can be translated into user effectiveness. My expertise integrates both of these critical components that are key in the Product Specialist role.

The Product Specialist position promises challenge and a high level of professional commitment that I am prepared to embrace. However, based upon the value I can bring ABC, plus the knowledge that the annual salary range for this type of position in our industry normally falls between $34,000 and $46,000, I must request that you reconsider your starting offer of $35,000. I am more than happy to assume all of the responsibilities necessary to meet the expectations of the Product Specialist position at a starting salary of $40,000. Of course, I appreciate the generous benefits package that you provide.

I look forward to your response, and hope that we can reach an agreement that will enable me to begin my career with ABC on June 4.

Sincerely,

Mary Martin

Mary Martin
MM

Resignation Letter (CCU Nurse)

This situation was sensitive. A lot of names and dates were needed to explain the events leading to the decision to resign. Notice how Elizabeth apologizes so she doesn't burn her bridges.

Elizabeth Dixon, RN

33 Leo Street ▪ Brentwood, NY 11717 ▪ (631) 555-0220 ▪ criticalcare@med.net

April 26, 20–

Ms. Dorothy Powell
Director of Special Care
Good Health Hospital
1024 Montauk Road
Brentwood, NY 11717

Dear Ms. Powell:

As requested by Joan Larson, Nursing Manager, I am submitting this letter as written confirmation of my resignation as a per-diem on-call CCU nurse with Good Health Hospital.

My employment with Good Health was scheduled to begin April 7th as a permanent part-time CCU nurse; however, in the interim, I accepted a permanent full-time position with Long Island Hospital to begin May 1st. On April 3rd I met with Gretchen Miller, Human Resources Administrator, to inform her of my decision. I expressed a desire to honor my commitment with the understanding that the need for flexibility in my schedule would be taken into consideration. Ms. Miller contacted Joan Larson to discuss an alternative employment arrangement. Subsequently, my status from permanent part-time was changed to per-diem on-call.

Immediately upon completion of the mandatory two-week orientation period, I was faced with a schedule conflict. As a result of an apparent miscommunication, I was scheduled to do my floor orientation from April 21st through 25th. I approached Diane Willis, Nursing Manager, to resolve the conflict and learned that she was completely unaware of both my situation and agreement between Joan Larson, Human Resources, and myself. As a result, my resignation seemed to be the logical solution.

Ms. Powell, it was never my intention to cause problems within your administration; therefore, please accept my apology for any inconvenience experienced. Thank you for the opportunity to be a part of your staff.

Sincerely,

Elizabeth Dixon

Elizabeth Dixon

Resignation Letter (Care Coordinator)

Marilyn was offered a new position with another organization, and this letter helped her make a positive exit from her current employer.

Marilyn Cummings

19 Blueberry Circle
Valhalla, NY 06077
(914) 776-3455

April 9, 20–

Ms. Karen Lawrence, R.N.
Patient Care Manager
Community Care Center, Inc.
56 Murray Lane
Valhalla, NY 06077

Dear Karen:

This letter will confirm my resignation from the position of Care Coordinator. I have accepted a new position as Supervisor of Client Services at a growing medical center in New Jersey.

My last day of employment will be on Friday, May 9, 20–, which should provide sufficient time to complete existing projects and assist with the transition to a new coordinator

The past 10 years at the Center have been both professionally and personally rewarding. Thank you for your trust and support over the years. I have appreciated the opportunity to expand my skills and work with many talented individuals.

Thank you, sincerely,

Marilyn Cummings

Marilyn Cummings

Resignation Letter (Management)

A very firm resignation, where a company needs encouragement to live up to obligations.

ROBERT McINTYRE
9803 Clinton Avenue
Lubbock, TX 79424

home: 806.783.9900
cell: 806.698.0451
robertmcintyre@crpn.com

November 11, 20–

Tim Johnson, President
XTC, Inc.
500 Indiana Avenue
Lubbock, TX 79314

Dear Mr. Johnson:

I am writing this letter as a follow-up to the resignation notice I submitted on Wednesday, November 5, 20–. Given the sensitive nature of the events leading to my resignation, I feel it is in everyone's best interest to resolve any issues remaining as quickly as possible.

In this respect, I hope that you will demonstrate swift compliance in delivering to me the management severance package guaranteed as a result of my employment with your firm. I wish to move ahead in my career and put the past several months behind me, as I am sure you can understand; therefore, I am certain you will act upon this request in a professional and forthright manner.

Please be advised that, in the event there is an attempt to withhold or deny this severance package to me, I will have no other alternative but to seek legal remedy for this situation. **Again, I believe that you will act as a man of integrity concerning this issue**, and I only mention the possibility of legal action in the unlikely event that my request is rejected or delayed.

I can assure you that I, like you, would like for this to be resolved without further complications or additional steps—and as quickly as possible.

Mr. Johnson, I thank you in advance for your swift attention and cooperation in this matter.

Sincerely,

Robert McIntyre

Robert McIntyre

Resignation Letter (Sales Representative)

.... **Gerard Carlisle**

(Date)

Phillip _____
(Title)
ABC Corporation
1 Industry Plaza
Idaho Falls, ID 83726

Dear Mr. _____:

Please accept my resignation of my position as Sales Representative in the _____ area, effective January –, 20–. I am offering two weeks' notice so that my territory can be effectively serviced during the transition, with the least amount of inconvenience to our clients.

While I have enjoyed very much working under your direction, I find now that I have an opportunity to further develop my career in areas that are more in line with my long-term goals. I thank you for the sales training that I have received under your supervision. It is largely due to the excellent experience I gained working for ABC Corporation that I am now able to pursue this growth opportunity.

During the next two weeks, I am willing to help you in any way to make the transition as smooth as possible. This includes assisting in recruiting and training my replacement in the _____ territory. Please let me know if there is anything specific that you would like me to do.

Again, it has been a pleasure working as a part of your group.

Best regards,

Gerard Carlisle

Gerard Carlisle

GC

....
5555 State Street • Boise, Idaho 83701 • (208) 555-5555

Resignation Letter (Vice President)

David R. Chang

2491 Goodman Street, San Francisco, CA 94080 / (650) 258-6911
changvp@earthlink.com

(Date)

Emily _____
(Title)
ABC Corporation
1 Industry Plaza
San Francisco, CA 94082

Dear Ms. _____:

As of this date, I am formally extending my resignation as _____. I have accepted a position as Vice President of _____ at a university medical center in _____.

My decision to leave ABC Corporation was made after long and careful consideration of all factors affecting the institution, my family, and my career. Although I regret leaving many friends here, I feel that the change will be beneficial to all parties. My subordinate staff is readily able to handle the institution's operations until you find a suitable replacement. I intend to finalize my business and personal affairs here over the next several weeks and will discuss a mutually acceptable termination date with you in person.

Finally, I can only express my sincere appreciation to you and the entire board for all your support, cooperation, and encouragement over the past several years. I will always remember my stay at ABC Corporation for the personal growth it afforded and for the numerous friendships engendered.

Yours truly,

David Chang

David Chang

DC

Resignation E-mail (General)

From: John Billingsly [systemsoperator@hotmail.com]
To: nbraun@mis.augsburg.edu
Cc:
Subject: With regrets but many thanks

Dear Mr. _____:

This email is to notify you that I am resigning my position with ABC Corporation effective Saturday, March 26, 20–.

I have enjoyed my work here very much and want to thank you and the rest of the MIS Department for all the encouragement and support you have always given me. In order to achieve the career goals that I've set for myself, I am accepting a higher level Systems Operator position with another company. This position will give me an opportunity to become more involved in the technical aspects of setting up networking systems.

Please know that I am available to help with any staff training or offer assistance in any way that will make my departure as easy as possible for the department. I want to wish everyone the best of luck for the future.

Sincerely,

John Billingsly
(516) 555-1212
systemsoperator@hotmail.com

POWER PHRASES

Consider using adaptations of these key phrases in your resignation letters.

I am offering two weeks' notice so that my territory can be effectively serviced during the transition, with the least amount of inconvenience to our clients.

While I have enjoyed very much working under your direction, I find now that I have an opportunity to further develop my career in areas that are more in line with my long-term goals. I thank you for the sales training that I have received under your supervision. It is largely due to the excellent experience I gained working for ABC Corporation that I am now able to pursue this growth opportunity.

During the next two weeks, I am willing to help you in any way to make the transition as smooth as possible. This includes assisting in recruiting and training my replacement in the _____ territory. Please let me know if there is anything specific that you would like me to do.

Again, it has been a pleasure working as a part of your sales force.

I have thoroughly enjoyed the work environment and professional atmosphere at _____. Your guidance and counseling have been the source of great personal and career satisfaction, and I am grateful.

These _____ years have made a considerable contribution to my career and professional development and I hope that I have likewise contributed during this time to the growth and development of ABC Corporation. I am grateful for the kind of associates I have had the opportunity to work with and the substantial support I have consistently received from management.

Thank-You Letter (after hire) (General)

Matilda Vixard
310 Sweetwater Lane ▪ Milwaukee, WI 53172 ▪ (414) 555.3471

(Date)

Phillip _____
(Title)
ABC Corporation
1 Industry Plaza
Madison, WI 53182

Dear Mr. _____:

I want you to be among the first to know that my job search has come to a very successful conclusion. I have accepted the position of _____ Director at _____, Inc., located in _____.

I appreciate all the help and support you have provided over the last several months. It has made the job search process much easier for me. I look forward to staying in contact with you. Please let me know if I can be of any assistance to you in the future. Thank you.

Sincerely,

Matilda Vixard

Matilda Vixard

MV

Thank-You E-Mail (after hire) (Software Manager)

From: Shane Franklin [softwarespecialist@yahoo.com]
To: hr@surrex.com
Cc:
Subject: Great News! Thanks for the help ;-)

Dear Ms. _____:

I am happy to inform you that I received and accepted an offer of employment just after Thanksgiving. I am now employed by the _____ Corporation.

I would also like to thank you for all your help the past several months not only in my search for employment but also by your understanding and friendly words of encouragement.

My duties include responsibility of all Dun & Bradstreet software (General Ledger, Accounts Payable, Accounts Receivable, and Fixed Assets) for _____ worldwide plus the first-year training of several entry-level employees.

I am enjoying my new responsibility and being fully employed again, although at times I feel overwhelmed with all I have to learn.

If there is ever anything I can do for you please call me. I hope you and your family have a wonderful holiday season and much luck and happiness in the new year.

Sincerely,

Shane Franklin
(516) 555-1212
softwarespecialist@yahoo.com

POWER PHRASES

Consider using adaptations of these key phrases in your thank-you letters.

I am writing to share this good news with you and to thank you for your efforts on my behalf. If there is ever anything that I can do for you, please do not hesitate to call on me.

Thank you for all your help. I have accepted a position as a _____ for _____.

I want you to be among the first to know that my job search has come to a very successful conclusion.

I appreciate all the help and support you have provided over the last several months. It has made the job search process much easier for me. I look forward to staying in contact with you. Please let me know if I can be of any assistance to you in the future.

I would like to extend my sincere thanks to you for your kind help and encouragement during my job search. If I can be of any assistance to you in the future, please do not hesitate to contact me. I was often reminded during the past few months that we too easily lose contact with old friends. Let's try to stay in touch.

If you ever get a chance to visit _____, on business or pleasure, please be sure to let me know.

If there is ever anything I can do for you please call me. I hope you and your family have a wonderful holiday season and much luck and happiness in the new year.

Just a quick note to bring you up to date with what I am doing.

Special Reports

Once in a very long while a new idea comes along in the world of job-hunting. The special report is one of those ideas. It presents you as an expert in your field without overtly saying you are job-hunting, and as such gets the reader to create an initial impression of you that is very different from that of a typical job seeker. A special report is not for everyone, but if you really know your business and you like to write, this can be a very helpful tool to add to your job-hunting arsenal.

A special report has the appearance of a newspaper, newsletter, or trade magazine article that focuses on a commonly recognized challenge in your profession; but rather than mass publication it is created by you to send directly to end users. You create it by using your professional knowledge and packaging it in a written document. Just about anyone in your field who receives one will read a well-written and properly edited special report, and at the end they'll get to read the resume of the person who created it. While a resume gets very little initial time investment, your report can have the reader building a respectful relationship with you even before they know you are available and looking. Special reports have titles like:

Computer conversion: Plan it, move on it, and roll it out!

Three simple things you can do that double the effectiveness of your school resource center

Research reveals little used sales technique that dramatically improves product sales in financial investment market

Ten simple actions any FCM, BD, Bank, Prop Trading, and/or Treasury Director can take to head off trouble at the pass

Seven Secrets of the Successful Waitperson

Special reports all aim to help the reader solve problems, make money, save money, or save time. Think of them as departmental reports, position papers, or articles (whichever works best for you), where the goal is to give the reader some useful information they can actually use. This is why a special report is not for everyone. You have to know your stuff and enjoy the writing process, but as I always say, anyone can write so long as they don't have a so-called life! If this is you (at least the part about having an affinity for writing) read on, you will not only learn a new job hunting technique you'll be contributing to your professional credibility and visibility in ways that reach well beyond this job hunt.

In the space available here, I can't show you how to write short, job-hunting-oriented, nonfiction articles—a.k.a. special reports. Instead, I'll explain the basic structure and packaging and then refer you to a couple of additional resources.

What goes into a special report?

- A benefit-oriented title
- An introduction
- The body copy usually in the form of "tips" or "mistakes to avoid"
- Author info (usually, your resume)
- A binding

The key to this Trojan horse approach is to include your resume with contact information in the author information section. If your resume isn't right for the job, you can use a biography that highlights information you feel is more relevant to the reader; in this instance you'll be able to cut and paste one of your broadcast letters without the salutation.

The proper length is up to you, and opinions differ. Some will tell you that special reports can be as long as you like, and I have seen some that run to 6,000 words (about ten pages). Personally, I think you should keep your report to between 600 and 1,000 words—in other words about the length of a regular newspaper column (or the length of this section on what goes into special reports, which runs about 1,000 words).

There is another benefit to this approach. Job offers usually go to the person who turns a one-sided examination of skills into a two-way conversation between professional colleagues. The nature of the special report goes a long way toward defining you as someone quite different to almost every other candidate.

If you look at the examples below and think that this might be a useful approach for your needs, but you feel you need more help, go to *www.salary negotiations.com*, the Web site of long-time career consultant Jack Chapman, who developed the whole special report idea. You'll find information about his book *Special Reports: Amazing New Job-Search Technology with 100 Times the Impact of [Even the Best] Résumé or Cover Letter*. The book contains instructions and ten examples of the many ways a special report can be done.

If you do try this as an additional approach for your job hunt, you will be able to re-use the fruits of your efforts. You can submit your article for publication to professional newsletters and magazines, and you can turn it into a presentation. In fact, your notes for the special report simultaneously form the outline of a business presentation. So even outside of the context of your job hunt, this approach of putting your professional expertise into a different delivery medium can have a significant impact on your professional visibility and credibility.

Now look at these samples.

SPECIAL REPORT EXAMPLE #1: WAITRESS

BACKGROUND:

With NO experience directly as a waitress, Christine, a college freshman, got hired. She had only been a hostess at "23"—Michael Jordan's Restaurant near the University of North Carolina. She had observed waiters and waitresses, and she had definite ideas about what differentiated the satisfactory from the excellent. She wanted to "jump over" the menial waitress positions and get hired by an upscale, four-star restaurant (read: big tips!). This way, she positioned herself as an exceptional waitress who had the boss' viewpoint of the job.

TITLE: Christine's Four Keys to an Excellent Waitperson

EXCERPT FROM INTRODUCTION:

Excellent waiter, waitress? It's not all that complicated to be just a satisfactory waitperson. Practically anyone can write down an order and bring food to the table. Surprisingly, it's not all that hard to be an outstanding waitperson, either—but not everyone does it. I've put down my thoughts, here, on the 4 keys to excellence on the job as I see it. It will help you get an idea of my philosophy.

EXCERPT FROM RULES SECTION:

Key #3 There's always a way to get people what they want.

When you know that customers want more than just food, that they want a pleasant time as well, possibilities arise. As hostess at 23, wait-staff would often complain to me about customers ordering things not on the menu, or prepared a certain way. When, out of curiosity, I checked it out with the cooks they almost always said, "no problem." So it was the waitperson creating a problem for a customer—that problem didn't exist! I find that if you put your mind to it, there's always a way to keep the customer satisfied.

OUTLINE OF THE REST OF THE REPORT:
Key #1) Remember that your job is not "things to do" but people to take care of.
Key #2) The friendlier you are, the friendlier the customers will be.
Key #3) There's always a way to get people what they want.
Key #4) It's a job for you, but it's a business for your boss.
Summary

RESULTS: Christine leapfrogged into a fine-dining (and fine tipping) job.

SPECIAL REPORT EXAMPLE #2: SALESMAN

Mike's success at sales came from meticulous attention to detail (read: boring!), but he turns that dull skill into a reason to be hired! His report shows how astoundingly elementary your report "rules" can be and still make an indelible impression. (His first rule is, "Answer the Phone.") He focused on software sales to financial investors, but this type of report could be applied to almost any type of sales. Mike also got the Hiring Decision Makers' attention in the cover letter by mentioning that theirs was one of the firms he called in his "secret shopper" research.

TITLE: Research Reveals Little Used Sales Technique that Can Dramatically Improve Sales [to the Financial Investment Market].

EXCERPT FROM INTRODUCTION:
Recently I undertook a research project to determine how companies might improve their sales. I called several companies and said, "I would like to buy your software."

It was astonishing to me that from over twenty companies, I only reached someone knowledgeable about the product only 14% of the time. Equally surprising was that only 28% of the organizations had someone return my call. Almost 40% didn't bother to send me any information. And even when they did, only 4% followed up with a phone call.

This confirmed my hunch. Just by applying a sales principle I've used for 18 years, namely follow-up consistency, any one of these firms could experience a dramatic increase in sales. Here is how consistent follow-up can be easily applied in five areas to increase sales. I'm embarrassed at how basic these actions are, but remember—only 14% of my calls reached a salesperson!

EXCERPT FROM RULES SECTION:

Follow-up Consistency Rule #1: ANSWER THE PHONE.

Having a dedicated line that is answered by a knowledgeable, helpful, friendly, live human being is essential in sales. No voice mail allowed! Not every line needs to be answered this way (although that's nice if you can afford it), but each and every call from potential customers must receive this follow-up consistency.

On one of my calls an operator informed me she could not take my name and address for information—that would have to be handled by a salesperson. She then informed me that she could not transfer me to a salesperson because they were all gone for the rest of the day. It was 11 a.m.!

QUESTION: Have you called your own sales line recently? What happened next?

OUTLINE OF THE REST OF THE REPORT:

Rule #2) Return messages;

Rule #3) Send the materials;

Rule #4) Don't just call the prospect, get through;

Rule #5) Never discard the names of prospects.

Summary

RESULTS: Mike got interviews with EVERY ONE of the 20 firms he had called as a "secret shopper." He got job offers from two of them.

SPECIAL REPORT EXAMPLE #3: FINANCIAL INVESTMENT SERVICES CFO

BACKGROUND:

Scott was seeking a high six-figure CFO job in the investment field. Billion dollar scandals at Enron, MCI WorldCom, and Tyco had just occurred so his report caught people's attention. His simple techniques to prevent these catastrophes were powerfully linked up with the war-stories attached to each rule.

TITLE: How to Uncover Financial and Operational Trouble Before Your P&L Blows Up... Ten simple actions any FCM, BD, Bank, Prop Trading and/ or Treasury Manager or Director can take to head off trouble at the pass.

EXCERPT FROM INTRODUCTION:

When a company is in, or about to be in trouble, there are <u>always</u> flashing yellow warning lights. The good news is that <u>problems rarely travel alone</u>.

Usually they create a pattern of circumstances that aren't individually recognized as problems, but when the puzzle pieces are assembled—wham! It's an open invitation to red ink. It may be up to you to recognize enough of those pieces in time to stop the entire puzzle from being completed.

For the past 20 years, as a trouble-shooter CFO or COO at financial services firms, I've learned to read the signs. And what are some of those signs?

EXCERPT FROM RULES SECTION:

***Rule #2:** Pay attention to your checks after they're cashed and cleared.*
How are they endorsed?

Your employees? The ones who can't trade because you won't let them, why is one or more of their checks endorsed over to a third party or brokerage firm—hidden trading account in their own name?

Your customer? Why are multiple checks for identical amounts drawn on a single customer's account and endorsed over to multiple third parties? Unregistered pool? What if one of those third parties is your employee in a position to allocate trades or initiate commission rate or brokerage rate changes in your computer system?

Your vendor? Why are checks always endorsed to the name of a company you don't recognize? Is it an innocent d/b/a or are you dealing with a middleman who is marking up goods or services you could get for less by going direct?

OUTLINE OF THE REST OF THE REPORT [FOUR SAMPLES OF THE TEN RULES):

Rule #1) Periodically, sort your name and address file. Look for dual-identity payments.

Rule #3) Review a month of original trade tickets, blotters, out-trade sheets... Slowly. It's worth it.

Rule #6) Use simple line graphs to compare periods. It's easy to be caught up in the day-to-day.

Rule #9) Regularly review IB/RR/AP/Broker/Trader Payouts. Without exception, the most consistent source of hidden losses is linked in some way to Payouts.

RESULTS: Scott's report opened doors to networking interviews with "heavy hitters" in his field, which led to his new job.

PROFESSIONAL RESUME WRITING SERVICES

As part of your job search, you might feel the need for extra help from a professional resume writer. A professional in the field may be able to help you develop a more polished layout or present a particularly complex background more effectively.

The big question is, "Who should I use?" As in any other profession, there are practitioners at both ends of the performance scale. I am a strong believer in using the services of resume writers who belong to the field's professional associations. They tend to be more committed, have more field experience, and have an all-around higher standard of performance.

Resume writers who are members of the appropriate professional associations are more likely to be able to help you fine-tune your resume into an effective marketing tool. Depending on the help you need, the cost of their services can range from $50 to $1,500. (Don't gasp—the higher up the professional ladder you are aiming, the more important a polished and professional-looking resume becomes, and the more complex the task!)

There are three major associations in the field: the Professional Association of Résumé Writers (PARW, at *parw.com*), the National Résumé Writers' Association (NRWA, at *nrwa.com*), and Career Masters Institute (CMI, at *www.cminstitute.com*).

All have hundreds of members and provide ongoing opportunities for members to gain mentoring experience and additional training. They all offer resume-writing certification and operate e-mail list servers for members with access to e-mail. The professional training programs range from how to handle specific resume challenges to issues related to running a resume service. The associations build camaraderie between members and offer them access to the expertise of hundreds of other professional resume writers; a fair number of professional resume writers belong to more than one association (just as you should in your own field). Each organization holds an annual convention with workshops on industry issues. NRWA is the only nonprofit organization in the group.

The following is a list of professional resume writers who have contributed to the *Knock 'em Dead* books and who are members of one or more of the above groups.

Ann Baehr
Best Resumes
122 Sheridan Street
Brentwood, NY 11717
tel: (631) 435-1879
fax: (631) 435-3655
E-mail: *resumebest@earthlink.net*
Web: *www.e-bestresumes.com*

Beverly Baskin, Ed.S, NCCC, MCC, CPRW
Mitch Baskin, MMS, PE
BBCS Counseling Services
6 Alberta Drive
Marlboro, NJ 07746
tel: (800) 300-4079 Toll-free
Web: *www.baskincareer.com*
additional office locations in Woodbridge and Princeton

Rosie Bixel
A Personal Scribe
Resume Writing and Design
tel: (503) 254-8262
fax: (503) 255-3012
E-mail: *aps@bhhgroup.com*
Web: *www.bhhgroup.com/resume.asp*
Member: National Résumé Writers' Association

Arnold G. Boldt, CPRW, JCTC
Arnold-Smith Associates
625 Panorama Trail, Building Two, Suite 200
Rochester, NY 14625
tel: (585) 383-0350
fax: (585) 387-0516
E-mail: *Arnie@ResumeSOS.com*
Web: *www.ResumeSOS.com*
Member: Career Masters Institute
Member: Professional Association of Résumé Writers & Career Coaches
Member: National Résumé Writers' Association

Tracy A. Bumpus, CPRW, JCTC
Executive Director
RezAMAZE.com
Austin, TX
tel: (512) 291-1404 or (888) 277-4270
fax: 208-247-2542
Web: *www.rezamaze.com*

Diane Burns, CPRW, IJCTC, CCM
President
Career Marketing Techniques
5219 Thunder Hill Road
Columbia, MD 21045
tel: (410) 884-0213
E-mail: *DianeCPRW@aol.com*
Web: *www.polishedresumes.com*

(Ms.) Freddie Cheek, MS Ed., CPRW, CWDP
Cheek & Cristan Phonelo Career Connections
4511 Harlem Road, Suite 3
Amherst, NY 14226
tel: (716) 839-3635
fax: (716) 831-9320
E-mail: *fscheek@adelphia.net*

Norine T. Dagliano, CPRW
Inspirations
616 Highland Way
Hagerstown, MD 21740
tel: (301) 766-2032
fax: (301) 745-5700
E-mail: *ndagliano@yahoo.com*

Lori Davila, Career Coach
LJD Consulting, Inc.
1483 North Springs Drive
Atlanta, GA 30338
tel: (770) 392-1139
E-mail: *loritil@aol.com*

Deborah Wile Dib, NCRW, CPRW, JCTC
President
Advantage Resumes of New York
tel: (631) 475-8513
Web: *www.advantageresumes.com*
Member: NRWA, PARW, AJST, CPADN, CMI

Kirsten Dixson, JCTC, CPRW, CEIP
New Leaf Career Solutions
tel: (866) NEW-LEAF (639-5323)
Toll free: (914) 961-9779
Web: *www.newleafcareer.com*
Certified Career Coach and Resume Writer
Certified Employment Interview
Professional
Career Planning & Development Certificate
from NYU
Strategies To Recession-Proof Your Career
(2002, McGraw-Hill)
Member: PARW/CC, NRWA and IACMP

Jacqui Barrett Dodson, CPRW
Career Trend
7501 College Boulevard, Suite 175
Overland Park, KS 66210
tel: (913) 451-1313
fax: (913) 451-3242
E-mail: *dodson@careertrend.net*
Web: *www.careertrend.net*

Daniel J. Dorotik, NCRW
100PercentResumes
9803 Clinton Avenue
Lubbock, TX 79424
tel: (806) 783-9900
eFax: (214) 722-1510
E-mail: *dan@100percentresumes.com*
Web: *www.100percentresumes.com*

Nina K. Ebert, CPRW
A Word's Worth Resume and Writing Service
25 Oakwood Drive
New Egypt, NJ 08533
tel: (609) 758-7799
fax: (609) 758-7799
Web: *www.keystosuccessresumes.com*

Susan Eckert, MA, CCM, CPRW
Advance Career & Professional
Development
138 Concourse East
Brightwaters, NY 11718
(Long Island area)
tel (local): (631) 666-3224
Toll-free: (800) 824-6611
fax: 631-980-7846
Web: *www.advancecareerdevelopment.com*

Cory Edwards, CRW
Partnering For Success
109 Country Road
Sterling, VA 20165
tel and fax: (703) 444-7835
E-mail: *ResumeWriter@aol.com*
Web: *www.Resumes4Results.com*

Debbie Ellis, CPRW
President, Phoenix Career Group, LLC
"Fax your resume for a professional
evaluation!"
(800) 876-5506 (toll-free inside U.S.);
(888) 329-5409 (toll-free 24-hour fax
inside U.S.);
(859) 236-4001 (worldwide voice);
(859) 236-4001 (worldwide 24-hour fax)
Web: *www.phoenixcareergroup.com*
Certified Professional Resume Writer (CPRW)
Resume Expert for www.CareerFolios.com
Member: Professional Association of
Résumé Writers (PARW)
Member: International Certification Board,
PARW

Donna M. Farrise, JCTC
Dynamic Résumés of Long Island, Inc.
300 Motor Parkway, Suite 200
Hauppauge, NY 11788
tel: (631) 951-4120
fax: (631) 952-1817
E-mail: *donna@dynamicresumes.com*
Web: *www.dynamicresumes.com*

Dayna Feist, CPRW, JCTC
Gatehouse Business Services
265 Charlotte Street
Asheville, NC 28801
tel: (828) 254-7893
fax: (828) 254-7894
E-mail: *Gatehous@aol.com*
Member: Certification Board, PARW
Member: Career Masters Institute

John Femia, BS, CPRW
Custom Resume & Writing Service
1690 Township Road
Altamont, NY 12009
(Albany area)
tel: (518) 872-1305

Joyce Fortier, CCM
Create Your Own Career
23871 W. Lebost
Novi, MI 48375
tel: (248) 478-5662
fax: (248) 426-9974
E-mail: *careerist@aol.com*
Web: *www.careerist.com*

Roberta Gamza, JCTC, CEIP, JST
Career Ink
Louisville, CO
tel: (888) 581-6063
fax: (303) 955-3065
E-mail: *roberta@careerink.com*
Web: *www.careerink.com*

Louise Garver, CMP, JCTC, CPRW
Career Directions
115 Elm Street, Suite 203
Enfield, CT 06082
tel: (888) 222-3731
fax: (860) 623-9473
Web: *www.resumeimpact.com*

Wayne M. Gonyea, MS, CCM
President
Gonyea Career Marketing, Inc.
1810 Arturus Lane
New Port Richey, FL 34655
tel: (727) 375-0489
E-mail: *online@resumexpress.com*
Web: *www.resumexpress.com*
Founding Member: Career Masters Institute

Susan Guarneri, CPRW, CEIP, JCTC, NCCC,
CCMC
Guarneri Associates
1905 Fern Lane
Wausau, WI 54401
tel: (866) 881-4055 Toll-free
fax: (715) 355-1936
E-mail: *Resumagic@aol.com*
Web: *www.resume-magic.com*

Michele J. Haffner, CPRW, JCTC
Managing Director
Advanced Resume Services
1314 W. Paradise Ct.
Glendale, WI 53209
tel: (877) 247-1677
fax: (414) 247-1808
Web: *www.resumeservices.com*

Beate Hait, CPRW, NCRW
Résumés Plus
80 Wingate Road
Holliston, MA 01746
tel: (508) 429-1813
fax: (508) 429-4299
Web: *www.resumesplus.net*

Cheryl Ann Harland, CPRW, JCTC
Resumes By Design
25227 Grogan's Mill Road
The Woodlands, TX 77380
tel: (281) 296-1659
fax: (888) 213-1650
E-mail: *cah@resumesbydesign.com*
Web: *www.resumesbydesign.com*

Beverly Harvey, CPRW, JCTC, CCM
Beverly Harvey Resume & Career Services
P.O. Box 750
Pierson, FL 32180
tel: (386) 749-3111;
Toll-free: (888) 775-0916
fax: (386) 749-4881
E-mail: *Beverly@harveycareers.com*
Web: *www.harveycareers.com*

Maria Hebda, CPRW
Career Solutions, LLC
tel: (877) 777-7242
E-mail: *careers@writingresumes.com*
Web: *www.WritingResumes.com*
Professional Association of Résumé Writers
& Career Coaches
National Résumé Writers' Association
Professional Résumé Writing and Research
Association
Career Masters Institute

Peter Hill, CPRW
Distinctive Resumes
Honolulu, HI
tel: (808) 306-3920
E-Mail: *distinctiveresumes@yahoo.com*
Web: *www.peterhill.biz*

Jan Holliday, MA, NCRW, Certified
Webmaster
Arbridge Communications
Harleysville, PA
(Philadelphia Area)
tel: (215) 513-7420
Toll-free, U.S.: (866) 513-7420
E-mail: *info@arbridge.com*
Web: *www.arbridge.com*

La-Dana Renée Jenkins
LRJ Consulting Services
Staten Island, NY
tel: (718) 448-5825
fax: (718) 448-5825
E-mail: *lrjconsulting@hotmail.com*
Web: *www.lrjconsulting.net*

Bill Kinser, CPRW, CEIP, JCTC
To The Point Resumes, Inc.
Fairfax, VA
tel: (703) 352-8969
Toll-free: (866) RESUME1 (737-8631)
Web: *www.tothepointresumes.com*

Cindy Kraft, CPRW, JCTC, CCM
Executive Essentials
"Helping clients achieve career success"
tel: (813) 655-0658
Toll-free: (888) 221-0441
fax: (813) 653-4513
Web: *www.exec-essentials.com*
Credentialed Career Master

Bonnie Kurka, CPRW
Resume Suite
85B Schofield Circle
Fort Riley, KS 66442
tel: (785) 375-6981
fax: (785) 717-3289
Web: *www.resumesuite.com*

Louise Kursmark, CPRW, JCTC
Best Impression Career Services, Inc.
Cincinnati, OH
tel: (513) 792-0030
Web: *www.yourbestimpression.com*

Richard A. Lanham, CCM, M. Div., MRE,
and MA
RL Stevens and Associates
Indiana Region-General Manager
8888 Keystone Crossing Blvd., Suite 950
Indianapolis, IN 46240
tel: (888) 806-7313
E-mail: *rlanham@rlstevens.com*
Web: *www.interviewing.com*
Career Masters Institute
Professional Résumé Writing and Research
Association

Rolande L. La Pointe, CPC, CIPC, CPRW,
IJCTC, CCM
President/Founder
RO-LAN Associates, Inc.
725 Sabattus Street
Lewiston, ME 04240
tel: (207) 784-1010
fax: (207) 782-3446
E-mail: *RLapointe@aol.com*

Denise M. Larkin, CPRW, CEIP, CHT
ResumeRighter.com
PO Box 10944
Oakland, CA 94610
tel: (510) 891-0200
fax: (510) 891-0157
E-mail: *denise@resumerighter.com*
Web: *www.resumerighter.com*

Mary Laske, MS, CPRW
ExecPro Résumé Service
1713 Park Blvd.
Fargo, ND 58103
tel: (866) 232-0239
fax: (707) 760-3951
Web: *www.execproresumes.com*

Lorie Lebert, CPRW, IJCTC, CCMC
"Helping professionals write the next chapter of their career."
The Loriel Group
CoachingROI :: RésuméROI
Resumes For Results, LLC
P.O. Box 267
Novi, MI 48376
Toll-free: (800) 870-9059
tel (local): (248) 380-6101
E-mail: *Lorie@DoMyResume.com*
Web: *www.DoMyResume.com* and *www.CoachingROI.com*

Diana C. Le Gere
Executive Final Copy
PO Box 171311
Salt Lake City, UT 84117
tel: (866) 754-5465
fax: (626) 602-8715
Web: *www.executivefinalcopy.com*

Cherie Lynch, Ed.M.
Certified Professional Resume Writer
Portfolio – Career Solutions
Newburyport, MA (Boston/
New Hampshire Area)
tel: 1-978-235-8998
E-mail: *clynch@portfolio-pro.com*
Web: *www.portfolio-pro.com*

Ross Macpherson, CPRW, CJST, CEIP
Career Quest
1586 Major Oaks Road
Pickering, ON, Canada
tel: (877) 426-8548
fax: (905) 426-4274
Web: *www.yourcareerquest.com*

Linda Matias
34 East Main Street #276
Smithtown, NY 11787
Phone and fax: (631) 382-2425
E-mail: *careerstrides@bigfoot.com*
Web: *www.careerstrides.com*

Nicole Miller, CRW, IJCTC, RRP
Mil-Roy Consultants
1729 Hunter's Run Drive
Ottawa, ON K1C-6W2, Canada
tel: (613) 834-4031
E-mail: *resumesbymilroy@hotmail.com*

Stacy Moore
Less Is Moore Resumes
8448 Angwin Place
Charlotte, NC 28262
tel: (704) 904-6794
fax: (704) 988-0860
Web: *www.lim-resumes.com*

Melanie Noonan
Peripheral Pro, LLC
560 Lackawanna Avenue
West Paterson, NJ 07424
(New York/New Jersey Metropolitan Area)
tel: (973) 785-3011
fax: (973) 256-6285
E-mail: *PeriPro1@aol.com*

Debra O'Reilly, CPRW, JCTC
Resumewriter.com
16 Terryville Avenue
Bristol, CT 06010
tel: (860) 583-7500
fax: (860) 585-9611
E-mail: *debra@resumewriter.com*
Web: *www.resumewriter.com*
Charter Member: Career Masters Institute
Member: Professional Association of
Résumé Writers
Member: National Résumé Writers'
Association

Don Orlando, MBA, CPRW, JCTC, CCM
The McLean Group
640 South McDonough
Montgomery, AL 36104
tel: (334) 264-2020
fax: (334) 264-9227
E-mail: *yourcareercoach@aol.com*

Tracy M. Parish, CPRW
CareerPlan, Inc.
P.O. Box 507
Kewanee, IL 61443
Toll-free: (888) 449-2200

Sharon Pierce-Williams, M.Ed., CPRW
The Résumé.Doc
609 Lincolnshire Lane
Findlay, OH 45840
tel: (419) 422-0228
fax: (419) 425-1185
Web: *www.TheResumeDoc.com*

Edie Rische, NCRW, JCTC
Write Away Resume
5908 73rd Street
Lubbock, TX 79424-1920
tel: (806) 798-0881
fax: (806) 798-3213
Web: *www.writeawayresume.com*

MeLisa Rogers, CPRW, MSHRD
Ultimate Career
"Creating Strategies to Increase
Your Worth"
270 Live Oak Lane
Victoria, TX
tel (local): (361) 575-6100
Toll-free: (866) 5résumé (1-866-573-7863)
Serving the entire South Texas and Coastal
Bend Areas
Web: *www.ultimatecareer.biz*

Jane Roqueplot
JaneCo's Sensible Solutions
194 North Oakland Ave.
Sharon, PA 16146
tel: (888) 526-3267
E-mail: *info@janecos.com*

Jennifer Rydell, CPRW, CCM
Simplify Your Life Career Services
6327-C SW Capitol Highway PMB 243
Portland, OR 97201-1937
tel: (503) 977-1955
fax: (503) 245-4212
E-mail: *simplify@spiritone.com*
Web: *www.simplifyyourliferesumes.com*

Janice M. Shepherd, CPRW, JCTC, CEIP
Write On Career Keys
Top of Alabama Hill
Bellingham, WA 98226-4260
tel: (360) 738-7958
fax: (360) 738-1189
E-mail: *Janice@writeoncareerkeys.com*
Web: *www.writeoncareerkeys.com*

Karen M. Silins, CRW, CTAC, CCA
A+ Career & Resume
Kansas City, MO
tel: (816) 942-3019
fax: (816) 942-1505
Web: *www.careerandresume.com*

Tammy J. Smith
Professional Image Design LLC
7030 Marshall Road
Olivet, MI 49076
tel: (877) 588-7459
Web: *www.professionalimagedesign.com*

Billie Ruth Sucher, MS, President
Billie Ruth Sucher & Associates
7177 Hickman Road, Suite 10
Urbandale, IA 50322
tel: (515) 276-0061
fax: (515) 334-8076
E-mail: *betwnjobs@aol.com*

Gail Taylor, CPRW, CEIP
A Hire Power Résumé Services
21213-B Hawthorne Blvd #5224
Torrance, CA 90503
tel: (310) 793-4122
fax: (310) 793-7481
Web: *www.call4hirepower.com*

Gina Taylor, CPRW
Gina Taylor & Associates, Inc.
1111 W. 77th Terrace
Kansas City, MS 64114
tel: (816) 523-9100
E-mail: *ginaresume@aol.com*

Julie C. Thomas
Julie's Typing & Notary Service
1134 West Olive Street
West Monroe, LA 71292
tel: (318) 322-2199
Member: National Résumé Writers'
Association

Patricia Traina-Duckers CPRW, CRW, CEIP
The Resume Writer
P.O. Box 46
Port Reading, NJ 07064
tel: (732) 500-6330
fax: (800) 887-3467
Web: *www.theresumewriter.com*

Donna Tucker
Career*PRO* Résumé Center
10210 N. 32nd Street #204
Phoenix, AZ 85028
tel: (602) 788-3121
fax: (602) 788-1999
Web: *www.4greatresumes.com*

Ilona Vanderwoude
The Vanderwoude Advantage
"Expert Résumés"
Riverdale, NY
tel: (914) 376-4217
fax: (646) 349-2218
E-mail: *info@YourResumeWriter.com*

Vivian Van Lier, CPRW, JCTC, CEIP
Advantage Resume & Career Services
(Los Angeles, CA)
CuttingEdgeResumes.com
tel: (818) 994-6655
fax: (818) 994-6620
E-mail: *Vivian@CuttingEdgeResumes.com*
Web: *www.cuttingedgeresumes.com/
home.html*
Certified Professional Resume Writer
Internationally Certified Job & Career
Transition Coach
Certified Employment Interview Professional

Janice Worthington, MA, CPRW, JCTC, CEIP
Worthington Career Services
6636 Belleshire Street
Columbus, OH 43229
tel: 1-877-9Resume (973-7863)
Web: *www.worthingtonresumes.com*

Linda Wunner, CPRW, CEIP, JCTC
Career & Resume Design/Linda's Page Works
"Advanced career development concepts
that WORK!"
E-mail: *Linda@successfulresumes.com*
Web: *www.successfulresumes.com*

Debra Feldman
21 Linwood Avenue
Riverside, CT 06878
tel: (203) 637-3500
E-mail: *DebraFeldman@JobWhiz.com*
Web: *www.JobWhiz.com*
Debra Feldman is an executive talent agent
representing candidates to prospective new
employer opportunities. Debra arranges for
JobWhiz clients to be introduced to company
insiders, making them privy to news
about internal restructurings and special
circumstances that produce job leads.

ONLINE RESOURCES

General Job Sites

Career Builder

www.careerbuilder.com

In partnership with Tribune and Knight Ridder (two major newspaper publishing chains), CareerBuilder is the recruitment service provider for major metropolitan newspapers throughout the United States and provides jobs and career resources for more than thirty-five of the country's online version of local newspapers and information sites. CareerBuilder provides a unique combination of local, national, and niche career audiences. In addition to the standard job bank and resume bank, new job seeker services include a Career Resource Center, Resume Distribution, Brainbench Skills Certification, and Personal Salary Reports. Although improvements are needed, especially to the Resource Center, the site is big and free to job seekers.

Monster.com

www.monster.com

The name of this growing site is becoming more apropos. The site offers areas catered to specific types of job seekers. ChiefMonster caters to the executive and charges fees for access to its exclusive jobs and career assistance. MonsterTRAK is specifically for college students and remains free for them. Explore this site's home page and discover the growing specialty niches offered to guide you down your career path. My Monster Premium is a fairly new service allowing any job seeker to "upgrade" their service. For less than $7 a month, additional services and information are provided, such as resume enhancement, a job search tutorial, and the Harvard ManageMentor for managing your career. The free ride may be nearing an end for the more unique and exclusive information for job seekers.

Hotjobs

www.hotjobs.com

This site has recently become a wholly owned subsidiary of Yahoo! The site offers job-seeking professionals a one-stop job search resource, job bank, and resume bank—at no cost. Besides keyword searches, jobs can be searched by category, company, staffing firm, U.S. location, and international locations.

Candidates create a personalized career management page called MyHotJobs, which provides tools to help in a job search. Features include access to HotJobs.com's central resume database where companies search for candidates.

Other general job sites:

www.flipdog.com
www.americasjobbank.com
www.net-temps.com
www.vault.com
www.4jobs.com
www.job.com
www.employment911.com
www.nationjob.com
www.employmentguide.com
www.careerboard.com
www.careersite.com
www.directemployers.com
www.topusajobs.com
www.jobbankusa.com
www.wetfeet.com
www.snagajob.com
www.jobwarehouse.com
www.careermag.com
www.truecareers.com
www.bestjobsusa.com
www.localcareers.com
www.sologig.com
www.jobfind.com
www.hiregate.com
www.careershop.com
www.career.com
www.summerjobs.com
www.employmentspot.com
www.americanjobs.com

www.4work.com
www.worklife.com
www.worktree.com

College Job Sites

www.collegegrad.com

CollegeGrad.com is one of the original "Big Three" in the college jobs space, in business since January of 1995. They offer loads of free resources for job seekers, including one of the most valuable lists in the field: their list of the Top Entry Level Employers.

NACElink

www.nacelink.com

NACElink is a site combining the resources of NACE (National Association of Colleges and Employers) and DirectEmployers.com, which is a nonprofit site representing a recruitment portal for a growing number of blue chip companies. Lots of job postings and links to the blue chips.

Other college job sites:

www.collegejournal.com
www.experience.com
www.ecampusrecruiter.com
www.collegerecruiter.com
www.campuscareercenter.com
www.collegecentral.com
www.aftercollege.com
www.jobpostings.net
www.gradunet.co.uk
www.careerfair.com
www.collegejobboard.com
www.aboutjobs.com
www.entryleveljobs.net
www.collegeclub.com

www.collegegrad.com
www.blackcollegian.com
www.experience.com
www.ednet.com
www.graduatingengineer.com
www.internshipprograms.com
www.jobtrak.com
www.jobweb.com
www.planetedu.net
www.snagajob.com
www.a1education.com

Executive Job Sites

www.6figurejobs.com

Executives I consult with speak well of 6figurejobs. Just as its name implies, the site is geared to those making six-figure salaries. Submit your resume, search jobs, research companies, find an executive recruiter, and use the extensive resources and tips.

There is a fee for membership, depending on how long you want to have access to the site. The site is definitely worth considering if you are an executive.

www.careerjournal.com

This site brings with it the vast resources of the *Wall Street Journal* with articles, surveys, and options for accessing the interactive *Wall Street Journal* in addition to its national and international job bank and resume bank. To apply for a job opening you must create a profile and enter your resume into the resume bank. However, it remains there unless you consent to have it released to a specific company or recruiter.

This is a site with a wealth of information for many types of professionals including those who are considering international careers.

Other executive job sites:

www.execunet.com
www.chiefmonster.com
www.spencerstuart.com
www.ekornferry.com
www.netshare.com
www.futurestep.com
www.MBA-exchange.com
www.mbajungle.com

Diversity Job Sites

www.latpro.com

LatPro.com is the number-one employment source for Spanish- and Portuguese-speaking professionals in North and South America, and the site can be viewed in English, Spanish, or Portuguese. Features both resume and job banks.

www.hirediversity.com

HireDiversity.com links multicultural and bilingual professionals with both national and international industry sectors. Clients primarily consist of Fortune 1000 companies and government agencies.

Other diversity job sites:

www.imdiversity.com
www.eop.com
www.diversitylink.com
www.quintcareers.com/diversity_resources.html
www.bilingual-jobs.com

www.blackcollegian.com

www.bwni.com (business women's network)

www.christianjobs.com

www.experienceworks.org

www.gaywork.com

www.destinygroup.com

    (#1 post-military careers site)

www.taonline.com

    (military transition assistance)

http://janweb.icdi.wvu.edu

    (Job Accommodation Network)

www.business-disability.com

International Job Sites

www.workopolis.com (Canada's #1 job site)

www.jobstreet.com (Asia-Pacific's #1 job site)

www.monster.ca/ (Monster Canada)

www.seek.com.au/ (Australia's #1 job site)

www.monster.co.uk/ (Monster UK)

    (England's #1 job site)

www.gojobsite.co.uk/

www.reed.co.uk

www.jobserve.com

www.totaljobs.com

www.careerone.com.au/

www.eurojobs.com

www.joblinks.f2s.com/index_eng.htm

www.jobpilot.com

www.jobsbazaar.com

www.overseasjobs.com

www.stepstone.com

www.topjobs.co.uk

Career Sites

www.acinet.org/acinet

www.backdoorjobs.com

www.careerhunters.com

www.careers.org

www.job-hunt.org

www.jobweb.com

www.phoenixcareergroup.com

www.rileyguide.com

www.quintcareers.com

www.myreferences.com

Recruiter Lists and Staffing Firms

www.rileyguide.com

www.randstad.com

www.kellyservices.com

www.kornferry.com

www.manpower.com

www.recruitersonline.com

www.worktree.com

www.snelling.com

www.spherion.com

Niche Job Sites

Advertising, public relations, and graphic arts

www.adage.com (Ad Age)

www.amic.com

    (Advertising Media Internet Center)

www.adweek.com (Adweek Online)

www.creativehotlist.com

    (Communication Arts)

www.prweek.net (PR Week)

Agriculture and horticulture

www.agricareers.com

www.hortjobs.com

www.fishingjobs.com

Aerospace and aviation

www.aerojobs.com

www.avjobs.com (Airline Ass't Corps)

www.avcrew.com

www.spacejobs.com

Business, finance, and accounting

www.jobsinthemoney.com

www.careerbank.com

www.accounting.com

www.bankjobs.com

www.businessfinancemag.com

www.careerjournal.com

www.efinancialjobs.com

www.fei.org

www.financialjobs.com

Broadcast, communications, and journalism

www.womcom.org (AWC Online)

www.b-roll.net

www.cpb.org/jobline (Corporation for Public Broadcasting)

www.crew-net.com

www.journalismjobs.com

www.telecomcareers.net

Education

www.academic360.com

www.academiccareers.com

www.chronicle.com

www.higheredjobs.com

www.petersons.com

www.phds.org

www.teacherjobs.com

www.ujobbank.com

Engineering

www.engineeringcentral.com

www.engineeringjobs.com

www.engineerjobs.com

www.asme.org

Entertainment, TV, and radio

www.tvjobs.com

www.tvandradiojobs.com

www.castingnet.com

www.entertainmentcareers.net

www.eej.com (Entertainment Employment Journal)

www.showbizjobs.com

www.themeparkjobs.com

Health care

www.healthcaresource.com

www.jobscience.com

www.healthjobusa.com

www.dentsearch.com

www.hirehealth.com

www.mdjobsite.com

www.medcareers.com

www.nursingspectrum.com

www.physemp.com

www.allnurses.com

www.nursetown.com

www.nursingcenter.com

Human resources

www.jobs4hr.com

www.hrjobnet.com

www.hrworld.com

www.shrm.org

www.tcm.com/hr-careers

IT/Programming, and MIS

www.dice.com

www.computerjobs.com

www.computerjobsbank.com

www.gjc.org

www.mactalent.com

www.techemployment.com

www.tech-engine.com

www.techies.com

Law

www.legalstaff.com

www.emplawyernet.com

www.ihirelegal.com

www.law.com

www.theblueline.com

Nonprofit

www.execsearches.com

www.naswdc.org/JOB.HTM

www.idealist.org/career.html

www.nonprofitcareer.com

www.opportunityknocks.org

Real estate

www.realtor.org

Retail, hospitality, and customer service

www.coolworks.com

www.hcareers.com

www.allretailjobs.com

www.Leisurejobs.com

www.chef2chef.net

www.chefjobsnetwork.com

www.resortjobs.com

Sales and marketing

www.salesjobs.com

www.salesheads.com

www.marketingpower.com

www.careermarketplace.com

www.jobs4sales.com

www.marketingjobs.com

www.marketingmanager.com

Science, chemistry, physics, and biology

www.medzilla.com

www.hirebio.com (bio/pharm)

www.bioview.com (bio/pharm)

www.biocareer.com

www.biomednet.com

www.biospace.com

www.biotech.deep13.com

Telecommuting

www.homeworkers.org

www.tdigest.com

www.tjobs.com

www.jobs-telecommuting.com

INDEX

A

Accounting position letters, 101, 127, 145, 200, 233
Accuracy, 83
Action, eliciting, 4–6
Action verbs, 28
Administrative position letters, 99, 103, 193–94, 222, 224
Alumni associations, 48
Appearance, of letters, 34–38. *See also* Electronic cover letters
    brightening page, 35–36
    checklist, 38
    fonts, 35, 71
    formatting electronic letters, 80
    layout, 34–35
Assessment coordinator letter, 98
Assistant director of college housing letter, 162
Associations, 48
Attack plan. *See also* Electronic cover letters
    business/trade magazines, 50–51
    carpet-bombing strategy, 54–55
    direct-research opportunities, 45–48
    employment agencies/recruiters, 48–50
    following up, 55–57
    goals, 52
    help-wanted ads, 41–42
    marketing schedule, 54–55
    multiple letters for, 53, 69–71
    networking, 42–45
    online job postings, 40–41
    sending letters, 51–53
    targeted approach, 53–54
Attention, grabbing, 2, 74–75
Auditing letter, 233

B

Banking position letters, 86, 137
Brevity, of letters, vii–ix, 21–22, 31–32
Brightening page, 35–36
Broadcast letters, 12–14, 160–92
Business magazines, 50–51

C

Care coordinator letter, 267
Carpet-bombing strategy, 54–55
Checklists, 23, 32–33, 38
Chief financial officer letter, 198
Cold responses
    to employment agencies/recruiters, 144–59
    to potential employers, 108–43
Community empowerment team director letter, 240
Concierge associate letter, 216
Construction manager letters, 221, 244

Consultant position letters, 183–84, 205, 256
Contact information, proofing, 32
Contact tracker, 56–57
Cover letter importance, v–ix, 1–2, 17–18
CPA letter, 145
Credit account specialist letter, 127
Customer service position letters, 93, 113

D

Desire, creating, 3–4
Direct-research opportunities, 45–48

E

Electronic cover letters
    accuracy, 83
    attaching resume to, 80
    content, 66–69
    customizing, 75–77
    "fake" real stationery for, 81–82
    formatting, 71–74, 80
    keywords, 66
    multiple, 53, 69–71
    online job-hunting and, 65–66
    print cover letters vs., 66–69
    reaching right person, 80–81
    requirements, 66
    scannable letters and, 71
    sending, 77–80
Electronic signatures, 81–82
E-mail
    acceptance letter sample, 258
    accessibility with, 23
    follow-up letter samples, 201–2, 226–33
    free accounts, 61–63
    organizing, 63–65, 70–71, 79
    rejection of offer letter, 253
    resignation letter sample, 271
    response letter samples, 85–89, 137–39, 151–56, 186–90, 210–11
    resurrection letter samples, 246–48
    sending letters, 77–80
    subject line, 74–75, 78
    thank-you letter (after hire), 274
Employer interests, 20, 21–22
Employment agencies/recruiters
    categories of, 48–50
    letters, 15–16, 143–57
Entertainment industry letter, 117
Entry-level position letters, 94, 108, 109, 232, 245
Envelopes, 37–38
Executive assistant letters, 103, 222
Executive briefings, 10–12
Executive chef/hotel/restaurant manager letter, 165

F–H

Financial planning professional letter, 163
Following up, 55–57
  after face-to-face meetings, 213–37
  after phone contacts, 205–12
Fonts, 35, 71
Formatting electronic letters, 71–74, 80
Fundraising consultant letter, 205

General letters
  acceptance letter, 258
  cover letters, 7–9, 199
  follow-up letters, 210, 219, 226, 231
  negotiation letter, 261–62
  rejection of offer letter, 252
  resignation letter, 271
  thank-you letter (after hire), 273
Graphic design position letter, 230

Health care management letters, 90, 143
Heavy equipment operator letter, 164
Hiring decision process, vi–viii
Human resources position letters, 177–78, 201, 238
Hydrogeologist letter, 92

I–L

Interest, generating, 2–3
International operations letter, 150
International sales letters, 102, 136
Internet job search, 58–83. *See also* Electronic cover
  letters; E-mail
  benefits of, 58–59
  online job posting response letters, 85–89
  online job postings, 40–41
  online resources, 292–97
  privacy online, 60–61
  requirements, 59–60
Internship letters, 122, 139, 195
IT/computer position letters, 138, 147, 151–56, 167,
  181, 196, 247, 274. *See also* Network admin. letters

Keywords, 66
K.I.S.S. (Keep It Simple, Stupid), 29–30

Lab specialist letter, 264
Layout, of letters, 34–35
Legal profession letters, 87, 100, 207
Length, of letters, 31–32. *See also* Brevity, of letters
Library position letters, 109, 213, 220, 250
Lift line driver position letter, 239
Loan processor letter, 215
Logistics position letter, 189

M

Magazines, 50–51
Mail, ix. *See also* E-mail
Mailing lists, purchasing, 47–48
Maintenance mechanic letter, 166

Management information systems letter, 223
Management position letters. *See also specific senior
  management titles*
  cover letters, 110–11, 118, 149–50, 154, 175–76,
    179, 181, 188, 193, 197
  follow-up letters, 209, 211, 229
  rejection of offer letter, 253
  resignation letter, 268
  resurrection letters, 243–44
Manufacturing position letter, 88
Marketing position letters, 187–88, 243, 255
Media position letter, 130
Medical biller letter, 95
Mental health position letter, 112
Merchandise manager letter, 217
Multilingual sales manager letter, 173–74
Multiple letters, 53, 69–71

N, O

Negotiation letters, 261–65
Network admin. letters, 108, 144
Networking, 42–45, 193–204
Newspaper ad responses, 41–42, 90–107
Nursing position letters, 116, 266

Objectives
  of cover letters, 2–6, 32–33
  daily mailings, 52
Office administrator letter, 99
Online job postings. *See* Internet job search
Online resources, 292–97
Organizing
  contacts, 56–57
  e-mail accounts/correspondence, 63–65,
    70–71, 79

P

Peace officer letter, 97
Personal profile, 18–21
Personal trainer letter, 115
Pharmaceutical sales position letters, 132, 180
Physician's assistant letter, 119
Power phrases
  acceptance letters, 259–60
  broadcast letters, 191–92
  employment agency/recruiter cold responses,
    157–59
  face-to-face meeting follow-up letters, 234–37
  networking letters, 203–4
  newspaper ad responses, 104–7
  phone contact follow-up letters, 212
  potential employer cold responses, 140–42
  rejection of offer letters, 254
  resignation letters, 272
  resurrection letters, 249
  thank-you letters (after hire), 275
Privacy online, 60–61
Product manager letter, 248
Product specialist letter, 265

Production supervisor letters, 89, 124
Professional profile, 18–22
Professional resume writing services, 282–91
Project management letters, 134, 185
Proofing steps, 32–33, 36–37
Publishing position letters, 135, 202
Purchasing position letters, 186, 208

Q, R

Quality assurance position letter, 146
Questionnaire, 25–27

R&D engineer letter, 171–72
Radiation safety officer letter, 120
Rail industry letter, 129
Recruiter position letter, 133
Recruiters. *See* Employment agencies/recruiters
Rejection of offer letters, 250–54
Research professional letter, 114
Resignation letters, 266–72
Resume, attaching, 80
Resurrection letters, 238–49

S

Salary information, 22
Sales management letters, 173–74, 227
Sales position letters. *See also* International sales
    letters
    cover letters, 85, 94, 126, 128, 132, 168, 180
    follow-up letters, 214, 218, 225
    negotiation letter, 263
    resignation letter, 269
    resurrection letter, 246
Sample letters. *See also specific job titles*
    broadcast letters, 14, 160–90
    employment agency/recruiter, 16, 144–56
    executive briefing, 11
    general cover letter, 8–9
    negotiation letters, 261–65
    networking letters, 193–202
    newspaper ad responses, 90–103
    online job posting responses, 85–89
    to potential employers, 108–39
    rejection of offer letters, 250–53
    resurrection letters, 238–48
    thank-you letters (after hire), 273–75
Scannable letters, 71
Schedule, marketing, 54–55
School board seat letter, 125
Sending cover letters. *See* Electronic cover letters
Sending letters. *See* Attack plan
Senior counselor letter, 228

Senior network control tech./administrator letter, 144
Skilled laborer letter, 96
Skills analysis questionnaire, 25–27
Social worker letter, 242
Special reports, 276–81
Stevedore letter, 241
Style, of sentences/letters, 27–32. *See also* Electronic
    cover letters; Writing cover letters
Subject line (e-mail), 74–75, 78
Successful letters, common thread, viii–ix

T

Targeted approach, 53–54
Teaching/faculty letters, 91, 123, 160–61, 206
Team supervisor letter, 251
Telecommunications position letter, 169–70
Telephone accessibility/voice mail, 23
Telephone calls
    follow-up calls, 56
    letters following, 205–12
Templates, vi, 25. *See also* Sample letters; *specific*
    position titles
Tense, of sentences, 30–31
Thank-you letters (after hire), 273–75
Traits, universally-admired, 18–20
Types of letters
    broadcast letter, 12–14
    employment agency/recruiter, 15–16
    executive briefing, 10–12
    general cover letter, 7–9

V

Veterinarian letter, 121
Vice president letters, 131, 148, 182, 190, 257, 270
Voice, of sentences, 30–31

W

Wholesale market manager letter, 243
Writing cover letters. *See also* Electronic cover letters
    action verbs for, 28
    appearance of letters, 34–38
    checklists, 23, 32–33, 38
    envelopes and, 37–38
    K.I.S.S. approach, 29–30
    letter length and, 31–32
    optimal sentences, 27–28
    preparation questionnaire, 25–27
    proofing steps, 32–33, 36–37
    varying sentence structure, 29
    voice/tense for, 30–31

READER QUESTIONNAIRE

Please help me to help you, and in turn help others in their job hunt, by answering these questions. You can copy this page, fill in your answers, and mail it to me at the address below.

1. How did you use *Cover Letters That Knock 'em Dead* in your job hunt, and how did it help you?

   _____

   _____

   _____

   _____

2. What additional topics would you like to see covered in future editions?

   _____

3. What do you see as your biggest career challenges over short/long term?

   _____

4. What advice would you give to other job hunters and career changers?

   _____

Contact info:

   Name _____

   E-mail _____

   Tel. # _____

   Address _____

Mail to: Martin Yate c/o Adams Media • 57 Littlefield Street • Avon, MA 02322

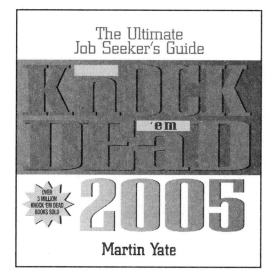